THE THEBAN EMPIRE

THE THEBAN EMPIRE

AGES IN CHAOS REVISITED

AGES IN ALIGNMENT SERIES, VOL. 3
SECOND AND REVISED EDITION

EMMET SWEENEY

Algora Publishing
New York

Library of Congress Cataloging-in-Publication Data —

Names: Sweeney, Emmet John, author.
Title: The Theban empire : Ages in Chaos revisited / Emmet Sweeney.
Other titles: Ages in Chaos revisited
Description: Second and revised edition. | New York : Algora Publishing,
    2020. | Series: Ages in alignment series; vol. 3 | Includes
    bibliographical references and index. | Summary: "Inspired by
    Velikovsky's reconstruction of ancient history, Emmet Sweeney
    demonstrates that an even more radical shift makes perfect sense.
    Archaeological evidence, the Amarna Letters, and records from the
    Mitanni, the Midians, the Hittites, from Egypt, Samaria, Jerusalem and
    elsewhere, depict matching events, matching biographies, and matching
    cultural artifacts . This demands we accept reality and revise our
    invented model of antiquity. This volume particularly emphasizes (and
    clarifies) mysteries centered on Thebes"— Provided by publisher.
Identifiers: LCCN 2020040589 (print) | LCCN 2020040590 (ebook) | ISBN
    9781628944372 (trade paperback) | ISBN 9781628944389 (hardback) | ISBN
    9781628944396 (pdf)
Subjects: LCSH: Egypt—History—New Kingdom, ca. 1550-ca. 1070 B.C. |
    Egypt—History—Errors, inventions, etc. | Middle East—History—To 622.
    | Middle East—History—Errors, inventions, etc. | Velikovsky, Immanuel,
    1895-1979. Ages in chaos.
Classification: LCC DT87 .S93 2020 (print) | LCC DT87 (ebook) | DDC
    932/.014—dc23
LC record available at https://lccn.loc.gov/2020040589
LC ebook record available at https://lccn.loc.gov/2020040590

Printed in the United States

Table of Contents

PREFACE TO THE SECOND EDITION   1

INTRODUCTION   3

CHAPTER 1: AN IMPERIAL AGE   9
Rise of the Thebans   9
The Land of Mitanni   12
15th Century or 7th Century?   14
Hittites and Lydians   17
Egypt and the Bible   19
The "Centuries of Darkness"   22

CHAPTER 2: HATSHEPSUT, THE QUEEN OF THEBA   29
A New Perspective   29
A Most Unusual Ruler   33
The Terms "Queen of Sheba" and "Queen of the South"   35
Sheba, City of the Sphinx   39
God's Land and Syria/Palestine   40
The Frankincense Terraces of Palestine   47
Thutmose III's List of Conquered Lands   49
Punt as a "Southern" Boundary?   52
The Flora and Fauna of Punt   55
Ethnic Identity of the Puntites   60
Eritrea and Somalia in Hatshepsut's Time: A Primitive Land   64
Recapitulation   65

CHAPTER 3: IMPERIAL EGYPT   69
Thutmose III and Shishak   69
Thutmose III Destroys Hatshepsut's Legacy   70
The Road to Kadesh   76

Jerusalem in the Time of Thutmose III: A Mighty Citadel 80
The Conquest of God's Land 83
The People, Flora and Fauna of God's Land 85
Shishak and Sesostris 87

CHAPTER 4: THE AMARNA LETTERS 91
Historical Setting 91
Jerusalem and Botrys 93
The Time of the Letters 95
Abdi-Ashirta, Grandson of Hiram 99
Labayu of Shechem 101
Aziru: Hadadezer I of Syria 103
The Captains of the King of Jerusalem 105
Aftermath 107
Ugarit 109
The City of Samaria 112

CHAPTER 5: THE FALL OF THEBES 119
Egypt and the Zoroastrian Fire Cult 119
The Heretic Pharaoh in Ancient Legend 123
Wars of the "Polluted Wretches" 127
A Pharaoh Deposed and Exiled 131
Tutankhamun's Reign 133
The Wily Vizier 137
Horemheb 139
An Asiatic Interlude 142
Chronological Considerations 145

CHAPTER 6: ARCHAEOLOGY AND CHRONOLOGY—
THE STRATIGRAPHIC GAP 149
Mitannians and Neo-Assyrians 149
KINGS OF THE MEDES 152
Hittites, Hurrians and Urartians 152
The Strategic Land of Northern Syria 155
The Kings of Carchemish 158
The Archaeology of Carchemish 161
The Art of War 163
The Alphabet and Phoenician Sarcophagi 171
Semitic Influences on the Egyptian Language 176
Scarabs and Pottery 177
The Nimrud Ivories and the Tombs of Enkomi 182

CHAPTER 7: IN THE DAYS OF SETI I AND RAMSES II   187

An Egyptian "Renaissance"   187
The Egyptian–"Assyrian" Alliance   189
Sardanapalus and the Battle of the Nations   190
Egypt and the Battle for Assyria   192
Shamshi-Adad V and Semiramis   194
Ramses II and Alyattes of Lydia   197
Adad-Nirari III (Astyages the Mede)   202
Croesus and His Time   206

CHAPTER 8: THE NINETEENTH DYNASTY AND THE HEBREW MONARCHIES   209

Seti I's Asiatic Wars   209
The "Wretched Foe"   213
Ramses II Secures the Borders of Israel and Judah   216
The "Israel Stele" of Merneptah   220

APPENDICES   225

The Medes   225
Tukulti-Ninurta I and Tukulti-Ninurta II   227
Kassites and Chaldaeans   229
Arame of Urartu   234
The Princess of Bactria   236

EPILOGUE   239

BIBLIOGRAPHY   243

Books   243
Articles   245
Classical Texts   249
Abbreviations   249

INDEX   251

PREFACE TO THE SECOND EDITION

My book *Empire of Thebes* was first published by Algora in 2006. Since that time, so much more supporting evidence has appeared that an update of this book would be warranted. Other factors too made me realize that a new edition was necessary. *Empire of Thebes* represented a radical rewriting of ancient chronology — a rewriting of a past never before accurately chronicled. Other historians of ancient times hold tenured posts at prestigious universities, and they are afforded all the resources and help those august institutions can offer. My researches, by contrast, were conducted alone and unfunded. As such, it was inevitable that minor errors would occur, and these I freely admit. None of those errors, however, undermines the central argument of *Empire of Thebes*, whose narrative I have found no reason whatsoever to alter. On the contrary, the new evidence mentioned above has only made it more watertight.

Another reason for an update was the somewhat circuitous reasoning of the final two chapters, a situation that demanded a clearer and more linear presentation.

And finally, there was the question of illustrations. The ancient Near East was home to some of the most colorful civilizations in history. Their artwork and architecture was often spectacular and always instructive. Since a great part of the argument of *Empire of Thebes* centered on art styles and their development, the inclusion of illustrations, as well as maps and other charts, was not only helpful but even essential. In my eagerness to publish *Empire of Thebes* in 2006, I had neglected these indispensable aids; a neglect I now make good.

INTRODUCTION

The work that follows represents the third volume of a general recon-struction of ancient history which I have named *Ages in Alignment*. As the term suggests, our chronology of ancient civilizations has hitherto been out of alignment, out of joint. Kingdoms, empires and individuals in the different regions and cultures of the ancient Near East have been set down in the history books in a completely chaotic order, with the result that kings in Israel, for example, who were contemporary with pharaohs of the Egyptian New Kingdom (Eighteenth and Nineteenth Dynasties), have been placed centuries after those same pharaohs. Thus the "history" of the ancient East, found in the voluminous learned textbooks of the great libraries of the world, is little more than an elaborate fiction.

Those with an interest in these things will know that the first person to identify this error was Immanuel Velikovsky, who, beginning in 1952, sought to rectify the mistake with a series of books entitled *Ages in Chaos*. Volume 1 of *Ages in Chaos* was followed by *Peoples of the Sea* (1977) and *Ramses II and His Time* (1978). Velikovsky died before he could completely reach his goal, namely a complete reconstruction of ancient history; a series of books of his, most notably *The Assyrian Conquest* and *The Dark Ages of Greece*, remain to this day unpublished (though these can now be viewed on the Internet Archive housing his works).

My own series of books, *Ages in Alignment*, is directly inspired by *Ages in Chaos* and seeks to complete the work of reconstruction which commenced in 1952. Readers of my other books will know that whilst in general I agree with the main thrust of Velikovsky's work, there are significant differences.

Most importantly, *Ages in Alignment* calls for a much more radical short-ening of ancient chronology than anything envisaged even by Velikovsky. It became clear to me that Velikovsky had been unable to complete the work of reconstruction because he had placed too much reliance on the Bible as a chronological measuring rod. Some of his works, such as *Peoples of the Sea* and (to some degree) *Ramses II and His Time*, shortened Egyptian New Kingdom chronology by a full seven to eight centuries in order to make it conform to the chronology outlined by the classical and Hellenistic writers. Other volumes, however, such as *Ages in Chaos* Vol.1, shortened Egyptian history by just over five centuries in order to make it conform to the chronology of the Israelite kings, as outlined in the Old Testament. Thus a 200-year gap was opened up between the two parts of the reconstruction; and this gap was inserted by Velikovsky between the Eighteenth and Nineteenth Dynasties.

Critics of Velikovsky were quick to point out that such a gap could not be supported, in terms of either archaeology or historiography. There seems little doubt that Velikovsky in his later years became aware of the contradic-tions involved, and that it was these that stalled the completion of his great work.

The insights provided in the 1980s by Professor Gunnar Heinsohn of Bremen University were however to cast an entirely new light on things. Heinsohn argued that chronology had to be reconstructed solely on the strength of stratigraphic evidence, and when this was done, he said, the history of the ancient East began to conform precisely to the history of the region found in the classical authors. Thus for Heinsohn, Velikovsky had made a mistake in bringing the Eighteenth Dynasty down the time scale by only five centuries (into the 10th and 9th centuries BC), when he should have brought it down a full seven centuries to place it in the latter 8th and 7th centuries, and make it directly precede the Nineteenth Dynasty which Velikovsky himself had in any case placed in the 6th century (in *Ramses II and his Time*).

I follow Heinsohn's lead on this and place the Eighteenth Dynasty in the 8th and 7th centuries. I do not however follow Heinsohn in thereby aban-doning the reconstruction put forward in *Ages in Chaos* Vol.1. For me, the character identifications and synchronisms established by Velikovsky in the latter work were on the whole valid; only the absolute chronology needed altering. For this reason, I had not originally intended to cover the period of the Eighteenth Dynasty. What Velikovsky wrote in *Ages in Chaos* Vol.1 is excellent and cannot, in many ways, be improved upon. Nevertheless, I grad-ually came around to the idea that a separate volume dealing with the epoch would be necessary. There were a number of reasons for this.

To begin with, whilst the historical synchronisms established in *Ages in Chaos* Vol.1 are on the whole correct, the historical setting, as I have said, is wrong. Bringing the great pharaohs of the Eighteenth Dynasty, as well as the Hebrew kings with whom they interacted, down into the 8th/7th century BC is not simply a question of dates. The entire cultural context is radically altered, and the great empires of the time, with whom the Eighteenth Dynasty pharaohs interacted, such as the Mitanni and the Hittites, reveal themselves to be very different from the nations and characters imagined both by orthodox historians and by Velikovsky.

Secondly, whilst most of the character identifications made by Velikovsky in the first volume of *Ages in Chaos* are absolutely correct (such as for example Hatshepsut = the Queen of Sheba and Thutmose III = Shishak), these have been attacked in detail by his critics, and the impression put abroad is that they have been debunked. Part of the reason for this was Velikovsky's overconfidence in the ability of historians to see the wider picture. This they have failed to do; and since Velikovsky neglected to defend these pivotal character identifications in the depth necessary to rebut such critics, I propose to perform that task here.

Thirdly, whilst *most* of the synchronisms and identifications outlined in *Ages in Chaos* Vol.1 were correct, some were not. This applies most notably to the chapters dealing with the Hyksos, at the beginning of the book, and with the Amarna Letters, at the end. The Hyksos were identified by Velikovsky with the Amalekites, biblical enemies of the Hebrews. In this, as we shall see, he was mistaken. The other important error centered around the Amarna Letters, documents said by Velikovsky to have been written during the time of Ahab of Israel and Jehoshaphat of Judah. These texts do not in fact date from the time of the latter monarchs, and the errors identified here were a major reason for the jettisoning of the whole Ages in Chaos project. As a matter of fact, as we shall see in the pages to follow, Velikovsky got it very nearly correct with the Amarna Letters. He was "out" by only a single generation. The correspondences appear to have been written a generation or so earlier than he thought, apparently in the time of Baasha's son Elah, King of Israel and whoever it was sat on the throne of Judah at that time (officially King Asa, but this is not possible).

Fourthly, the end of the Eighteenth Dynasty, in the chaotic events which followed the reign of Akhnaton, is one of the most intriguing episodes in the entire history of the ancient world. Velikovsky dealt with this, to some degree, in his *Oedipus and Akhnaton* (1960), but he left the work half-finished and outside its proper historical context. This I hope to rectify.

Finally, in *Ramses II and His Time*, which really should be regarded as a direct follow-on from *Ages in Chaos* 1, Velikovsky — although correctly placing the Nineteenth Dynasty and Ramses II in the 6th century — made a number of major miscalculations with regard to the characters with whom this pharaoh interacted. These mainly concerned biblical history which, according to accepted ideas, places the epic struggle of the kingdom of Judah with the Babylonians under Nebuchadrezzar in the 6th century. Velikovsky did not question this scheme and accordingly identified Ramses II's Hittite enemy Hattusilis with the Babylonian king Nebuchadrezzar. But the Hittite center of power was Anatolia, far to the north and west of Assyria, and no Babylonian king ever ruled or claimed to rule in that region. In fact, as we shall see, the Hittites are much more properly identified with the real great power of sixth century Anatolia, the Lydians.

These then are some of my reasons for devoting a whole volume to the time of the Eighteenth (or more properly Theban) Dynasty, and thereby, in the process, expanding the *Ages in Alignment* project to four volumes (or five, if *Arthur and Stonehenge* is taken into account).

Evidence of many different types has been called upon in order to complete the picture here presented. The much-neglected ancient historians have been an invaluable source of evidence, and I have found myself quoting them alongside up-to-date modern scholars. Very frequently the cuneiform and hieroglyphic sources do not present enough information to properly reconstruct a history; and we are compelled to turn to the ancient authors to bring the whole thing to life. This is normal practice. We should know precious little (actually nothing at all) of the Persian War against Greece, or Alexander's conquest of Persia, if we had to depend on the contemporary monuments of either land. In my reconstruction of a history hitherto unknown, I have therefore found it necessary to turn to the ancient authors. The chapter on the fall of the Eighteenth Dynasty for example could not have been written without the combined insights provided by Manetho and various Greek traditions, as well as the hieroglyphic documents of Egypt herself.

Throughout the work I have made frequent use of the evidence presented in ancient art. The design of chariots, for example, went through a very definite evolution, an evolution accurately depicted by the artists of the time. Examination of this type of evidence may help us to date the reign of a king with a high degree of accuracy. Thus, for example, artistic and technological parallels prove beyond question that the so-called Neo-Assyrian Empire established by Ashurnasirpal II was contemporary with the latter Eighteenth and Nineteenth Dynasties of Egypt.

It is evident that in a pioneering work such as this, mistakes are inevitable. What is presented here is by no means an exhaustive or definitive history. Rather, it is a broad outline, a blueprint along whose lines a new understanding of the ancient Near East's past can be built. Some people, particularly those with a little knowledge, will object to much of what they will read. Many will perhaps reject the whole concept of royal alter egos, a concept central to the reconstruction herein advanced. I have stated that the Mede kings used Assyrian names in their capacity as kings of Assyria. To those who might instinctively be opposed to this concept, we must ask the following: Do they thereby suggest that ancient kings had but a single name (though we know that pharaohs regularly had dozens), or that they did not employ different names in the different regions and cultural areas over which they ruled? Tiglath-Pileser III called himself Pul as king of Babylon, and Ashurbanipal named himself Kandalanu as ruler of the same city. Did the Semitic-speaking Assyrian subjects of Cyaxares (Khwashatra) really call him by this name — a name which was for them meaningless and probably unpronounceable? Ancient kings derived their legitimacy from posing as earthly representatives of the gods. Is it so hard to believe that the Assyrian people would have had their own titles for Cyaxares and the other Mede rulers, titles that meant something to them?

But even establishment academics accept the ancient use of multiple names. No one denies for example that in the Amarna Letters Amenhotep III is referred to as Nimmuria and Akhnaton as Naphuria (both names have in addition a number of variant spellings): And how many Bible historians would object to the identification of Azariah of Judah with Uzziah?

So the objections, I contend, which may initially seem to rest on powerful foundations, will be seen to be not nearly so solid as they appear; and this has been my own experience in writing and researching the present work. Following the broader picture, which clearly demands a great reduction in antique chronology, the details have one by one, sometimes to my own astonishment, fallen into place. Bringing together all the evidence, from whatever source, the picture has gradually become almost crystal clear. What I have been left with, basically, is a synthesis of the written history, as it appears in the classical and Hellenistic writers, with the archaeology. It is, I suggest, a reclaiming of ancient history along the lines understood by the ancients themselves.

It only remains for me to say that I hope the reader of these pages will derive as much pleasure from them as the author derived from researching and writing them.

CHAPTER 1: AN IMPERIAL AGE

Rise of the Thebans

The Old Assyrian Empire tottered and fell. From the ruins of this kingdom, whose greatest rulers were named Sargon and Naram Sin, there arose two mighty empires: that of the Hittites, who controlled the vast region of central Anatolia around the Halys River, and that of the Mita, or Mitanni, who took control of the Assyrian heartland itself as well as all of northern and central Syria.

It was in fact the Mitanni, under their king Parattarna, who first challenged the Assyrians, apparently in the time of Naram Sin. Even as he did so, far to the south, the people of Egypt were involved in a titanic struggle of their own. This was against the hated Hyksos, the "Rulers of Foreign Lands," whose kings bore Semitic names and who had introduced the chariot, a Mesopotamian invention, into Egypt. And that was not the only Mesopotamian invention introduced by the "Shepherd Kings," whose symbol, the shepherd's crook (afterwards carried also by the pharaohs), was the symbol *par excellence* of the sheep-rich land of Assyria.

Much has been written about the Hyksos. Whole volumes have been devoted to examining their origins and identity. Yet for all that, little in the way of facts has emerged. In the 1950s, Immanuel Velikovsky argued that the Shepherd Kings should be identified with the nomadic Amalekites, an Arabian tribe encountered by the Israelites as they fled their bondage in Egypt.[1] Others have suggested that they were Hittites from Anatolia; still

---

[1] See Velikovsky, *Ages in Chaos* (1952)

others that they were Minoans from Crete. Some, perhaps in despair at ever finding an answer, declared them to be fictitious: an imaginary creation of Egyptian scribes.

But scholars should have paid greater heed to the archaeology; for this evidence, that of the spade and trowel, points insistently to Mesopotamia, the Land of the Two Rivers.

The cultural links between the Hyksos and Mesopotamia are actually all pervasive. A granite lion of Khyan, one of the most powerful Hyksos pharaohs, was discovered in Baghdad,[2] and during the Hyksos epoch large numbers of cultural innovations specifically connected with Mesopotamia were introduced to the Nile Valley. Thus the bronze scimitar, known to have a Mesopotamian origin, was brought to Egypt by the Shepherd Kings.[3] A very specific type of cylinder-seal, portraying a bull-headed hero, is associated with the Akkadian epoch; yet such seals appear in Hyksos-age strata in Palestine/Syria.[4] Pottery of the Akkadian age offers precise parallels with Hyksos pottery.[5] Architecture of the two peoples, supposedly separated in time by over seven centuries, offers further comparisons. Thus the peculiar defensive triple-gate of the Akkadian Age is copied in exact detail by the Hyksos.[6] In the same way, the cults of Ishtar and Bel made their first appearance in Egypt in the time of the Hyksos, whilst many of the Hyksos rulers and officials had names that were quite evidently Semitic.

One of the most enduring legacies of the Hyksos epoch appears to have been the establishment of the Akkadian language as the *lingua franca* of diplomacy throughout the Near East — a situation that we find already at the beginning of the New Kingdom. In the famous Amarna documents, for example, we find Syrian vassal kings of Amenhotep III and Akhnaton corresponding with their master by means of letters written in Akkadian — an Akkadian strikingly similar to that used by Sargon I and Naram Sin.[7] Even Mesopotamian diplomatic protocols are preserved, with royal correspondences written in cuneiform upon clay tablets and concealed within clay envelopes.

Amongst Egyptologists, the question of who taught the Egyptians the Akkadian language still prompts lively debate. Yet proof positive

---

[2] W. C. Hayes, "Egypt: From the Death of Amenemmes III to Seqenenre II" in *The Cambridge Ancient History*, Vol.2 part 1 (3rd ed.), p.60

[3] H. Bonnet, *Die Waffen der Völker des Alten Orients* (Leipzig Germany 1926), p.94

[4] See eg Gunnar Heinsohn, "Who were the Hyksos?" *Sixth International Congress of Egyptology* (Turin, 1991), pp.10-12

[5] Ibid., pp.18-27

[6] Ibid., pp.32-5

[7] Ibid., p.32

that the Hyksos used Akkadian, and were therefore almost certainly the nation responsible for making it the language of commerce and diplomacy throughout Palestine/Syria, came with the discovery at Hazor in Israel of some jugs of Hyksos date, one of which bore an inscription in Akkadian cuneiform. "Three jugs belonging to Middle Bronze Age II were found *in situ* in Locus 6175. On one of them (C339/1) an inscription was found incised in cuneiform, the earliest in this script to be discovered hitherto in Palestine."[8] It was understood that "the historical conclusions connected with the fact that the grammatical form of the name is Akkadian and not Western Semitic" would be far-reaching. One scholar noted that "it is instructive that the first element of the name, whose reading is plain, has the Akkadian form *is-me* (i.e., 'he has heard') and not the West Semitic form one would expect: *iasmah*, as in the name Iasmah-Adad known from Mari."[9]

Thus the experts expressed their puzzlement and discomfort at the apparently anomalous and anachronistic appearance of the Akkadian language amongst the Hyksos.

All in all, the evidence increasingly demonstrates that the Hyksos were a mighty and cultured people, closely connected to Mesopotamia, and not the ignorant barbarians portrayed by the Egyptians. They described themselves as "Rulers of Nations" — a term held to be "suggestive of worldwide domination."[10] Strange indeed that such an awesome imperial power should have escaped the attention of everyone but the Egyptians! Not only were they great conquerors, their technological innovations are now justly recognized. "Through their Hyksos adversaries the Egyptians probably first became acquainted with the composite bow, bronze daggers and swords of improved type, and other advances in the equipment and technique of war, as well as with some of the important western Asiatic innovations in the arts of peace which we encounter in Egypt for the first time under the Eighteenth Dynasty."[11] Such benefits of civilization could force only one conclusion about those responsible: "However we may evaluate them, they were evidently not the ruthless barbarians conjured up by the Theban propagandists of the early New Kingdom and the Egyptian writers of later periods."[12]

So, the Hyksos epoch was one of high civilization. Fresh ideas from the east flooded into Egypt, and we cannot doubt that international trade, as well as diplomacy, was a characteristic of the age. Literature — in the form of the

---

[8] Y. Yadin et al. Cited from Heinsohn, loc. cit., p.31
[9] A. Malamat "Hazor, 'The Head of all those Kingdoms" *Journal of Biblical Literature* Vol. LXXIX (1960), p. 18
[10] Hayes, loc. cit., p.61
[11] Ibid., p.57
[12] Ibid., p.55

"Prophetic" and "Pessimistic" treatises — flourished, as did art and architecture. The Hyksos kings it seems built great monuments throughout Egypt, and they poured substantial resources into beautifying the nation's temples and shrines. Put simply, the archaeological record demonstrates that Egyptian civilization suffered not at all from the Hyksos occupation, and that, on the contrary, it was greatly enriched by the infusion of Asiatic influence.

It is no coincidence that the various cultural features linking the Hyksos to Mesopotamia are associated with the Mesopotamia of the Akkadian epoch. Two of the most important of the Akkadian kings were named Sargon and Naram-Sin; identical to the names of the two greatest of the Old Assyrian kings. This might lead the casual observer to wonder whether the Akkadians and Old Assyrians (as well as the Hyksos) were the same people; and in fact it can be shown, by the irrefutable weight of a great body of evidence, that the Hyksos kings of Egypt were identical to the Old Assyrians, and that the Mitannians and Egyptians had been involved in a great war against a common foe.

The Land of Mitanni

In the late 1980s, Professor Gunnar Heinsohn of Bremen University began to suggest that the Old Assyrians, as well as the Hyksos, were identical to the Imperial Assyrians of the classical authors.[13] In conformity with this conclusion, he also argued that their conquerors, the Mitanni, were one and the same as the Medes, the Iranian-speaking people whom all the ancient authors agreed had been the conquerors of the Assyrians. Archaeologists had been unable to discover the Medes in the Late Iron Age strata in which they were sought; and this problem, along with many others, said Heinsohn, was solved if we equated them with the Bronze Age Mitanni.

Could it be that the Mitannians, whom conventional chronology normally places in the 16th and 15th centuries BC, rightfully belong in the 7th? Examination of the evidence suggests that Heinsohn was correct.

The actual conquest of the Old Assyrian kingdom is nowhere recorded in Mitannian documents, yet from the evidence available it would appear that Parattarna, their first important king, opened hostilities and succeeded in overrunning a great portion of the Assyrian Empire. During his time there were established in northern Syria a large number of potentates bearing Mitannian names and owing allegiance to him.[14] But it was left to Parattarna's successor Shaushtatar, son of Parsatatar (who may have been the same as

---

[13] Heinsohn, *Die Sumerer gab es nicht* (Frankfurt, 1988)
[14] Margaret S. Drower, "Syria c. 1550–1400 BC." in *The Cambridge Ancient History* Vol.2 part 1 (3rd ed.), p.422

Parattarna), to complete the conquest of the Assyrian heartland, and we hear in a document of a later time how Shaushtatar plundered the city of Ashur and took the silver and golden doors of the royal palace to adorn his own residence in Washukanni.[15] The influence of Mitanni now made itself felt over a large section of the Near East. Members of the Mitannian aristocracy, the *Mariyanna*, assumed positions of power and authority throughout Syria and Palestine, a circumstance strongly suggesting that these regions too had been conquered by them. So prominent was this folk that the pharaohs of the latter Eighteenth Dynasty regularly sought wives from them. These were obtained, after much courtship on the part of the Egyptians, from the time of Thutmose IV onwards.[16] The kings of Mitanni gloried in the title Great King, and they were so named in the various political correspondences of the period.

Shaushtatar's successors remained in control of the Assyrian land for the next three generations, and we find Tushratta, a contemporary of Akhnaton, sending the pharaoh the cult-figure of the goddess Ishtar of Nineveh.[17]

From the personal names of the Mitanni kings, we know that they were of a race who spoke a language closely related to Persian[18] — virtually identical, in fact, to the Indo-Iranian language of the Medes. The text of a treaty between Mitanni and the Hittite land shows that Mitra, Varuna, and Indra, deities of Indo-Iranian origin, comprised the Mitanni pantheon. Indo-Iranian technical terms appear with great frequency in the Mitanni vocabulary.[19] True, another racial and linguistic group, designated Hurrian, is evinced in Mitannian documents and personal names. The exact relationship between the Hurrian and Iranian elements is unclear, though it would appear that the Iranian group was dominant, for all the Mitanni kings had clearly Iranian names. Hurrian is non-Indo-European and is closely related to the language of Urartu, the region of eastern Anatolia immediately south of the Caucasus. From the Iranian royal names and the Indo-Iranian gods worshipped by the Mitanni, it seems certain that the Mitanni kingdom was comprised of an Indo-Iranian aristocracy who had subdued, and ruled over, a largely non-Indo-Iranian population. Confirming this is the fact that the Mitanni warrior-class bore an Indo-Aryan name, *Mariyanna*, a term recognized as related to the Sanskrit *marya*, a nobleman.

---

[15] Ibid., p.464

[16] Ibid., p.463

[17] Ibid., p.489

[18] W. F. Albright, "The Amarna Letters from Palestine" in *The Cambridge Ancient History* Vol.2 part 1 (3rd ed.), pp.109-10

[19] eg. W. F. Albright, *The Archaeology of Palestine: From the Stone Age to Christianity* (Baltimore, 1940), p.153

One thing is clear: The original Mitanni kingdom occupied almost exactly the same position as historical Media. Even the name Mitanni, or more correctly Mita, is indistinguishable from that of the Medes, the Madai; and Herodotus, in the 5th century BC, names Matiene as a province of the Persian Empire located very close to Media.[20]

The capital city of Mitanni is generally given as Washukanni or Washuganni — a name which could perhaps be related to Sanskrit *vashu-khani*, "mine of wealth." The ancient capital of the Medes was named Ecbatana (modern Hamadan), which is apparently the Old Persian *hagmatana*, "gathering place." Washukanni, the Mitannian capital, has never been identified; but if it is the same place as Ecbatana, the mystery of its location is solved. It would appear that Washukanni and Hagmatana were two names for the same place. In the same way, Shaushtatar (or Shaushattra), the conqueror of the Old Assyrians, must be Cyaxares (Khwashatra), the Median conqueror of Assyria, and his predecessor Parattarna must be Phraortes, who, according to Herodotus,[21] had earlier waged an inconclusive war against the Assyrians.

But the Medes were not the only people around in the 7th century. In the testimony of the classical writers, there were great population movements at the time; one of these saw a savage race from the steppes, the Scythians, enter the civilized lands of the Near East. Do these people too occur in the documents and archives of the period we are dealing with?

15th Century or 7th Century?

At this point we must stop and consider an important question. Could it really be that conventional chronology, as found in the textbooks, is so dramatically wrong? That the Mitanni people, normally placed in the 15th and 14th centuries BC, really were the Medes, the "Mighty Medes" of the 7th century BC, who destroyed the Assyrian Empire and who controlled much of the Near East before the rise of the Persians? Could it be also that their contemporaries, the pharaohs of the Eighteenth Dynasty, actually belong to so recent a time in history?

If the Mitannians were the Medes and their enemies, the Old Assyrians, were the Empire Assyrians, then the destruction of the latter kingdom must have taken place in the 7th century BC. We know from the classical authors that the Medes conquered the Assyrians about a century before the rise of the Persians, whose first Great King, Cyrus, flourished in the middle of the 6th century BC. According to the story outlined by Herodotus, the Assyr-

---

[20] Herodotus, v,50
[21] Ibid., i,103

ians were, to begin with, assisted by an army of nomadic Scythians, who had arrived in the Near East in hot pursuit of their arch enemies the Cimmerians. These hordes the Assyrian king unleashed on Phraortes' Medes, and for a while, the tide of war was turned.[22] Only by a ruse did the next Mede ruler Cyaxares break their power, inviting their tribal chiefs to a banquet at which they were set upon and butchered. In spite of this, bands of the nomad warriors continued to harass the peoples of the Near East for many years, and they ranged far and wide in pursuit of plunder. All of Mesopotamia was harried, and Egypt was only spared their depredations by the payment of a huge bribe.[23] After the latter incident, we are told, most of the invaders returned north, though a few remained in Syria to pillage.[24]

If the Mitanni were the Medes and they truly belong in the 7th century, then the Scythians should figure prominently in the documents of the period. Their presence should make itself felt everywhere. They should, for example, probably appear in the Amarna Letters, political correspondences of the latter Eighteenth Dynasty, most of which concern Syria and Palestine. Their activities should certainly be noted in Mesopotamian documents. Above all, however, they should be extremely prominent in the records of the Hittite Empire, a state which was contemporary with the Mitannians and which must surely have borne the brunt of the Scythian onslaught. If the Scythians do not figure prominently in the records of, say, Suppiluliumas I, the Hittite king who reigned contemporary with Akhnaton, then we must seriously question whether they truly belong in the age to which we have assigned them.

The biography of Suppiluliumas I, written by his son Mursilis, was among the cuneiform documents unearthed at Boghaz-koi. From it we learn that a barbarian race named the Gasga (Ga-as-ga, or Ga-as-ga-as), had brought the Hittite nation to the verge of complete destruction. Such was the situation faced by Suppiluliumas upon his ascent of the throne, and we are told that the first twenty years of his reign were taken up in a desperate struggle for survival against the barbarians. That the Gasga were nomads is evident from the description of their activities. They burned, they looted, and they pillaged. The capital of the Hittite kingdom itself was destroyed.[25] But they did not hold on to any of the cities or country they took. Furthermore, their organization was tribal. In one part of the biography, they are described as a

---

[22] Herodotus, i,104-6
[23] Ibid., i,105
[24] Ibid., i,105
[25] A. Goetze, "Anatolia from Shuppiluliumash to the Egyptian War of Muwatallish," in *The Cambridge Ancient History* Vol.2 part 2 (3rd ed.), p.117

group of twelve tribes. In another battle described elsewhere, they are said to have assembled nine tribes.

The power of these nomads, who devastated large areas of Anatolia, has led scholars to question their country of origin. By and large, it is agreed that they must have come from the north, probably north of the Caucasus.[26]

The word Gasga, or Ga-as-ga-as, calls to mind the Akkadian name for the Scythians, which we know from monuments of the Persian period to be Ashguzai, or Ashguza.[27] The Hebrew name for the Scythians, Ashkenaz, was apparently derived from an erroneous rendering of the latter word. Since vowels in Akkadian are entirely conjectural, the term we find transliterated from the Persian monuments as Ashguza, could equally well be rendered Shagaz, or Sagaz; and indeed this very name, usually given as Sa.Gaz, features very prominently in another set of documents from the time of Suppilu-liumas, the Amarna Letters. The period during which the Amarna Letters were composed was a time of great disturbance throughout Syria and Pales-tine. The pharaoh's correspondents never tire of complaining of brigands and marauders, who seem to infest the countryside. Even important officials sent by the Hittite or Babylonian kings were not safe, and the petty kings of the region viewed with increasing alarm the activities of these bandits.[28] The latter are divided into two main groups: there are the Habiru, who seem to be situated east of the Jordan, and the Sa.gaz, or habatu, who are reported in various areas. These marauders are apparently total outsiders and are greatly feared by all parties. Notwithstanding the attempts of various scholars to associate these people with the early Hebrews in the time of Joshua, it seems clear that the barbarous Sa.gaz of the Amarna documents, as well as the *habiru* and *habatu* (both of which can be translated as "marauders" or "cut-throats") can be little other than the Ashguza of the Persian inscriptions.

It would appear then that the words Ga-as-ga-as and Sa.gaz, as well as Ashguza, are all local variants of the name Scyth (Saka, in the Persian language). These are different versions of the same name, rendered by scribes whose native languages were other than Akkadian.

There was another nation of nomadic marauders active, chiefly in Meso-potamia, in the period under discussion. These were the Gutians, a people whose name is also rendered as Quti or Cuthi. Now the Guti are held to be one of the most mysterious peoples of antiquity. An inscription of Cyrus the Great indicates that they were active as late as the 6th century BC.[29]

---

[26] Ibid., p.118
[27] See eg. H. W. F. Saggs, *The Greatness that was Babylon* (London, 1962), p.117
[28] W. F. Albright, "The Amarna Letters from Palestine," loc. cit., pp.112-3
[29] eg. J. Pritchard, *Ancient Near Eastern Texts* (Princeton, 1950), p.315

What puzzles historians is that the Guti occur in the same role apparently two thousand years earlier, at the collapse of the Akkadian Empire. A whole series of documents from throughout Babylonia, which relate to the Akkadian period, speak of the depredations of the Guti, who are very clearly portrayed as barbarous nomads.[30] How could a race of barbarians remain so after two thousand years amongst the civilized peoples of Mesopotamia?

Since we have already identified the Akkadian (or Old Assyrian) Empire with the Assyrian, it is clear that the Guti, who play a major role in its destruction, must be another name for the Scythians, with whom they are admittedly associated on the inscription of Cyrus.

As we have said, the Guti also feature prominently in the records of the Kassite and Middle Assyrian kings — contemporaries of Akhnaton and his successors. So, as well as being active at the beginning and end of native Babylonian civilization, these marauders are also active in the middle. Yet another anomaly for orthodox scholarship to grapple with.

Hittites and Lydians

Ancient writers insisted that during the period of Median supremacy, most of Anatolia formed part of the Lydian kingdom; and indeed the Lydians were great rivals of the Medes. The monuments and diplomatic correspondences of the Mitanni period apparently make no mention of the Lydians, though they do refer repeatedly to a mighty rival power that controlled Anatolia. This was the kingdom of Hatti: the Hittite Empire.

In the early days of archaeology, travellers to Anatolia did in fact attempt to identify the Hittite monuments of the region with the Lydians, and several carved bas-reliefs at Yazilikaya, just outside Boghaz-koi, were actually linked to specific events from Lydian history. Thus, for example W. J. Hamilton in his *Researches in Asia Minor, Pontus and Armenia* (1842) remarked that in his opinion one of the major reliefs commemorated a treaty signed by Croesus with Cyrus around 550 BC. "I am rather inclined to think that it represents the meeting of two coterminous kings, and that it was intended to commemorate a treaty of peace concluded between them. The Halys, which is not many miles distant, was long the boundary between the kingdoms of Lydia and Persia and it is possible that in the figure with the flowing robes we may recognize the king of Persia, and that in the other the king of Lydia, with his attendants, Lydians and Phrygians, for their headdress resembles the well-known Phrygian bonnet. This spot may have been chosen to commemorate the peace."[31]

---

[30] Ibid.
[31] W. J. Hamilton, *Researches in Asia Minor, Pontus and Armenia* (London, 1842), 393-95

Another scholar of the same period also identified the monuments as Lydian, but he inclined more to the view that the bas-relief commemorated a treaty signed by Croesus' predecessor Alyattes with the Medes under Astyages.[32] According to Herodotus, these two kings had met with their armies near the river Halys, but fighting broke off when the sun was eclipsed.[33] Afterwards, through the efforts of the kings of Babylon and Cilicia, a peace was negotiated and signed.

The more our knowledge of Hittite civilization and history has grown, the more clear-cut the Lydian connection has become. The Boghaz-koi documents, for example, showed that a number of Hittite kings had borne the name Mursilis — identical to the name (Myrsilos) given by Herodotus to one of the greatest kings of Lydia. The language of the Hittite Empire, known as "Hittite" to us but actually called "Neshili" in the Boghaz-koi texts, was found to be Indo-European. Further research into the linguistic make-up of ancient Asia Minor found that Lydian too was an Indo-European dialect — a dialect identical to "Hittite." In the words of one scholar, "Linguistically Lydian is related to the Hittite-Luwian group, but the curious thing is that unlike most of its contemporaries it seems to be Hittite rather than Luwian."[34] In other words the Lydian language is one and the same as that of the Hittites in their Cappadocian heartland — Nesha/Neshili — rather than Luwian, a related tongue employed by many other peoples of Asia Minor and Anatolia, such as the Phrygians and Lycians. In explanation of this strange anomaly, the writer quoted above continues, "One has to assume that in the disturbances following the collapse of the Hittite Empire a central Anatolian group had seized power among the ruins of Arzawa, and a memory of this may be preserved in the Herodotean story of a Heraclid dynasty with eastern connections which gained power in Lydia about 1200 BC."[35]

Arzawa, of course, is the name given to the Lydian district in the Hittite documents, and indeed the word may be identical to Lydia, given the interchangeability of "l" and "r" and the conjectural nature of vowels in cuneiform. Arzawa may reasonably be reconstructed as "Lyzawa."

The relationship between Arzawa/Lydia and the greater Hittite world has in fact caused considerable confusion amongst scholars, a confusion highlighted in the following statement: "And so we reach the final position that the language originally known as Arzawan [Lydian] is in fact the

---

[32] H. Barth, "Versuch einer eingehenden Erklärung der Felssculpturen von Boghaskoei in alten Kappadocien" *Monatsberichte der Königlichen Preussischen Akademie der Wissenschaften* (Berlin, 1869), pp. 128-75

[33] Herodotus i,74

[34] J. G. MacQueen, *The Hittites* (London, 1975), p.59

[35] Ibid.

language of the Hittites, while the language written in 'Hittite Hieroglyphs' is a dialect of the language of Arzawa."[36]

The Lydian and Hittite kingdoms therefore used the same language, occupied the same geographical space, and were, as we shall argue, contemporary.

It is generally presumed that the Hittite Empire took in only the eastern part of what was later to constitute the Lydian kingdom — a domain supposedly centered more on western Asia Minor. However, it is untrue to say that Hittite rule did not extend as far as the Aegean coast. The documents of Boghaz-koi show quite clearly that the regions comprising Lycia, Caria, Ionia and Aeolia were considered to be part of the Empire, and this has been confirmed by the discovery of Hittite monuments at Karabel near Smyrna and on Mount Sipylus overlooking the Aegean.

If then we accept the Hittites as Lydians, how do they fit into the history of the period, and do the historical records of the Hittite period speak of events known to us from the classical authors? Do the two histories match?

An examination of the lives and careers of the last two Hittite emperors, Hattusilis III and Tudkhaliyas IV, to be attempted at a later stage, will reveal a close match with the lives and careers of the last two Lydian kings, Alyattes and Croesus.

Egypt and the Bible

There seems to be strong evidence then to suggest that the entire epoch of the Eighteenth Dynasty needs to be brought forward in time by a staggering seven centuries or thereabouts. All the great pharaohs of this time, along with all the epic events associated with them, seem to belong squarely in the late 8th and 7th centuries BC. It is only by this dramatic reduction that Egyptian history can be made to square with the history of the ancient world as outlined by the classical authors.

It should be noted here that this margin of reduction agrees very well with the scenario outlined by Immanuel Velikovsky in his *Peoples of the Sea* (1977). In this volume, the Twentieth Dynasty, of Ramses III, was revealed to be the line of pharaohs who battled against the Persians in the 4th century BC. Thus, *Peoples of the Sea* reduced New Kingdom Egyptian dates by around eight centuries. Combining *Peoples of the Sea* with what has been discussed thus far in the present work therefore suggests that all New Kingdom dates need to be reduced by a span of roughly seven to eight centuries. This means, in addition to an Eighteenth Dynasty in the 8th/7th century, a Nineteenth

---

[36] Ibid., pp.24-5

Dynasty in the 6th, which of course is exactly where Velikovsky did place the latter line in his *Ramses II and his Time* (1978).

Clearly then, in terms of absolute chronology, the Egyptian New Kingdom belongs between the 8th and 4th centuries BC.

Yet now we encounter a difficulty, for that is only half the story: There remains the problem, first tackled by Velikovsky, of trying to "tie in" the history of Egypt with that of the Bible. Bringing the Theban Dynasty down into the 8th/7th century, into the age of the Medes, ties it into the history of antiquity as reported by the classical authors. It still however leaves us with the task of integrating it with the history found in the Old Testament.

Now, of course, making Egyptian history agree with that of the Bible has been something of the holy grail of orientalists throughout the centuries. The process of trying to "fit" the two histories together actually began in antiquity, with the highly polemical works of Apion, Manetho, Josephus and others. With the translation of the hieroglyphs in the early 19th century, scholars fervently hoped that the perennial questions would soon be answered. Which pharaoh made Joseph his vizier? Which pharaoh enslaved the Israelites? Which plundered Solomon's temple? Sadly, in the years that followed Champollion's historic breakthrough, cold reality took hold. Nowhere, it seemed, in the native records of Egypt, were the children of Israel even mentioned. One or two minor documents, it was periodically claimed, may have alluded to the Hebrews, but even these were uncertain.

In time, all attempts to make the two histories agree were abandoned.

It was all the more shocking then, when Immanuel Velikovsky made the surprise announcement in the early 1950s that he had answered all of the above questions; that he had achieved a real synchronization of Egyptian and Hebrew histories; and, most importantly, that other scholars had failed to make the two histories match because they had been blindly accepting a chronological framework that was completely distorted and which twisted the whole of ancient history out of recognition.

The history of the ancient world, Velikovsky said, as found in the great libraries of the world, is a complete fiction. In his *Ages in Chaos*, which appeared first in 1952, he argued in great detail that the pharaohs of the glorious Eighteenth Dynasty actually belonged in the same epoch as the early kings of Israel, from Saul and David through to Jehoshaphat and Ahab. Using a wide range of evidence, from art forms to language, epigraphy and religion, he demonstrated in great detail how the pharaohs of the Eighteenth Dynasty interacted with their Hebrew royal counterparts. Thus he suggested that Hatshepsut, Egypt's famous female "pharaoh," was actually the Queen of Sheba, whose visit to Solomon in Jerusalem forms one of the most romantic episodes of biblical history. He argued too that Hatshepsut's successor, Thutmose III, was the mighty conqueror Shishak, whom the Book of Kings names as the plunderer of Solomon's temple.

These "synchronisms" demanded a reduction in the length of New Kingdom history of roughly five centuries; and it has to be stated that the arguments presented by Velikovsky here were, for a long time, regarded as his most attractive and robust.

Nevertheless, not everyone was convinced, and when Velikovsky eventually unveiled his "sequel" to *Ages in Chaos* I, namely *Ramses II and his Time* — where he outlined the history of the Nineteenth Dynasty — the storm broke. In *Ramses II and his Time* Velikovsky proposed a gap of over two centuries between the end of the Eighteenth Dynasty and the beginning of the Nineteenth, a gap which neither historiography nor archaeology could support. In *Ramses II and his Time* Velikovsky placed the Nineteenth Dynasty squarely in the late 7th and 6th centuries BC, whereas he had brought the Eighteenth Dynasty to an end in *Ages in Chaos* I near the end of the 9th century. Where had he gone wrong?

In the pages to follow, I will argue that the problem lay in something totally unsuspected. Hebrew history, in its later parts at least, is generally taken to be well established. Thus, no one questions that the prophet Isaiah, for example, lived in the 8th century BC, and was a contemporary of the Assyrian king Tiglath-Pileser III, who flourished in the same period. It is, in fact, generally agreed that Hebrew history is in harmony with the scheme outlined in the classical authors, and the chronology of the Old Testament, at least from the time of the early Hebrew kings onwards, is regarded as well established. But all of that has now changed. Following the revolutionary work of Professor Gunnar Heinsohn, it became clear, from the late 1980s onwards, that Old Testament chronology was itself no more reliable than that of Egypt. It too had its anomalies and dark ages. Heinsohn demonstrated that roughly two- to two-and-a-half centuries, roughly the period of the Persian Empire, was missing from Hebrew historiography. In essence, this meant that Old Testament history was not aligned accurately with that of the classical world; and that Isaiah, for example, normally reckoned to have flourished in the mid-8th century, actually flourished in the mid-6th.

This then was where Velikovsky had gone wrong. *Ages in Chaos* vol. 1 had brought Egyptian history down by five centuries to make it harmonize with biblical history. Yet *Peoples of the Sea* had brought another part of Egyptian history down by eight centuries to make it harmonize with classical history. Velikovsky inserted the resulting two or two-and-a-half centuries' discrepancy between the end of the Eighteenth and the start of the Nineteenth Dynasties; hence the problem.

Unfortunately for Velikovsky, and for the reconstruction of ancient history in general, no one at the time understood this. Having welcomed *Ages in Chaos* 1 with open arms, many people, particularly a group of British scholars, tried to hold onto this part of his work, whilst rejecting his later efforts. These writers wanted to have the Nineteenth Dynasty follow the Eighteenth directly in the latter years of the 9th century BC. This scheme was presented at the Society for Interdisciplinary Studies "Ages in Chaos?" conference in Glasgow in 1978 and came to be known as the "Glasgow Chronology." Yet within a short time of the latter's appearance, holes were being picked in the identifications argued in *Ages in Chaos* Vol.1; and by the mid-80s all three of the above-mentioned scholars had abandoned it, too. In its place a series of chronologies were produced which reduced the age of Egyptian history by a much smaller margin than the five centuries proposed therein. Thus Peter James would take just over two centuries from the age of the Eighteenth Dynasty, whilst David Rohl makes it roughly three.

I believe that the British scholars made a grave mistake in abandoning *Ages in Chaos* 1 and the "Glasgow Chronology." All that was needed was to move the whole of *Ages in Chaos* 1 — all the characters and events, lock, stock and barrel, a further two centuries or so down the time scale, so that Hatshepsut's meeting with King Solomon occurred in the late 8th century rather than the latter 10th, whilst Thutmose III's sacking of Solomon's temple occurred around 690 BC rather than 920 BC.

Before going into these events in more detail, however, I want to take a broader look at the evidence for deleting five centuries from the history of the Eighteenth Dynasty in order to make it tie in with the history of the Bible.

The "Centuries of Darkness"

There exists a great body of evidence, some of it missed even by Velikovsky himself, which indicates that the "dark age" gap between the Late Bronze Age of the second millennium and the Early Iron Age of the first (the latter dated according to the Bible) is in fact around five centuries long. This is demonstrated in numerous ways, not least by stratigraphy, where, in the land of Israel, for example, the hiatus (occupation gap) between Late Bronze 2b (end of the Nineteenth Dynasty) and the beginning of the Iron Age (contemporary in Israel with the Neo-Assyrian kings Tiglath-Pileser III and Sargon II) lasts just under 500 years. This was admitted and even argued for in the 1970s by John Bimson and Peter James (e.g., John Bimson, "Can there be a Revised Chronology without a Revised Stratigraphy?" *Society for Interdisciplinary Studies: Proceedings. Glasgow Conference* (April, 1978).

But there is a great deal of other evidence, either missed by Velikovsky and his supporters or not yet published, which fully supports the 500-year gap. Let's look at just a small sample (and I emphasize that it is a small sample) of this material. Most of the material below is covered in much greater detail in my *Ramessides, Medes and Persians* (2001), the volume of *Ages in Alignment* subsequent to this:

- Thutmose III (c.1480 BC.) plunders a temple in Palestine belonging to a city named Kadesh. This sounds like the plundering of Solomon's temple in Jerusalem (also called Kadesh, the "holy") by pharaoh Shishak (c. 925 BC) Gap of c. 555 years.[37]
- Abdi-Ashirta of Amurru (Syria), a contemporary of Amenhotep III (c.1360 BC), has a name identical to Abdastartus (c. 880 BC), a king of Tyre mentioned by Menander of Ephesus. Gap of c. 490 years.[38]
- In Assyrian remains dating from the time of Neo-Assyrian kings Ashurnasirpal II and Shalmaneser III (c. 860 BC) were found scarabs and other artefacts of Eighteenth Dynasty kings, especially of Thutmose III and Amenhotep III (c.1480-1350 BC). Gap of c. 500-600 years.[39]
- Cavalry first shown in the Memphis tomb of Horemheb (c.1310 BC) and in action on the Hypostile Hall of Seti I at Karnak (c.1280 BC) are identical (in terms of equipment and deployment) to the first next appearance of cavalry in the bas-reliefs of Ashurnasirpal II (860 BC). Gap of c. 440 years.[40]
- Full-length mail shirts used in the time of Ramses II (c.1270 BC) are identical to the first next appearance of full-length mail shirts in the time of Shalmaneser III (c.850 BC). Gap of c. 420 years.[41]
- Hilani-house of Nikmepa of Ugarit, a contemporary of Seti I (c.1280 BC), identical in design to next-known hilani-house, of Kilamuwa of Zincirli, a contemporary of Shalmaneser III (c.820 BC). Gap of c. 460 years.[42]

---

[37] The evidence for this is presented in Velikovsky's *Ages in Chaos* (1952).

[38] For Abdastartus of Tyre see Josephus, *Against Apion* i,122

[39] A. H. Layard, *Discoveries in the Ruins of Nineveh and Babylon* (London, 1853), p.282

[40] The cavalry of Ashurnasirpal II is described thus by Gaston Maspero; "The army [of Assyria] ... now possessed a new element, whose appearance on the field of battle was to revolutionize the whole method of warfare; this was the cavalry, properly so called, introduced as an adjunct to the chariotry." *History of Egypt* Vol.VII (London, 1906), p.8. The Hittite cavalry shown on Seti's Hypostile Hall are also deployed as an adjunct to the chariotry.

[41] The long mail shirts illustrated by Ramses II at Karnak are mainly worn by his Hittite opponents, whilst the "Neo-Assyrian" troops of Shalmaneser III are, as I would argue, actually Mitannians. (See my *Ramessides, Medes and Persians*, (New York, 2008), pp.24-9)

[42] See e.g., Ekrem Akurgal, *The Birth of Greek Art* (London, 1968), pp.69-71

Hittite Great King Tudkhaliyas IV, a contemporary of Merneptah (c. 1210 BC), is mentioned regarding preparations for a royal marriage, in Carchemish inscription dating from time of Sukhis II or his son Katuwas — believed by Turkish archaeologist Ekrem Akurgal to be a contemporary of Tiglath-Pileser III (c. 740 BC). Gap of c. 470 years.[43]

Cilician inscription of Azitawatas, mentioning his overlord Awarkus ('Wrks) in Hittite style of 13th century BC but known to date from time of Tiglath-Pileser III (c. 740 BC) because Awarkus is also mentioned (as Urukki) in Assyrian inscriptions of this king. Gap of c. 500 years.[44]

Career of Marduk-apil-iddin (Merodach-Baladan) I (c.1170 BC) a Babylonian prince, virtually identical to that of Marduk-apil-iddin III (c.730–710 BC). Gap of c. 450 years.[45]

Aton-city of Palestine, Hanaton, built by Akhnaton (c.1340 BC) mentioned in Amarna letters and next mentioned in inscription of Tiglath-Pileser III (c. 730 BC). Gap of c. 610 years.[46]

Seti II, a great warrior-pharaoh (c.1200 BC) mentioned by Herodotus (there named Sethos) as being an enemy of Sennacherib (c. 700 BC). Gap of 500 years.[47]

Seti II, who bore the Golden Horus name Aa-neru-emtaunebu (Inaros), had a namesake who was also a warrior-hero during the time of Esarhaddon, and who is mentioned in documents of Ashurbanipal. Gap of 520 years.

Seti II was also called Usikheprure and had a fort named for him at the northeastern border of Egypt — defending the Asiatic frontier. This is mentioned by Esarhaddon (who calls it Ishhupre) (c. 680 BC) and by no one else. Gap of 510 years.[48]

Esarhaddon carves an inscription of his Egyptian conquests at the Dog River immediately beside one of Ramses II recalling his Asiatic conquests, with obvious ironic intent. Gap of c. 580 years.[49]

---

[43] Peter James et al., *Centuries of Darkness* (London, 1991), p.136

[44]   J. D. Hawkins, "The Neo-Hittite States in Syria and Anatolia," in *The Cambridge Ancient History* Vol.1 part 3 (2nd ed), pp.430-1

[45] Merodach-Baladan I lived during the time of Tukulti-Ninurta I and briefly reasserted Babylonian independence after the Assyrian conquest (C. H. W. Johns, *Ancient Babylonia* (Cambridge, 1913), p.102) In the same way, Merodach-Baladan III lived during the time of Tiglath-Pileser III and briefly reasserted Babylonian independence after the Assyrian conquest. Johns. Ibid., p.120

[46]   A. T. Olmstead, *A History of Assyria* (New York, 1923), p.201

[47] Herodotus, ii, 141

[48] Albrecht Alt, "Ishupri" *Orientalistische Literarzeitung* (1925) Nr. 9/10

[49] In *Ramses II and His Time*, Velikovsky mentions the Dog River inscriptions but, contrary to accepted ideas, makes Ramses II's carving come after that of Esarhaddon. This is because he accepted the traditional date of Esarhaddon (early 7th century) whilst placing Ramses II in the early 6th century. I however, in accordance with my proposal of combining the Glasgow Chronology with that of Heinsohn, would place Ramses II in the 6th century

A prince called Wenamon is sent to Byblos by Herihor (c.1080 BC) during a time when Egypt is held in no great esteem abroad and is perhaps a conquered territory. Another prince Wenamon (Unamon) is installed in power by Ashurbanipal immediately after his conquest of the country (c.660 BC). Gap of 420 years.[50]

The reader will note how actual persons (as opposed to art styles, artefacts, etc.) are always almost exactly 450–470 years apart. The apparent exception is Thutmose III and his plunder of the Kadesh ("holy") Temple in Canaan, which is placed almost precisely 555 years after the plunder of Solomon's Temple in Jerusalem.[51] Thus a discrepancy from the other examples of 80–90 years. This can be explained, I believe, by the biblical chronologists according grossly inflated reign-lengths to both Solomon and his father David (each about 40 years). The likelihood of a father and son reigning 80 years consecutively is extremely low, and it is probable that, their epoch being remembered as something of a golden age, their reigns were "expanded" to the numeralogically-sacred span of 40 years. But the inflation of Solomon's and David's reigns knocked early Hebrew history "out of sync" and led later chroniclers to balance things by shortening or even omitting the reigns of several of their successors. This has made it more difficult to establish a precise synchronicity between Egyptian and Hebrew histories in the years between Rehoboam and Jehoshaphat. Nonetheless, it is clear that the evidence cited above, added to the volumes of evidence presented by Velikovsky in *Ages in Chaos* 1 and the other historical works, confirms beyond reasonable doubt that a gap of roughly four and a half to five centuries separates the New Kingdom of Egypt and the parallel history of the Hebrew and Neo-Assyrian kings; a gap that needs to be removed.

(as per Velikovsky), but would see Esarhaddon as an alter ego of Artaxerxes I and would place him in the mid-5th century. Therefore, it was Esarhaddon who was being ironic, as conventional history believes.

[50] For Ashurbanipal's mention of Wenamon, see F. Petrie, *A History of Egypt* Vol.3 (London, 1905), p.299. It should be noted here that a third Wenamon, a contemporary of Darius II, is also known, and is referred to by Velikovsky in *Peoples of the Sea*, pp.129-140. This character triplication calls to mind Gunnar Heinsohn's arguments about the triplication of history, as explained for example in his *Die Sumerer gab es nicht* (Frankfurt, 1988). The triplication, he contends, occurred because the ancient history of the Near East was constructed upon three quite distinct and contradictory dating blueprints; the first millennium being (by and large) dated according to classical sources; the second millennium being dated according to Egyptian Sothic sources, whilst the third millennium dates were supplied by biblically dated Mesopotamian sources.

[51] Wenamon too presents an exception, being only 420 years before his Neo-Assyrian-Age namesake. This is explained, I contend, by the fact that modern historians have placed Wenamon's Twenty-First Dynasty after the Twentieth, whereas in reality it should come, in some cases at least, before. The evidence for this is examined at length by Velikovsky in his *Peoples of the Sea* (1977).

And the above merely scratches the surface. We could, for example, have gone into the detailed evidence from Ugarit (cited in *Ages in Chaos* 1), where texts in alphabetic cuneiform supposedly of the 14th century were composed in a Phoenician dialect virtually indistinguishable from biblical Hebrew of the 8th and 7th centuries. Much scholarly debate has gone into this apparent anomaly, as Velikovsky himself noted. Consider also the precise parallels with 8th/7th century Hebrew in the letter of Amenemope (reign of Ramses II) and the dedicatory inscription in the tomb of Ahiram in Byblos, which also contained artefacts from the time of Ramses II. The debate which raged around these was discussed at some length by Velikovsky in *Ramses II and his Time*. Or we could have gone into the details of Hittite archaeology. The great "Neo-Hittite" cities of northern Syria, dating from supposedly the 9th and 8th centuries, are actually indistinguishable from the Hittite Empire settlements, supposedly of the 15th and 14th centuries. Even worse (and this was fully admitted by Peter James in his "Chronological Problems in the Archaeology of the Hittites" *Society for Interdisciplinary Studies: Proceedings. Glasgow Conference* (April, 1978)), although the Syrian cities were incorporated into the Hittite cultural sphere during the time of the Hittite Empire (by Suppiluliumas I in fact), not a single Syrian city can show an Imperial Hittite stratum underlying the Neo-Hittite stratum. If Imperial Hittite remains are found (e.g., those bearing the name of a Hittite Great King), these are invariably found in a Neo-Hittite context, and the anomaly explained away in some manner or other.

But this brief summary can in no way do justice to the evidence and its quality; for the more deeply we examine each point, the more strongly the original *Ages in Chaos* I position is reinforced.

Consider for example the 500-year gap between the hilani-house of Nikmepa of Ugarit and that of Kilamuwa of Sam'al (modern Zincirli). Nikmepa, a contemporary of Horemheb and Seti I, must have been at the beginning of adopting an architectural style then becoming popular throughout the region of northern Syria and Cilicia. Other princes and potentates from a slightly later period, perhaps contemporary with Ramses II and Merneptah, must also have built hilani-houses. But these have never been found. Why? Is this a problem for the *Ages in Chaos* argument? Quite the contrary, it constitutes powerful evidence in its support.

One of the fundamental principles of *Ages in Chaos* I is that the changeover from the Eighteenth to the Nineteenth Dynasty (during the time of Nikmepa) represents just the point at which the archaeology of northern Syria ceases to be dated along Egyptological lines and commences being dated according to the chronology of Assyria. This is because, following the reign of Akhnaton, Egypt lost her control and influence in the region, with her place being taken first by the Hittites under Suppiluliumas I and later by the Assyrians under Shalmaneser III. From the time of Shalmaneser III, Assyria becomes dominant politically and the art and culture of Mesopotamia prevails. However, this of course is the ruler placed by Velikovsky at the time of the declining Eighteenth Dynasty.

So, the hilani-houses built immediately after those of Nikmepa are indeed found in great abundance throughout the region. They are the hilani-houses raised in the time of Shalmaneser III's immediate successors — in the days of Adad-Nirari III and Tiglath-Pileser III. But these of course are also the houses contemporary with Ramses II and Merneptah.

It is the same with all the evidence. The more closely one investigates each point, the more overwhelming becomes the argument for eliminating a full five centuries.

But even that is not all. It is not simply the strength of each individual point of evidence upon which the *Ages in Chaos* Vol.1/Glasgow edifice is based. Rather, it is the infinitely more powerful accumulated force of all of these together. Even one provable reoccurrence of an individual or an art form after a gap of 500 years would, in itself, be compelling grounds for eliminating these five centuries. However, when such evidence is repeated again and again, one generation after another, in parallel sequence, the accumulated weight of the argument becomes almost irresistible. Each new concurrence does not simply add to the improbability of error but multiplies it by many orders of magnitude. The increase is therefore of a geometric character.

This too was a point stressed by Velikovsky all those years ago, and (like most of what he said) it was ignored by his critics.

CHAPTER 2: HATSHEPSUT, THE QUEEN OF THEBA

A New Perspective

Moving Egyptian history five centuries closer to the present era, to make it agree with biblical time scales, has startling consequences. Characters and events that fill the pages of the Old Testament, whose existence could never be confirmed by archaeologists, now emerge into the full light of day; and the sight is astonishing.

Before looking at these, however, something must be said about the situation in Egypt itself.

The Egypt that emerged from the shadow of Hyksos rule was a revitalized nation. But although Ahmose and Amenhotep I were great warriors, they stopped short at the borders of their own land. There is little if any evidence that these pharaohs sent armies into Asia. It is true that Ahmose had pursued the Hyksos into Avaris, a fortress located in the northeastern corner of the Nile Delta. In addition, it is accepted that some of the action against the Hyksos took place in southern Palestine. Nevertheless, aside from this, neither Ahmose nor Amenhotep I undertook any significant military campaigns in Asia.

In line with his proposed reduction of Egyptian dates by over five centuries, Velikovsky had made the founding of the Eighteenth Dynasty contemporary with the rise of the first kings in Israel, with the time of Saul and David. It was for this reason that he had equated the Hyksos with the Amalekites: these, after all, were the main enemies of Saul and David. Whilst the simple equation of Hyksos = Amalekites was mistaken, it does, nevertheless, seem to be true that Ahmose and the early Eighteenth Dynasty pharaohs had friends and allies in Palestine and that they co-operated with those allies in the war against the Hyksos.[52]

About thirty or so years after the war of liberation, Egypt came to be ruled by a woman. This was Hatshepsut, the stepmother of the underage Thutmose III. And it is here that we come to one of the most spectacular of Velikovsky's synchronisms: For if we remove five centuries from New Kingdom history, we find that Hatshepsut must have been a contemporary of Solomon, the fabulously wealthy and powerful son of King David. It was, for Velikovsky, but a short step from placing Hatshepsut at the same time as Solomon to making her identical to Solomon's famous royal visitor, the Queen of Sheba.

There is no question that Velikovsky's equation of Hatshepsut with the Queen of Sheba was one of his most attractive and dramatic insights. Few biblical characters have captured the imagination of successive genera-tions quite like this woman. For centuries the identity of the queen, who appears but briefly in the Book of Kings, has prompted endless speculating and romanticizing. Whole mythologies have been built around her. For the people of Ethiopia, she is — along with her host Solomon — the ancestor of the native monarchy. The southern Arabs vie with the Ethiopians in claiming her; and they too regard her as their royal forebear. The passing centuries have not diminished her allure, and to this day she holds a unique fascination for many people. Every year sees the publication of new studies propounding supposedly fresh insights into the identity of the bewitching queen. Yet for all that, precious little is known about her. Theories proliferate, but hard facts remain hard to come by.

Our only real knowledge of the Queen comes in a very brief description of her visit to Solomon in the Book of Kings. She is simply identified as the ruler of Sheba who, having heard of the fame of Solomon, came to "try him with hard questions" (I Kings 10:1). She is said to have entered Jerusalem in a great train carrying enormous quantities of treasure. She was then shown around the city, after which Solomon answered her questions. Everything she saw and heard impressed her; and, after being presented with a great quantity of gifts, she departed to her own country. And that is all. The entire story occupies no more than thirteen biblical verses.

---

[52] There is in fact good evidence to suggest that both Amalekites and Philistines were close allies of the Hyksos. This question is examined in some detail in my *Pyramid Age* (1999). Furthermore, the Amalekites mentioned in the Book of Samuel may well have been identical to the Hyksos, as Velikovsky argued, but these have to be differentiated from the "Amalekites" who attacked the Israelites at Rephidim in Arabia, shortly after the Exodus.

With such meager information to go on, it is little wonder that the mythologists and romanticizers have had such scope. Even worse, archaeo-logical investigations over the past century failed to discover anything that could confirm either the queen's or even her host's existence. This must be emphasized. A century of excavation in the lands of the Bible has, far from confirming the existence of David's and Solomon's kingdom, brought it into question. By the time of the publication of *Ages in Chaos*, many biblical scholars had already consigned these two supposedly great kings to the same fairy-land as the Queen of Sheba herself. It was into this climate that, in 1952, Velikovsky produced his dramatic hypothesis. Not only did the Queen of Sheba really exist, but she was one of the most powerful monarchs of her age; and not only her monuments but actual portraits of her remain! If this were to be correct, if the Queen of Sheba really was identical to Hatshepsut, then Velikovsky, by this discovery alone, had made one of the greatest contribu-tions ever to the understanding of ancient Near Eastern history. An achieve-ment worthy of a literary Indiana Jones!

As might be imagined, the reading public was captivated by Velikovsky's hypothesis; and among his academic supporters the identification was long regarded as one of his strongest, as well as most attractive, points. But things were to change. During the late 1970s and early 1980s various criticisms of the identification were published, some by supporters of Velikovsky's ideas, and one at least by a mainstream Egyptologist, David Lorton.[53] By the middle of the 1980s, even some of Velikovsky's hitherto closest academic allies began to question various of the claims made in *Ages in Chaos;* and in 1986 the bomb-shell was dropped. John Bimson, an erstwhile ally of Velikovsky, who had himself produced much evidence in favor of the Ages in Chaos argument, now formally repudiated the "Hatshepsut = Queen of Sheba" equation; and in a trenchant article published in the *Society for Interdisciplinary Studies Review* he systematically demolished, one by one, the arguments Velikovsky had used for the identification.[54] One of the most sturdy pillars of the Ages in Chaos edifice, it seemed, had been pulled down.

In retrospect, there can be no doubt that Bimson's article proved to be a turning point in the whole Velikovsky debate. In the years that followed, no effective rebuttal of Bimson ever appeared. In time, it came to be almost part

---

[53] D. Lorton, "Hatshepsut, the Queen of Sheba, and Immanuel Velikovsky" (1984). Other criticisms were by William H. Stiebing, in *Pensee* 5 (Autumn, 1973) 10-12; Peter James, in *Society for Interdisciplinary Studies Review* 3 (1979), pp. 48-55; and Michael Jones, in *Society for Interdisciplinary Studies Review* 6/1-3 (1982), pp. 27-33

[54] J. Bimson, "Hatshepsut and the Queen of Sheba: A Critique of Velikovsky's Identification and an Alternative View," *Society for Interdisciplinary Studies Review*, 8 (1986)

of accepted wisdom, amongst the British Velikovskians at least, that *Ages in Chaos* had been "debunked."

Yet this was far from being the case. Although detailed and cogently argued, Bimson's case was deeply flawed, and I hope to demonstrate, as we proceed through the present investigation, that his entire thesis rests on a single erroneous proposition.

Fig. 2. Hatshepsut, whose throne-name was Maat-ka-re (pronounced roughly Makare), identified by Velikovsky as the Queen of Sheba.

In the pages to follow, I will not take up the reader's time simply in reiterating the various arguments used by Velikovsky in *Ages in Chaos* for supporting the Hatshepsut = Queen of Sheba equation. That would be superfluous. However, some of the arguments he advanced were unfairly criticized; and where this occurred I will try to set the record straight. I shall also have occasion to look at a great quantity of new evidence, of which Velikovsky himself was unaware, which greatly strengthens the Hatshepsut/Queen of Sheba identification. The reader will find, I hope, that some of this new material will place the latter identification on very solid ground indeed.

A Most Unusual Ruler

The argument for equating Hatshepsut with the Queen of Sheba is given fairly detailed treatment in *Ages in Chaos* Vol.1, but the main points may be summarized as follows:

(1) The archaeology showed that Hatshepsut lived roughly at the same time as Solomon.

(2) She was a female ruler whose kingdom was, basically, to the south of Israel.

(3) One of the most important events of her life was an expedition to a mysterious land called Punt — a region which archaeologists had at one time located in Asia.

(4) Punt was also called the Divine Land, or Land of the God; and Velikovsky argued that this was a general name for the Palestine/Phoenicia region. Thus the expedition to Punt was most probably the same as the Queen of Sheba's expedition to Israel.

(5) One ancient writer, Josephus, claimed that the Queen of Sheba had been the ruler of Egypt and Ethiopia (as was Hatshepsut, who ruled Nubia as far as the Second Cataract).

(6) Ethiopian tradition also claimed the Queen of Sheba as one of theirs; and they named her Makeda, a name not far removed from Hatshepsut's throne name Makera.

Of the above, points (2), (3), (5), and (6) are contested by no one. Everyone accepts that Hatshepsut's kingdom lay more or less to the south of Israel; that one of the most important events of her life was an expedition to a mysterious land called Punt; that Josephus described the Queen of Sheba as ruler of Egypt and Ethiopia; and that the Ethiopian name for this queen, Makeda, is reminiscent of Makera. Nevertheless, although these points are not denied, their importance and significance as evidence is. Thus, John Bimson suggested that Josephus' source for his claim that the Queen of

Sheba ruled Egypt may have been late and corrupt, whilst both he and David Lorton held that the similarity between Makeda and Makera was not close enough to be really significant.

Point (1), the idea that the archaeology demands a reduction of the date of the Eighteenth Dynasty by five centuries, certainly is contested by the critics; yet it is significant that neither Bimson nor Lorton proposed any counter-arguments on this issue. (Note: When writing his own critique of the Hatshepsut/Sheba equation, Bimson still supported Velikovsky's down-dating of the Eighteenth Dynasty, though this support was later withdrawn.) The failure to tackle this question is a crucial omission on the part of the critics, an omission which they have nevertheless failed to acknowledge. More on this below.

The most strongly contested point is (4), the equation of Punt with Israel; and indeed both Lorton and Bimson devote the great majority of space in their articles towards refuting this idea. Clearly they see this as the central question in the whole debate; and it is true that Hatshepsut's description of the expedition to Punt was an important factor leading Velikovsky to making the identification with the Queen of Sheba. Nevertheless, in focusing on the identity of Punt, Lorton and Bimson made a great mistake. This was *not* the most important evidence linking Hatshepsut to the biblical queen. Even if it could be proved beyond question that Punt was not the land of Israel, Hatshepsut's identification with the Queen of Sheba would still be almost certain if the archaeology really did demand down-dating the Eighteenth Dynasty by five centuries. In short, the most crucial evidence, that of absolute chronology, was completely ignored by the critics. In this, they were following a technique familiar from other critics of Velikovsky. Yet this is far from being an academically sound procedure. Part of the strength of Velikovsky's reconstruction — an immensely important part of it — lies in the fact that, following the removal of 500 years from the span of the Egyptian New Kingdom, the histories of Israel and Egypt then formed a precise match, generation by generation, for up to two centuries. Thus the force of the evidence was accumulative and individual points could not really be considered without allusion to the whole.

Consider the following.

It is an undoubted fact that, if a 500-year span is removed from the history of Egypt, Hatshepsut assumes a place in the 10th century BC and becomes a contemporary of Solomon. It is however an even greater certainty that her successor Thutmose III then becomes a contemporary of Solomon's successors Rehoboam and Jeroboam I, and that, as a consequence, he must be identical to the pharaoh named Shishak who plundered Solomon's temple. This cannot be stressed too strongly. Making Hatshepsut contemporary with Solomon may still leave some doubt as to whether she is the Queen of Sheba, but the very same adjustment leaves *no doubt at all* that her stepson Thutmose III is the biblical Shishak; for whereas the Queen of Sheba is nowhere explicitly identified as an Egyptian monarch (or so it is widely believed), Shishak is indeed unequivocally identified as such.

The one identification thus makes the other inevitable. And this is the whole point of *Ages in Chaos*. Even one proven reoccurrence or "matching" of a personality or cultural feature after a gap of five centuries would in itself present a powerful argument for removing those five centuries. But when such reoccurrences repeat themselves generation after generation, in parallel sequence, the force of the argument becomes almost irresistible.[55] Each new parallel does not simply add to the probability that the adjusted chronology is correct, but multiplies it by many orders of magnitude in a geometric progression. This too was a point made by Velikovsky all those years ago; and, like most of what he said, ignored by his critics.

Yet having said that, there is a case for looking at the different identifications proposed in *Ages in Chaos* on an individual basis; for if the picture presented by Velikovsky is correct, each identification should be able to withstand any cross-examination; and in fact, as I hope to demonstrate here (in spite of the assertions of Velikovsky's critics), the identification of Hatshepsut with the Queen of Sheba is rock solid.

Before doing that however I want to look very briefly at another important question: namely the Queen of Sheba's identity and her land of origin. The critics make a major point of denying any suggestion that she was Egyptian. But is this really the case?

The Terms "Queen of Sheba" and "Queen of the South"

In the Bible, Solomon's royal guest is known both as the Queen of Sheba (Book of Kings) and Queen of the South (Gospel of Matthew). Is it possible to identify the queen's origin from these titles? Commentators throughout the centuries have suggested various solutions, though there has never been any general agreement. There is a region in southern Arabia known as Saba, and the natives of that land have long claimed the queen as their own. Yet the people of Ethiopia make a similar claim, and the historian Josephus

---

[55] In *Ages in Chaos* Vol.1, Velikovsky produced literally hundreds of detailed links stretching over the five century gap. This number was added to by some of his erstwhile supporters, such as Peter James and John Bimson (e.g., *Society for Interdisciplinary Studies Review* I:3, II:3, III:1) and over the years by a great many other writers such as Martin Sieff, Alfred De Grazia, Lewis Greenberg, Eddie Schorr, among others. And more recently, in some detail, by myself in *Ramessides, Medes and Persians*.

named Saba as the capital of ancient Nubia (southern Egypt) and claimed that the Queen of Sheba hailed from there.[56] As we shall now see, this author, who is admittedly the oldest written source outside the Bible, was right on the mark: For the Queen of Sheba was almost certainly an Egyptian; and whether or not Hatshepsut, the female "king" who ruled Egypt during one of its most splendid periods was *the* Queen of Sheba and Queen of the South mentioned in the Bible, she was without question *a* queen of Sheba and *a* queen of the South.

Let's look first of all at the term Queen of the South. In his article, Lorton asks the question: "Why would [the Gospel writers] ... have said 'queen of the South' when they might so easily have said 'queen of Egypt'?" In the same vein, Bimson comments on what he describes as "the total lack of reference to Egypt in connection with the Queen of Sheba." "If the visiting queen was Hatshepsut," he says, "she should be described as the Queen of Egypt by the Old Testament writers."[57] If Lorton and Bimson had researched the question more thoroughly, they would have found that the name "ruler of the South" was a recognized biblical term for the Egyptian monarch. Thus for example in the Book of Daniel, the Ptolemaic pharaoh is repeatedly called the "King of the South." It is true that this was not the most common biblical designation for the Egyptian ruler, but its occurrence in Daniel, without any explanatory comments, proves beyond question that it was a well-recognized form.

> And the king of the south shall be strong ... and shall enter into the fortress of the king of the north ... and shall also carry captives into Egypt ... So the king of the south shall come into his own kingdom and return to his own land. (Daniel 11, v.5-9)

So, whether or not Hatshepsut was *the* Queen of the South mentioned in the Solomon story, she was very definitely *a* queen of the South.

She was also, as we shall now see, a queen of Sheba.

The capital of Egypt during the Eighteenth Dynasty was the mighty city of Thebes. Modern Egyptologists still use this name, which is derived from the Greeks. Where the Greeks got it has always been a mystery, since the native name of the metropolis, in the hieroglyphs, is read as *W-s.t* or Waset (the final 't' was unpronounced, so, generally rendered as something like Wase or Washe). Some years ago Lisa Liel of Israel, an authority on both hieroglyphic and cuneiform scripts, pointed out to me that in her opinion the word should be read as Se.wa or She.wa, since the spellings of hieroglyphic

---

[56] Josephus, *Jewish Antiquities* VIII, vi, 2
[57] Bimson, "Hatshepsut and the Queen of Sheba: A Critique of Velikovsky's Identification and an Alternative View," loc. cit., p.11

names vary and in addition are often written not precisely as they should be pronounced. In fact, spellings often had more to do with aesthetics or religious sentiment than with strict phonetics. Thus the name Tutankhamen is actually written as Amen-tut-ankh (since the god's name had to come first) and the names of the Senwosret pharaohs of the Twelfth Dynasty appear in the hieroglyphs as *Wsrt-sn*. One might also note that various pharaohs whose names are made up of the elements Ka-nefer-re are alternately named Nefer-ka-ra (in actual fact the name appears in the hieroglyphs normally as Ra-nefer-ka).

Now, if Thebes' Egyptian name is really Shewa (Sheba), then a whole host of hitherto mysterious facts become comprehensible. First and foremost, we now know where the Greeks got the word Thebes (Theba). A normal linguistic mutation (lisping) turns "s" or "sh" into "th." Thus for example the Persians called Assyria, *Athuria*. Secondly, we know why Josephus called the capital of Ethiopia (i.e., Upper Egypt/Nubia) by the name Saba or Shaba. Finally, we understand the significance of the name of another cult shrine of the god Amon — the oasis of Siwa.

Thus the two titles by which the Queen of Sheba is known in the biblical story clearly identify her as a queen of Egypt. It is simply untrue to say we don't know where she came from. But that is not all. For, as we have seen above, Josephus also described her as "Queen of Egypt and Ethiopia"; and it should be stressed here that in his time "Ethiopia" was the name given to Nubia, i.e., southern Egypt/northern Sudan. Again, in at least three places in the Old Testament Saba is linked to Egypt/Nubia. Thus Gen. 10:7 reads, "The descendants of Chus [Cushites-Nubians] are Saba, Hevila, Regma and Sabathacha." Isaiah 43:3 reports, "I have given Egypt for thy atonement, Ethiopia and Saba for thee," and Isaiah 45:14, "Thus saith the Lord: The labor of Egypt, and the merchandise of Ethiopia, and of Sabaim [people of Saba], men of stature shall come over to thee ..."

It is perhaps significant too, as Eva Danelius pointed out, that Josephus gives the Queen of Sheba's name as Nikaule.[58] Given the fact that the Egyptians had no separate "l" and "r," this could be read as Nikaure, which is reminiscent of Hatshepsut's prenomen Makare. The "Ma" part of Hatshepsut's name is derived from the goddess of truth Ma'at, who was portrayed in a characteristic headdress consisting of two high feathers. As Danelius noted, the only other goddess with a similar headdress was Neith, the great mistress of Sais. "In Josephus' time," she says "Neit had become the leading female deity in Lower Egypt, having absorbed most of the goddesses of an

---

[58] Eva Danelius, "The Identification of the Biblical 'Queen of Sheba' with Hatshepsut, 'Queen of Egypt and Ethiopia'," *Kronos* I, 4 (1977)

earlier period. Thus, it might have happened that the picture of a goddess with a peculiar high headdress, details of which were blurred on a cartouche carved about 1000 years earlier, was taken for the symbol of the goddess Neit and the first syllable of Hatshepsut's prenom read accordingly."[59] In short, read as Neit-ka-ra. Since the "t" was not pronounced, this would have been vocalized something like Ni-ka-ra — i.e., identical to Nikaule. Danelius notes also that "Wilkinson, one of the first Egyptologists to read the cartouches at Deir el-Bahari, thought, too, that the picture of the goddess was that of Neit, and read the queen's name accordingly: Neit-go-ri."

Fig. 3. Makeda (top) and Makera written in Phoenician (old Hebrew) script.

Although modern Ethiopia (Abyssinia) is not to be equated with Josephus' Ethiopia, the people of that region had much to say about the Queen of Sheba. According to them, the latter was ruler of both Egypt and modern Ethiopia — Abyssinia — and she returned to her home pregnant with Solomon's child. They too provided a name for the Queen: Makeda. Velikovsky of course drew attention to the close similarity between Makeda and Hatshepsut's throne-name Makare or Makera, but, as with his other arguments, this was dismissed as being irrelevant. The similarity, it was declared, was simple coincidence. However, in view of the fact that the Abyssinian source of this history, the Kebra Nagast, is known to contain much material actually derived from Egypt, as well as other regions in the Middle East, we should perhaps look again at what they have to say. It is an undoubted fact that much of what we find in the Kebra Nagast represents translations of translations from Egyptian, Hebrew, Aramaic, Arabic, etc; and, in this context, it is worth pointing out, is worth pointing out, as Don Stewart has remarked,[60] that in the early Phoenician or Hebrew script the letters "d" and "r" are strik-

---

[59] Ibid., p.11. Bimson (loc. cit., p.23) claims that Josephus' Nikaule is more probably derived from Herodotus' Nitokris. This is quite possible, but in no way does it invalidate Danelius' point, since Nitokris herself — identified by Herodotus as a sole queen among numerous male rulers — stands a very good chance of being another alter ego of Hatshepsut/Makere.

[60] Don Stewart, "Hatshepsut is the Queen of Sheba," December, 2008 at www.donstewart-research.blogspot. Stewart notes, in the same place, that evidence from the Old Testament shows that the two letters were in fact confused on several occasions by scribal editors. Thus in 2 Samuel 23:11, "Shammah...the Hararite" is "Shammah the Harodite" in 2 Samuel 23:25, whilst Hadar son of Ishmael in Genesis 25:15 is Hadad in I Chronicles 1:30.

ingly similar and could easily have been confused. Both are left-facing trian-gles, with the "r" sporting a small tail. However, on occasion, the "d" was also written with a short tail. As such, the two letters could easily have been confused — especially by a scribe whose native language was not Hebrew.

Before moving on, there is one more point that needs to be stressed. The context within which the Queen of Sheba story appears in itself constitutes evidence which cannot be ignored. The Queen of Sheba who visited Solomon was the ruler of an important and powerful kingdom. This is proved beyond question by the amount of space devoted to her in the biblical account and precludes the possibility that she was the queen of some desert principality in southern Arabia. Solomon no doubt entertained many princes and prin-cesses from Arabia and other areas, but their visits are not recorded because they lacked significance. From the importance placed on the Queen of the South's visit, it is evident that she must have been the ruler of an extremely powerful nation. This alone would point to Egypt and would, I suggest — even without the evidence mentioned above — be sufficient to identify her as an Egyptian monarch.

Sheba, City of the Sphinx

We have stated that Thebes seems to have originally been known as Sheba by the Egyptians and that Josephus gave the name Saba to the capital of Nubia. Biblical passages furthermore apparently connect "Saba" to the region of Nubia. Now the question must be asked: Was Sheba a Nubian name; and if so, what did it imply?

The Nubian provenance of the name "Shaba" or "Sheba" is rather obvi-ously illustrated by two of the great warrior-pharaohs of the Twenty-Fifth Dynasty, Shabaka and Shabataka. This would suggest that Sheba/Theba derived its name from the Nubian language, a fact which should come as no surprise, given the rather well-accepted Nubian origin of the Eigh-teenth Dynasty, the line of kings which had its home and base in Thebes.[61] So for example the blue war-crown or *khepresh*, which was introduced into pharaohnic iconography by the Eighteenth Dynasty kings, is widely believed to represent a negro hair-style.

Flinders Petrie was of the opinion that pharaoh Shabaka's name derived from a Nubian word meaning "wild cat" and that the word was actually pronounced something like "Shab" or "Shaba," given that the "ka" element

---

[61] See eg. F. Petrie, *The Making of Egypt* (London, 1039), p.155

was merely the definite article, an element usually omitted in common speech.[62] Could it be that Thebes was called after a species of wild-cat?

Greek legend told how the city of Thebes was plagued by a ferocious man-eating monster with a woman's head and the body of a lion or lioness. Velikovsky argued convincingly and in great detail that this legend — that of Oedipus — belonged in Egypt; that the city of Thebes referred to was the Egyptian metropolis and not its tiny Greek namesake.[63] Certainly no one denies that the sphinx is an Egyptian rather than a Greek creature. Now the sphinx, known in the Egyptian language as *Heru-em-akhet* (Harmachis), seems to have been originally identical to Sekhmet, a lioness pure and simple. The human head was a later refinement. Sekhmet was a much-feared deity, believed to represent the destructive power of Ra. In early representations the goddess is portrayed with a long serpentine neck, often intertwined with that of another long-necked feline. It is thus apparent that the beast was in some ways dragon-like or linked to dragon iconography.

The name sphinx is of course Greek, said to derive from the verb *sphingein*, "to bind tight," by reason of the creature's supposed reputation for killing by strangulation. This explanation seems somewhat strained, and it would lead us to look, perhaps, for an Egyptian etymology.[64] Yet the word cannot be derived from Sekhmet, which is what would be expected in the case of a borrowed Egyptian deity. It seems likely, in my opinion, that the term derives from the Nubian shaba, "cat," or rather shabak, "the cat."[65] What could be more appropriate than that the great metropolis, the home of a sphinx cult and sphinx-myth, should also derive its very name from the same creature?[66]

God's Land and Syria/Palestine

It may well then be that Hatshepsut was queen of the city Sheba and that, as ruler of Egypt, she would have been known — to the Jews of the

---

[62] "The present Nubian for the male wild cat is *Sab*, and *ki* is the article post-fixed. Hence in popular talk it is very likely that the king was known as Sab or Shab, just as the hieroglyphic name Pilak lost its article in the common mouth and became Philae." Petrie, *A History of Egypt* Vol.3, p.284. The "Shaba" part of Shabaka's name is admittedly spelled differently to that of the great metropolis. But this offers no real objection, as variant spellings are to be expected.

[63] Velikovsky, *Oedipus and Akhnaton* (1960).

[64] Nonetheless, since human beings were apparently sacrificed to the sphinx deity, the binding of such victims makes *sphingein* a very likely etymological origin of the word.

[65] But even should "sphinx" have a Greek etymology, this would not affect the likelihood that the city Sheba/Theba derived its name from the Nubian version of the creature, namely Shaba, the "wild cat."

[66] It should be remarked that the Egyptian crocodile-god Sebek bears a name similar to that of Shaba-ka. This may be more than coincidental, given the serpentine, dragon-like qualities of the early sphinx-creature.

first couple of centuries BC and AD — as a "queen of the south." But now we must ask the question: Was the queen of Egypt who visited Solomon one and the same as Hatshepsut? Velikovsky's proposed subtraction of five centuries from the Egyptian chronology made the identification absolutely essential. If Hatshepsut lived 500 years closer to our time, then she *must* have been a contemporary of Solomon.

Now it so happens that one of the most important events of Hatshepsut's life appears to have been a great expedition to a foreign land. It is quite evident that Hatshepsut regarded this journey as a seminal event of her reign, for she commemorated it (and very little else, aside from her divine birth) in her great funerary temple at Deir el-Bahri. The queen's description of this country, as found in the temple, verges on the ecstatic, and it is in many ways reminiscent of the language used by mystics. She calls it her "place of delight" and a "glorious region of God's Land." Whether or not the queen actually went on the journey has been debated for years, but if she did not, we must wonder why it was accorded such prominence in her own funerary monument. This alone strongly suggests that she did go on the trip (contrary to Lorton's and Bimson's suggestion that she did not).[67] It is also strongly suggestive in other ways. The prominent position occupied by this event in Hatshepsut's funerary monument in itself constitutes powerful evidence against the proposal of Velikovsky's critics that the destination of the expedition was a semi-primitive region near the southern end of the Red Sea.

The actual journey, which involved a sea voyage, was to a land alternately named Punt (*Pwene*) and the Divine Land (*Ta Netjer* — or, as Lorton has rightly translated, the Land of the God). Leaving aside for one minute the origin of the word Punt (to which Lorton and others devote an enormous amount of speculation), it needs to be stated here and now that the Divine Land or the Land of the God is unequivocally and unanimously identified by Egyptologists with the district comprising the territories between the Sinai Peninsula and Lebanon. Even Lorton himself admits the term to be a "reference to lands lying to the east of Egypt: especially Punt and the lands of incense, but not seldom also to Sinai and the Lebanon region."[68] I would, for further confirmation, direct the reader to the pages of the *Cambridge Ancient History*, where the country's location is discussed at some length. Thus in the words of Margaret S. Drower, "To the Egyptians, Byblos was the key to 'God's

---

[67] It is perhaps significant that 'Fragments of texts relating to a foreign campaign of Hatshepsut' have been found on the north side of Hatshepsut's lower colonnade. Gay Robins, *The Art of Ancient Egypt* (British Museum Press, 1997), p.126

[68] Adolph Erman and Hermann Grapow eds., *Wörterbuch der aegyptischen Sprache* Vol. V (Leipzig, 1926-1963), p.225.

Land, the Lebanon on whose steep slopes grew the timber they coveted."[69] The term Land of the God is unusual, and one popularly accepted suggestion is that the territory acquired its name by virtue of the resins and gums (from Lebanon cedars) which the Egyptians imported for use in embalming and other rituals. But the region's location in Palestine/Lebanon is not doubted, and is confirmed by literally scores, if not hundreds, of Egyptian texts. I will not burden the reader with an exhaustive overview of these, but two or three should serve to illustrate. Thus Thutmose III wrote:

> When my majesty crossed over to the marshes of Asia, I had many ships of cedar built on the mountains of God's Land near the Lady of Byblos.[70]

Again, an official of Thutmose III left an inscription of a commission which he undertook to secure cedar from Lebanon. He wrote:

> I brought away [(timber of) 60 cubits in [their] length ... I [brought] them [down] from the high-land of God's Land.[71]

An inscription of Thutmose IV tells of:

> Presenting the tribute of Retenu [Palestine] and the produce of the northern countries: silver, gold, turquoise, and all the costly stones of God's Land ...[72]

In order to get round this, Lorton suggests that God's Land (*Ta Netjer*) was a term used to describe many regions — much as one might describe any favorite locality as "God's country." So he asserts that "it cannot be argued from the fact that *ta-netjer* is attested in reference to Asiatic regions that Punt was located in Asia." And so, in these words, Lorton transforms *Ta Netjer* into a simple figure of speech. But this is intellectual sleight of hand. We cannot transfer the habits and usage of the profane modern age onto the Egyptians. The Egyptians would not have misused the word "god" in such a way; and certainly not on official royal and religious inscriptions (imagine an American president unveiling a monument in Washington DC describing his home state as 'God's Country'). Besides which, as Lorton himself is so keen to emphasize, *Ta Netjer* means the "land of the god." Which god? one might ask! This cannot be a generalized term like today's "God's country." This was a specific territory associated with a specific deity. But which deity?

---

[69] eg. Margaret S. Drower, "Syria Before 2200 BC," in *The Cambridge Ancient History* Vol.1 part 2 (3rd ed.), p.346
[70] Pritchard, op cit., p.240
[71] Ibid., p.243
[72] Ibid., p.249

The word netjer or "god" in Egyptian is said to be related to the word natron (Greek natrin), a substance used in the embalming process. Some at least of the materials used in embalming came from Phoenicia, specifically from the cedars of Lebanon. Now according to Egyptian tradition, the first being to be mummified was the god Osiris, whose body was floated down the Nile in a wooden casket and washed ashore at Byblos. For this reason, Byblos was a region sacred to the god and his cult. It was there that the body of Osiris was encased in the trunk of a tamarisk tree and it was there that his beloved wife Isis journeyed to retrieve it. But Osiris was also closely linked to the Arabah, the Valley of the Dead Sea. As Lewis Greenberg and others have noted, at least two of the essential ingredients of the mummification process were obtained there: bitumen and natron salt.[73] Furthermore, the Djed Column, which was viewed as the "spine" of Osiris, and was ritually covered in natron salt, seems to have been thematically connected with the salt-pillars found on the shores of the Dead Sea and associated in Jewish tradition with Lot's wife. And even the word natron is instructive; for it ultimately derived from the Egyptian netjer ("god"), a term particularly linked to Osiris. Thus in 1973 Siegfried Morenz found it "striking that the most human of gods, Osiris, is called netjer in a particular context: in quite a number of puns this word is used almost as though it were his name."[74]

So, in the Egyptian language the word netjer is linked to the god Osiris and also to natron, the salt used in mummification and largely derived from the Dead Sea, whilst in numerous other sources Byblos, the city sacred to Osiris, is linked to and considered to be the key to Ta Netjer, the Land of the God.

This alone should be sufficient reason to end the debate. Punt *is* the Land of Netjer (Osiris), and the Land of Netjer is Palestine/Lebanon. Yet, as we saw, whilst conceding that Ta Netjer is connected with Palestine/Phoenicia, Velikovsky's critics insist that the term was also used in connection with another, southern, land which they say is Punt. It is further asserted that whilst Ta Netjer is frequently identified as Palestine/Phoenicia, Punt is never so identified and is clearly a separate region lying to the south of Egypt. What are we to make of such claims?

---

[73]Lewis M. Greenberg, "The Land of Punt Redux," *Society for Interdisciplinary Studies, Review* No. 2 (2018). Greenberg (ibid.) even suggests that the name Zion may honor Osiris, as On (Wen) was one of Osiris' titles See also, Tine M. Niemi, Zvi Ben-Avraham, and Joel Gat, (eds.) *The Dead Sea: The Lake and Its Setting* (Oxford, 1997), p. 251. Also J. Rullkoetter and A. Nissenbaum, "Dead Sea asphalt in Egyptian mummies: Molecular evidence," *Naturwissenschaften* (2004).

[74] Siegfried Morenz, *Egyptian Religion* (Cornell University Press, 1973), p. 19.

A substantial body of evidence, generally ignored or dismissed by Velikovsky's critics, leaves us in no doubt that Punt is as strongly identified with Palestine/Phoenicia as is Ta Netjer.

Various statements in Egyptian literature clearly link Punt to Phoenicia and Palestine. Velikovsky himself noted an official of the Sixth Dynasty who casually remarked that he had visited Punt and Byblos eleven times,[75] and in fact no less than three Old Kingdom texts speak of Byblos and Punt in connection with each other.[76] In addition, and this is a point even Lorton has to concede, Punt is *always* described as being to the east of Egypt, whilst a whole series of documents, Bimson admits, place Punt in the north, and specifically associate the region with known cities in Syria.[77]

But Hatshepsut herself identifies Punt with Lebanon, and this is a fact strangely overlooked by the critics. Thus in one well-known inscription she writes;

> The myrrh of Punt has been brought to me ... all the luxurious marvels of this country were brought to my palace in one collection ... They have brought me the choicest products ... of cedar, of juniper and of meru-wood; ... all the goodly sweet woods of God's Land.[78]

Everywhere else when Hatshepsut uses the term God's Land, it is not denied that she is referring to Punt. But here, because she talks of the cedar of God's Land, it is claimed that on this occasion she is referring to somewhere else, namely Lebanon.

With equal clarity Thutmose III describes Punt as located in Palestine/Syria. Three years after his sixth campaign (in which he conquered northern Syria), the pharaoh returned to Palestine to gather the levy. Immediately after describing the tribute obtained from Shinar and Kheta and the land of Naharin (northern Syria), the register reads: "Marvels brought to his majesty in the land of Punt in this year: dried myrrh ..."[79]

---

[75] J. A. Montgomery, *Arabia and the Bible* (Philadelphia, 1934), p.176 n.28

[76] P. E. Newberry, "Three Old Kingdom Travellers to Byblos and Punt," *Journal of Egyptian Archaeology* 24 (1938). Newberry denies that these texts prove Byblos and Punt to be adjacent, and claims that they should be read as showing only that these travellers had been in the northernmost (Byblos) and the southernmost (Punt) parts of the world known to the Egyptians.

[77] Cf. R. Giveon, *Les Bédouins Shoshou des documents égyptiens* (Leiden, 1971) docs. 6, 20, 20b. Predictably enough, as Bimson tells us, Giveon tries to reinterpret the clear statement of the texts that Punt was in the north by claiming a scribal error. This is a familiar 'solution,' used also by Newberry to discount the testimony of the Sixth Dynasty official who claimed to have visited Punt and Byblos eleven times (though in the latter case Newberry argues that it was the error of a modern translator that was to blame).

[78] J. H. Breasted, *A History of Egypt* (2nd ed., London, 1951), p.280

[79] J. H. Breasted, *Ancient Records of Egypt* Vol. 2, Sec.486

One of the deities most closely identified by the Egyptians with Byblos was the goddess Hathor. In literally scores of inscriptions Hathor is described as the "Mistress (or Lady) of Byblos."[80] Yet a substantial number of Egyptian texts (and this is admitted by Lorton) also describe Hathor as the "Mistress of Punt." Thus, one oft-quoted poem to Hathor praises her thus:

> Your eyes have felled the Nubians,
>
> Oh, great mistress of Punt,
>
> Delightful source of the north wind,
>
> Mistress of the pleasant air.[81]

To the above we may also note an inscription in Wadi Gasus, which refers to Sesostris I as "beloved of Hathor, mistress of Punt."[82]

So, Hathor was equally the "Lady of Byblos" and the "Lady of Punt"; in much the same way as the Byblos region was "God's Land" and Punt too was "God's Land." But this begs the question: Why was Byblos/Lebanon thus specially linked to Hathor? In her own myth, Hathor was commissioned by Ra to destroy mankind. She set about the work so effectively that he repented of his action and devised a plan to save the remnants of the human race. A powerful beer, dyed red to resemble blood, was spilled over the earth. Hathor drank this and, believing it to be the blood of humanity, desisted from her work of destruction. It is surely significant in this context that the name "Phoenicia" is said to be derived from a word (Greek *phoinos*) implying "blood-red." This was probably a popular etymology relying on the fact that *phoinos* sounded a bit like Punt (*Pwene*), a land which, coincidentally enough, was also linked to a goddess who turned the world red.

Hatshepsut was a great devotee of the goddess Hathor and her journey to Punt was in large part a pilgrimage to the land of her tutelary deity. This is an extremely important factor to which we shall return when we come to consider the reporting of the expedition at Deir el-Bahri.

In addition to all this, a whole series of Egyptian documents, dating mainly from the New Kingdom, clearly and unequivocally place Punt in Palestine or Palestine/Phoenicia. John Bimson, we saw, was aware of this material but failed to quote from it in his critique of Velikovksy. David Lorton failed even to mention its existence, and Lorton's behavior is rather typical of mainstream Egyptologists. Bimson himself briefly explained why the texts were ignored, when he quoted R. Giveon as asserting they had to be the result of a scribal error (or errors).

---

[80] See for example, Pritchard (ed.) *Ancient Near Eastern Texts*, pp.240,243
[81] Paule Krieger (French trans. of Siegfried Schott), *Les chants d'amour de l'Egypte Ancien* (Paris, 1956), p.97
[82] El-Sayed Mahfouz, *Revue d'egyptologie* 29 (1977): 159-160.v

---

In more recent years these texts received a full-blooded reappraisal in the form of an article titled "Locating Punt" by author Dimitri Meeks in David O'Connor's and Stephen Quirke's *Mysterious Lands (Encounters with Ancient Egypt)* (2003). Meeks, who is not, by the way, a supporter of Velikovsky, goes to the original sources, bypassing conventional wisdom as found in the textbooks and guidebooks, and what he finds is most illuminating. He notes, to begin with, that "Texts locating beyond doubt in the south are in the minority, but they are the only ones cited in the current consensus on the location of the 'country.' All other texts [that locate Punt to the north or northeast], despite their large number, have been ignored."[83]

The texts placing Punt "beyond doubt" in the south will be examined in due course.

Meeks proceeds to highlight several toponym lists at Soleb, beginning with one of Amenhotep III, which clearly "locate Punt closely to the north of Egypt among places [where] Punt appears to be either between Pehal [in Transjordan] and Shosou, or in the sequence Mitanni, Shosou, Kadesh, Punt, Qutna, Tahse, Yenoam ..." "Curiously," says Meeks, "these sequences seem to have sometimes been taken unquestioningly to be the result of error on the part of scribes and sculptors ..." However, "Numerous [other] texts, from at least the Middle Kingdom onwards, describe Punt as the land of the rising sun and locate it in the East, equating it with the eastern horizon."[84]

Centuries after the time of Amenhotep III, Punt is mentioned again, in the monuments of the Ptolemies: "Once the construction of the temple of Edfu was completed, the priests decided to have inscribed on its walls an historic account of the events which marked the ... years that the work had taken. ... In connection with the dynastic feuds between Ptolemy IX Soter and Ptolemy X Alexander I, they note laconically in relation: 'he fled to Punt, his older brother took possession of Egypt and was crowned king again'.... Other sources record that Ptolemy X [then] fled to Cyprus, but Egyptologists have only mentioned the apparent [north-south] contradiction without further comment.... However ignorant one might assume Egyptian priests to be, they could scarcely have confused an island north of Egypt [Cyprus] with the depths of Africa."[85] Punt is mentioned again, this time in the Roman period, and once again it is clearly located in Syria/Palestine. Here the region is listed "between Upper Retjenou, corresponding to Palestine, and Pa Bekhen, the mountainous northern part of Mesopotamia ... on the one side and Beiber or Babylon (?) — or a place name in southern Palestine." In Meeks' words, "All

[83] Dimitri Meeks, "Locating Punt," in David B. O'Connor and Stephen Quirke (eds.) *Mysterious Lands (Encounters with Ancient Egypt)* (University of California Press, 2003), p. 58
[84] Ibid., pp. 56-7
[85] Ibid., p. 69

these texts agree in assigning Punt and its inhabitants to the Near East in more or less direct contact with the land of the Mediterranean coast."[86]

The obvious conclusion is that, "The hypothesis of an African location for the land of Punt is based on extremely fragile grounds. It is contradicted by numerous texts and has only become an established fact of Egyptology because no-one has taken into account the full range of evidence on the subject. ... The only way to reconcile all the data is to locate Punt in the Arabian Peninsula. The territory of Punt began quite close to that of Egypt, once Sinai had been crossed, in Arabia Petraea or the Negev [in southern Israel]."

That's fairly precise, but can we be even more so?

The Frankincense Terraces of Palestine

A major objective of Hatshepsut's expedition to Punt was the acquisition of incense trees (*anti*) for transplanting in Egypt. This is stressed again and again at Deir el-Bahri. Incense was of course essential to temple ritual and we cannot doubt that God's Land was so named at least in part because of its association with this sacred material. In the Deir el-Bahri reliefs the incense trees are depicted being loaded onto the Egyptian ships, whilst upon completion of the successful journey the inscription describes how "the best of myrrh is upon all her [Hatshepsut's] limbs, her fragrance is divine dew, her odour is mingled with that of Punt."[87]

Now, in modern times, frankincense grows wild in southern Arabia and north-east Africa, and this was one of the major reasons for looking south in the search for Punt. This is commonsense, since the shrub will only flourish in tropical conditions. However, as Velikovsky stated, there are very good reasons to believe that in antiquity the shrub was also cultivated in the Jordan Valley the lowest point on the surface of the earth, a stiflingly hot region where, to this day, plants otherwise associated with the tropics grow in abundance. Ancient literature, Egyptian, biblical and classical, repeatedly identifies Palestine as a source of incense. Thus after his fifth inspection of conquered Syria and Palestine, Thutmose III listed frankincense, oil, honey and wine as tribute. After his ninth visit he stated that he had received as "Retenu [Palestinian] tribute of this year" horses, chariots, various silver vessels of the workmanship of the country, and also "dry myrrh, incense 693 jars, sweet oil and green oil 2080 jars, and wine 608 jars."[88] Thutmose III again refers to the great amounts of incense he took from Palestine after his seventh campaign.

---

[86] Ibid., p. 65
[87] Breasted, *Records* Vol. 2, p.274
[88] Ibid., Vol. 2, Sec.451

Fig. 4. Hatshepsut's magnificent funerary monument, the Djeser-djeseru ('Splendor of Splendors'), where the incense trees from Punt were transplanted.

In the biblical Song of Songs, the enamored prince says to the little shepherdess, "Until the day break, and the shadows flee away, I will get me to the mountain of myrrh, and to the hill of frankincense" (4:6).

Where is the 'mountain of myrrh'?

Frankincense (olibanum) falls in clear drops which, when gathered and formed into balls or sticks, turn white. For this reason, the precious incense is called 'white' in various languages (Greek, Arabic) as well as in Hebrew/Phoenician (*lebana*, white). Velikovsky identified Lebanah, near Beth-el (Judges 21:19), with the 'mountain of myrrh' referred to in the Song of Songs, but it would appear that the entire Jordan Valley, whose steep sides descend over four hundred meters from the hill country of Judea and Samaria, was anciently covered in terraces devoted to the growing of frankincense and other exotic shrubs. Various classical sources refer to the intense production of incense in the region between Jericho and Jerusalem, where many of the ancient terraces are still visible and in use.[89] According to Yadin Roman, editor of Israeli natural history journal *Eretz*, "the Jordan Valley was a major

---

[89] Much of ancient Israel was heavily terraced for agriculture. See for example, L. E. Stager, "The Archaeology of the Family in Ancient Israel," *Bulletin of American School of Oriental*

center for the growth of these products [myrrh and frankincense]," whilst "Around Ein Gedi, Jericho, Phasaelis and other Jordan Valley sites extensive agricultural installations have been found for the cultivation of these spices... "[90] These "agricultural installations" were of course hillside terraces, which can be plainly viewed in the area to this day. Interestingly, although in my letter of enquiry to Mr. Roman I had made no mention of Hatshepsut and her "myrrh terraces," he nevertheless pointed out that the incenses and spices of the Jordan Valley led to it being "coveted by Queen Cleopatra of Egypt."

It is therefore untrue to state that southern Arabia was the only source of frankincense known to the ancient world: a far closer and richer source of the precious resin was found in Israel, a source apparently exploited as early as Egypt's Early Dynastic Age. And in this context we should note the passage in Genesis where the Ishmaelites who carry Joseph into Egypt are on their way from Gilead with "aromatic gum balm and myrrh" (Genesis 37:25). Gilead is recognized as the country on the east bank of the Jordan.

To recap briefly, not only were both Punt and Palestine/Lebanon specifically connected with the gods Osiris and Hathor, but both regions were also associated with terraced hillsides and incense trees. Even without the other evidence, these parallels would in themselves be sufficient to force an identification.

There remains to be mentioned the name Punt (*Pwenet*) itself, which, as Velikovsky stressed, has obvious parallels with the word Phoenicia. I will not on this issue address the hair-splitting and semantics of Velikovsky's critics, but will leave it to the reader to decide for himself whether he feels it likely that a link exists between the two names (remember, the Romans fought Punic wars against the Phoenician people of Carthage). Lorton, it should be remarked, was at great pains to point out that the "w" in Pwenet is a consonant, not a vowel, and that the word could not therefore be equated with "Phoenicia." He seems to have forgotten however that the word Punic in English is pronounced "pyunic," i.e., with the second letter being the consonant "y."

Thutmose III's List of Conquered Lands

Both Lorton and Bimson, as well as the entire Egyptological establishment, assert that the name Punt is found in Egyptian documents associated with a southern territory. Did the Egyptians know of a Punt in the south?

Research, Vol. 260, Issue 260 (1985); also Naomi F. Millar, *The Archaeology of Garden and Field* (University of Pennsylvania Press, 1984), p. 64
[90] Personal communication, 2nd October, 2009.

In actual fact, before the discovery of the Hatshepsut temple at Deir el-Bahri, it was universally assumed that Punt lay in Asia, with most authorities placing it somewhere in Arabia. However, the reliefs at Deir el -Bahri seemed to point to Africa, and this caused a rethink. All the evidence that had hitherto identified Punt with Asia was now either ignored or downplayed. Even worse, there was now a concerted effort to find inscriptional justification for this geographic relocation. In time, it became part of received wisdom that a number of Egyptian documents do indeed tell of a Punt in the south.

A search of the evidence shows that in fact there are but two, both of which shall now be addressed.

The more important of these is the famous victory lists of Thutmose III in the temple of Amon at Karnak, a series of documents whose importance was emphasized at great length by David Lorton. The lists in question, copied three times, record the names of all the foreign nations and city-states conquered by Thutmose III in his first year. The subjugated regions are not enumerated haphazardly but follow a definite sequence. In fact, they are named according to their geographical location. Thus, one of the lists, on the northwest facade of the seventh pylon, begins (following Lorton's translation):

> Summary of the foreign countries of Upper Retenu, which his majesty had shut up in the town of doomed Megiddo, and whose children his majesty had brought back as living captives to the town ... in Karnak, in his first campaign of victory, as his father Amon, who led him to the goodly roads, had commanded.

It would appear that Upper Retenu is the Egyptian term for the mountainous or upland regions of Palestine/Syria, very probably the Lebanese mountains. Megiddo itself is in the land of Israel, but a coalition of northern princes apparently had come to the aid of the people of Palestine.

After listing the conquered states and cities of Upper Retenu, Thutmose goes on to enumerate states closer to Egypt. He ends, according to Lorton (and this is accepted by Egyptologists in general), with a quite separate and corresponding list of southern states, similarly conquered in the first year. This list begins:

> Summary of these southern foreign countries of the Nubian 'Iwntyw — people of Khenthenopher whom his majesty had slaughtered, a massacre made of them, the numbers not known, all their inhabitants

brought back as living captives to Thebes to fill the workhouse of his father Amon-Re lord of the Two Lands.

Thus there appear to be two separate lists, one comprised of regions to the north of Egypt and the other of regions to the south of Egypt. Somewhat triumphantly, Lorton announces that in all three copies of these lists Punt is clearly and unequivocally placed as the forty-eighth land of the "southern" list. The evidence of these lists, he says, is "in and of itself sufficient to demonstrate that the thesis of Chapter III of *Ages in Chaos* [where Velikovsky claims Hatshepsut = Queen of Sheba] cannot be correct."

If the lists said what Lorton claims they say, then perhaps there would be some weight to his argument. But the fact is that they do not say what he claims. Before examining what the lists really say, let's look carefully at what he says about them.

First and foremost, he says that there are two separate lists, copied three times, of the northern and southern states conquered by Thutmose III.

Secondly, he says that the three lists are identical, and that they all clearly and unequivocally place Punt along with the southern (Nubian) states.

Statement (a) is in fact only partly correct. There are indeed two lists, but they are not entirely separate, in that one list always and only names northern states and the other always and only names southern states. More on this in due course. Statement (b) is quite simply untrue, and with this assertion Lorton is committing an act of *legerdemain* on his readers. Let's look at what he says about the lists. "The three lists," he claims, "are identical, the only differences among them being minor orthographic variations." He continues, "I have quoted the introductory passages at length to show that, despite some variation in wording and some loss of text, the variants are nevertheless explicit as to the fact that one of these is a list of northern countries and the other a list of southern countries."

It is with good reason that Lorton emphasizes the importance of the introductory passages, for it is there that we are told of the lists' contents. But the "minor variation" in wording of the introductions, which Lorton presumably hopes the reader will not question too much, is in fact a *major* variation in wording. Lorton, remember, bases his argument on the assertion that there are two entirely separate lists, one of the northern regions, the other of the southern, and that these lists are copied identically three times. But let's look at what the introduction to the register on the southwest facade of the seventh pylon says: "Summary of these *southern and northern* foreign countries whom his majesty had slaughtered." Lorton's comment gives the game away: "For reasons of space in this particular case, the last part of the northern list had to be placed with the southern list." This, I would suggest, hardly constitutes a "minor orthographic variation." The fact that "in this case" the last part of the northern list "had to be placed with the southern list" in fact invalidates his entire argument. Evidently there are not two separate lists, but one continuous list, beginning with Thutmose III's most northerly conquests and ending with his most southerly.

In order to properly understand these registers, the reader should consider the following. The vast majority of the territories and cities conquered by Thutmose III were in Asia, in the region of Syria/Palestine. Therefore, we must suppose that these would take up much more space in his inscriptions than the cities of Nubia. Therefore, quite probably in *all three* copies of the lists, we must expect that "for reasons of space" the "northern" list will overflow into the "southern." That this is so is, as we have seen, explicitly stated on one occasion. On another copy of the "southern" list the introduction, as Lorton himself admits, is lost. Which leaves only *a single list* to which Lorton can point to in support of his thesis.

The reader himself will by now, I am sure, be less certain of accepting anything Lorton has to say. His statement that three copies of the Thutmose III lists clearly place Punt to the south of Egypt is exposed as being simply untrue.

I would, at this stage, ask the reader to consider the following: In Velikovsky's theory Punt is identified as Palestine: in other words, the southernmost of Thutmose III's Asiatic conquests. Now if, as we say, these lists are in fact simply one long list, in a geographical north to south sequence, we must assume that in all of the copies Punt/Palestine will be placed right next to the cities of Nubia, which come next geographically to his southernmost Asiatic conquests: and this of course is exactly what we do find. On the other hand, there is a distinct possibility that the word 'Punt,' which would appear to come at the end of the list of northern territories, is a wide geographical designation intended to inform the reader to the effect that all the territories listed prior were in the region of Punt.

How then do we explain the one copy of the register where Punt is indeed apparently placed in the south? Since I myself have not seen the inscriptions in question, I have to take Lorton's word for certain things. Now one of the things he does stress is that in all three copies of the lists Punt is placed as the forty-eighth region of the second or so-called "southern" list. But if Punt occupies an identical position in all three copies, this must mean that all three copies are in fact, just as we surmised, an identical list of "southern and northern" regions. That one of these inscriptions is introduced as simply a list of southern regions can, I would suggest, be explained in the following way. The scribes and craftsmen had indeed originally intended to produce two separate lists, one of Thutmose's northern conquests and another of his southern. When it came to actually entering the names onto the prepared registers, it was found that there were far more northern names and these had to continue into the southern list. Having made the mistake once, the scribes corrected the error by describing the other two copies as a list of southern and northern states.

Punt as a "Southern" Boundary?

There is, it is said, one other written source — mentioned by Bimson and frequently alluded to in the literature — which is held to prove Punt a southern country. This is the famous inscription on the shaft of a fallen obelisk at Karnak where a passage celebrates Amon's goodness in establishing Hatshepsut's kingdom. The god, she says, has made her "southern boundary as far as Punt."

On the face of it, this seems to be fairly powerful evidence against Velikovsky's thesis. If that is truly what the inscription says, then everything else we have argued, powerful though the evidence might be, is brought into question. Before taking a more detailed look at the inscription and its interpretation, let's have a look at the fuller text:

> He [Amon] hath made my kingdom, the Black Land, and the Red Lands are united under my feet. My southern boundary is as far as Punt ...; my eastern boundary is as far as the marshes of Asia, and the Asiatics are in my grasp; my western boundary is as far as the mountain of Manu ... my fame is among the Sand-dwellers altogether. The myrrh of Punt has been brought to me ... all the luxurious marvels of this country were brought to my palace in one collection ... They have brought me the choicest products of cedar, of juniper and of meru-wood; ... all the goodly sweet woods of God's Land.[91]

A couple of things should be noted here:

First and foremost, whilst the queen supposedly here refers to her "southern" boundary (i.e., Punt), she apparently makes no mention of her northern boundary, but instead moves on immediately to her eastern boundary, which she declares to be as far as the marshlands of Asia. Her western (Libyan) border is next described, but she remains silent, apparently, about her northern boundary. This should immediately cause us to

---

[91] Breasted, *Records* Vol. 2, 321

pause. Of all her boundaries, those to the north of Egypt — from which direction she was most frequently attacked — were her most important. In that direction lay the mighty empires of Hatti, Mitanni and Assyria. It could of course be argued that the 'eastern' boundary by itself deals with all the lands of the Asiatics,; and certainly the queen claims to have the Asiatics in her "grasp." It may be argued also that the reference to the northern boundary could originally have been located in one of the lacunae. Nevertheless, it does seem strange that Punt is placed immediately next to the reference to the east, and that later on (as we saw earlier) Punt is named in conjunction with God's Land, which here however is said to be the source of cedar wood, the typical product of Lebanon. Even more to the point, the eastern border is here described as extending as far as the marshes of Asia. Now Punt itself is frequently described as to the east of Egypt (a fact admitted by all), whilst in numerous inscriptions (one of which, by Thutmose III, was quoted above) the "marshes of Asia" are clearly adjacent to God's Land and Byblos. Strange then that Hatshepsut too should mention the "marshes of Asia," of God's Land (Lebanon) next to Punt (also God's Land, but in this case supposedly to the south of Egypt).

Secondly, if Punt truly marked the southern extent of Egypt's rule, this means (according to conventional ideas) that Hatshepsut was claiming to rule everything to the south as far as Eritrea (or Somalia). Even taking into account the normal bombast and exaggeration of Egyptian royal inscriptions, this seems a fantastically improbable claim.

Still, the inscription, we are told, does apparently describe Punt as Egypt's "southern" border. If that is true, it constitutes an inescapable fact which no interpretation can get round. What then is the solution?

Assuming that Breasted translated the inscription literally (which he frequently did not),[92] the text, I would argue, still poses no real problem. It

---

[92] In one notorious example, highlighted by Eva Danelius, Breasted translated "bearded ones of Punt" as "southerners of Punt," a fact which should warn us to deal cautiously with the claims he makes. Danelius loc. cit. p.14 Danelius comments further "... it is commonplace to remark that translation is interpretation. But while interpretation has to be cut down to a minimum when translating, eg, from one modern European language into another, related one, interpretation becomes unavoidable when translating from Egyptian hieroglyphs into modern European diction. In the case of the Punt-reliefs, hieroglyphs fill the space left empty by the pictures, the 'letters' beings written in adaptation to the space available. They are partly arranged in horizontal lines — to be read from left to right, or from left to right — partly in vertical columns. There are no punctuation nor other diacritical marks. Thus, it is left to the reader to decide where a sentence ends and a new one begins; whether or not there is direct speech, and by whom, etc. Furthermore, while Naville translated line by line, Breasted broke the text up into sections not to be found in the original, and even added headings which are sometimes more confusing than helpful."

is apparent that Punt may here be used simply as a measure of distance. All the queen seems to be saying is that her southern border, in Nubia, is as far distant from Thebes as her northern border, in Punt. (scholars who were able to "explain" the Sixth Dynasty official's eleven visits to Punt and Byblos as a reference to eleven visits to the northern and southern extremities of the Egyptian world should have no quarrel with this interpretation). Since the Lebanon was a great distance to the north of Thebes, this would mean that she was claiming to rule Nubia probably as far south as Meroe.

Thus one can now assert that not a single Egyptian source unquestionably places Punt in the south. Contrast this with the scores of documents which beyond all doubt place *Ta Netjer* (according to Hatshepsut one and the same as Punt) in the vicinity of Byblos and the Lebanese mountains. Add to this perhaps a dozen or so other documents which specifically refer to Punt itself (sacred to the goddess Hathor) as being in the Byblos region (also sacred to Hathor) and I feel there should no longer be any reasonable doubt as to the country's true location.

Before moving on, I would like to put an open question to the supporters of the southern Punt theory. Considering the fact that Punt appears in a list of territories which Thutmose III claims to have conquered in his first year, this would compel Egyptologists to place it somewhere in Nubia. But of course it cannot have been located there, because the Hatshepsut reliefs clearly show, and refer to, a sea voyage. Thus Punt has to be, as the only other alternative, placed somewhere near the southern end of the Red Sea, say in Eritrea or Somalia (the latter two regions being in fact the favored location for Punt). But such a location causes immense problems, because Thutmose III states that Punt (along with the other areas mentioned) was a conquered territory. The list, after all, is introduced with the words, "Summary of these foreign countries of the Nubian people of Khenthenopher whom his majesty had slaughtered, a massacre made of them." No one in his right mind of course would suggest that Thutmose III or any other pharaoh conquered Eritrea or Somalia; but this is the unavoidable and inevitable consequence of placing Punt to the south of Egypt.[93]

It is a pity scholars do not always think out the consequences of their statements before making them.

---

[93] Nor was there in Eritrea or Somalia, in the time of Hatshepsut or Thutmose III, any civilization or culture of the type portrayed at Deir el Bahri that the Egyptians could have traded with. This topic, of fundamental importance to the whole debate, is examined in greater detail below.

The Flora and Fauna of Punt

Both Bimson and Lorton concentrated virtually all their efforts on the identity of Punt in an attempt to show that the expedition commemorated at Deir el-Bahri could not have been to Syria/Palestine. It cannot be emphasized too strongly that, even were this to be the case, if the chronological adjustment placing Hatshepsut beside Solomon was nevertheless correct, then Hatshepsut would still in all probability have to be identified with the Queen of Sheba. So, the most important issue, that of chronology, remained unaddressed; a fact which the critics signally failed to understand. In his paper Bimson examined the Deir el-Bahri reliefs in great detail and, on the strength of them, came to the conclusion that Punt had to be in Africa (Eritrea in fact was his place of choice).

Before saying another word, it should be remembered that this poses Bimson with the problem outlined directly above. But again, like Lorton, this was an issue he failed to address.

Nevertheless, the Deir el-Bahri reliefs do show a number of African people and apparently African animals, such as at least one rhinoceros and a giraffe. For Bimson, and for many of his readers, this was decisive evidence in proving an African location for the territory: Decisive enough to make them ignore or forget all the other evidence that clearly located Punt/the Divine Land in Palestine/Phoenicia. But if Punt really was Phoenicia, why then such an African influence? Why the large amount of space devoted to seemingly African animals and people with clearly negroid features? This is a question that cannot be ignored. Velikovsky himself suggested that the African elements were imports, and stressed that the Puntites themselves were not negroes but Semites or Hamites. This in fact is true. The Puntites look very much like the Egyptians and, curiously enough, sport long pointed beards of a type worn in Egypt only by the pharaoh.[94] (It should be noted also in this regard that the earliest Egyptian monarchy, the Horus kings of the First Dynasty, claimed to have originated in Punt, and this incidentally provides yet another dramatic connection with Asia: For, as David Rohl has illustrated (*Legend: The Genesis of Civilisation*: 1998), the god Osiris, from whom the Egyptian royalty claimed descent, was not only specifically linked to Byblos but was himself in origin a Mesopotamian god named Asar. Rohl also shows, in the same place, how the peoples of Lebanon also traced their origin back to Mesopotamia).[95]

---

[94] Abdel-Aziz Saleh, "Some Problems Relating to the Pwenet Reliefs at Deir el-Bahari," *Journal of Egyptian Archaeology* 58 (1972), 140-158

[95] According to Petrie the Land of Punt was "sacred to the Egyptians as the source of the race." *The Making of Egypt*, p.77. In my *Genesis of Israel and Egypt* (London, 1997) I have shown

But where then do the negroes and African animals come in? The answer is in two parts. First and foremost, whilst the negroes may indicate an African element, the animals very definitely *do not* belong to Africa. Giraffes of course are nowadays found only in Africa, and this has misled many people into seeing them as proof of a southern location for Punt. However, as Bimson himself admits, giraffes were found on the borders of Syria and Arabia in classical times — a fact noted by Diodorus.[96] Further-more, the Bible itself (Deuteronomy 14:5) speaks of giraffes (which it calls the "camel-leopard") in the region of Sinai and the Negev, whilst Alexandra Nibbi notes the occurrence of a rock-cut drawing of a giraffe in Sinai.[97] The giraffe then can at best show that Punt *may* have been in Africa.

The rhinoceros however more probably points to Asia. Once again, as with the giraffe, people have simply thought "Rhinoceros — Africa." But the rhinoceros portrayed at Deir-el Bahri appears to be of the Asian one-horned species *Rhinoceros unicornis*, and it cannot represent either of the two contem-porary African species, both of which have two horns. The one-horned rhinoceros has never been attested in Africa. Again, this is a fact that Bimson himself concedes.[98] A single-horned rhinoceros is portrayed on the Black Obelisk of Shalmaneser III, along with an elephant and an oryx, all of which are described as 'tribute' of Musri.[99] However, although Musri ("border land") was the normal Semitic appellation for Egypt (Hebrew *Mizraim*), in this case the border-region referred to was probably India, since a "water-ox," almost certainly a water buffalo, was listed as tribute from the same place. This does not however preclude the possibility that single-horned rhinos had at one time inhabited the Jordan Valley and Syria/Palestine, a territory remarkable for its mixture of African and Asian flora and fauna.[100] It should be remarked too, in this regard, that after his foray into Palestine and Syria, Thutmose II

---

in some detail how the migration from Mesopotamia which brought high civilisation to Egypt was identical to the 'Abraham' migration of the Book of Genesis. Everything about the Abraham story suggests that it should be placed at the very start of Egypt's First Dynasty. In effect, this means that the ruling class of Egypt, the *Iry pat*, were of the same stock as the Hebrews — which of course makes the Egyptian designation of Palestine/Phoenicia as the Land of the god all the more understandable.

[96] Diodorus, ii, 50-1

[97] Alessandra Nibbi, "The Shipwrecked Sailor Again" *Göttinger Miszellen* 24 (1977), p. 54

[98] Bimson, "Hatshepsut and the Queen of Sheba," (loc cit), suggests that the one-horned rhino may have once occurred in northern Africa, since early Egyptian hieroglyphs included a pictogram of such a creature. This is not impossible, since the rhinoceros, giraffe and elephant were all common in Egypt until near the end of the Early Dynastic period. But the same creatures also roamed Syria/Palestine, where they survived till much later owing to the more favourable climatic conditions.

[99] Olmstead, op cit., p.142

[100] See eg. H. C. Luke, "Palestine," in *Countries of the World* Vol.5 (Waverley Books, London), p.3072

records bringing back "horses" and "elephants."[101] Damien Mackey also drew attention to the fact that during the time of the Old Babylonian king Iarim-Lim, "there were herds of elephants in northern Syria, and tusks have been found in the palace of Alalakah..."[102]

In antiquity the entire Near East was home to most of the creatures associated nowadays only with Africa. It is well-known, for example, that lions occurred in great abundance throughout the region and were extensively hunted for sport by Assyrian kings as well as Egyptian pharaohs. What is not so well known is that in ancient times basically all of the animals now associated with the African savannah roamed throughout Syria/Palestine. These populations were remnants of an earlier time when the entire Sahara and Arabian deserts were well-watered grasslands.[103] Thus the *Illustrated Bible Dictionary*[104] supplies the following rather surprising information about the non-human inhabitants of the area in biblical times:

(a) Elephants. "The Asiatic elephant was once found as far west as the upper reaches of the Euphrates [northern Syria]." Vol.1 p.58

(b) Lions. "At one time lions were found from Asia Minor through the Middle East and Persia to India ... The last Palestinian lion was probably killed near Megiddo in the 13th century." Ibid.

(c) Leopards and Cheetahs. "It is possible that Heb. *namer* refers to both the true leopard and the cheetah, or hunting leopard, and also to one or two other spotted wild cats of Palestine." Ibid.

(d) Gazelles. "Two wild species [of gazelle] are found in Palestine: the dorcas and Palestine gazelles, both standing under 70 cm." Ibid.

(e) Hippopotami. The hippopotamus "lived in the lower Nile until the 12th century AD and, much earlier, in the Orontes river in Syria (and perhaps elsewhere in SW Asia) until after the time of Joseph, so it is well known in Bible lands." Ibid. p.61

(f) Ostriches. "The ostrich finds mention in several [Bible] passages ... Jb 39: 13-18 is clearly a description of the ostrich, a bird which once lived in the Middle East." Ibid. p. 62 (Note: An Assyrian portrayal of this bird is shown on the same page.)

---

[101] Breasted, *A History of Egypt*, pp.270-1

[102] J. R. Kupper, "Northern Mesopotamia and Syria," in *The Cambridge Ancient History* Vol.2 part 1 (3rd ed), p.19

[103] See eg K. W. Butzer, "Physical Conditions in Eastern Europe, Western Asia and Egypt Before the Period of Agriculture and Urban Settlement," in *The Cambridge Ancient History* Vol.1 part 1 (3rd ed), p.68 "Between the First and Fourth Dynasties, the second major faunal break, characterised by the disappearance of the rhinoceros, elephant, giraffe, and gerenuk gazelle in Egypt, culminated in the modern aridity."

[104] *The Illustrated Bible Dictionary* 3 Vols. (Hodder and Stoughton, 1980)

(g) Crocodiles. "In biblical times the Nile crocodile was found from source to mouth of the Nile. While its distribution north of Egypt in that period is unknown, returning Crusaders reported crocodiles in the Zerka river, which runs into the Mediterranean near Caesarea and is still known locally as the Crocodile river." Ibid. p. 65.

Even within the past hundred years Palestine/Lebanon was still home to the Syrian bear and the leopard, whilst the gazelle, ibex and hyena still occur, along with the wild pig, jackal and wild cat.[105]

So, far from proving Punt in Africa, the evidence of the fauna points once again to western Asia. The importance of this cannot be emphasized too strongly; for it was the appearance of supposedly African animals on the Deir el-Bahri reliefs that was most decisive in convincing scholars they should relocate Punt from Asia (where they had hitherto placed it) to Africa.

It is quite evident that in the time of Hatshepsut the exotic creatures displayed at Deir el-Bahri were still found in the less populated regions of Syria/Palestine, having been previously hunted to extinction in the more fertile parts. They were spotted by the royal expedition on its journey from the port of Eilat at the head of the Gulf of Aqaba as it made its way northward through the wild Arabah region.

The inscriptions at Deir el-Bahri make it quite plain that the Egyptian ships came ashore in a region of abundant date palms, where the inhabitants lived in rustic-looking houses on stilts. And these two details have been extensively highlighted by the proponents of the Punt in Africa hypothesis. Yet to this day the coast of Eilat, as Eva Danelius remarked, is fronted by numerous date palms whose roots are watered by underground springs issuing from the adjacent mountains of Edom and Sinai.[106] Furthermore, the entire coastland of Eilat/Aqaba acts very much as a funnel which brings together seasonal torrents issuing from those same uplands. Indeed, the towns of Eilat and Aqaba are periodically subject to severe flooding, as the wadis overflow with winter and spring rains. In such circumstances, houses on stilts would have been, for inhabitants, a very wise precaution.[107]

---

[105] Luke, "Palestine," loc cit.

[106] Danelius, "The Identification of the Biblical Queen of Sheba," loc cit.

[107] In Hatshepsut's time houses on stilts were common throughout the world, including in Europe, where entire villages were constructed upon lakes, mainly for defensive purposes.

Fig. 5. Fig. The houses on stilts near the shore of Punt, a sensible precaution in a region like Eilat/Aqaba, frequently subject to serious flash-flooding during the winter.

Having viewed these strange villages and been greeted by the Puntite governor Paruah, who presented the Egyptians with some of the produce of the region, including "green gold of the land of Amu" (which, as Eva Danelius remarked, can only be the copper ore which is still plainly visible in the rocks of the Arabah and the nearby Edomite hills), the queen with her entourage would then have made her way northwards to Jerusalem. At Timnah there existed an Egyptian temple (allegedly dating from the time of Seti I but remarkably similar in design to one of Amenhotep II) to the goddess Hathor, the "Lady of Punt," and it is virtually certain that Hatshepsut stopped here to pay homage. Just days north of Timnah, the Arabah valley descends into the tropical Dead Sea basin where the first of the myrrh terraces, possibly at Ein Gedi, would have been encountered. The rare and exotic creatures of the region, such as giraffe and single-horned rhinoceros, were occasionally spotted and recorded faithfully by the Egyptian artists.

Ethnic Identity of the Puntites

This brings us to the second supposedly irrefutably southern element present in Punt: namely, the negroes. Surely, it will be said, these at least must point to Africa. How are they to be explained if we locate Punt in Asia?

To begin with, let me reiterate an important point, one usually overlooked by Velikovsky's critics. The Puntites themselves were very definitely not negroes. This is a fact stressed by numerous Egyptologists. Quite the contrary, rather than being southern-looking, they are described as a "long-haired Hamitic people, similar in physical type to the Egyptians themselves."[108] Other writers see them as a mixture of Hamites and Semites,

---

[108] W. C. Hayes, "Egypt: Internal Affairs from Tuthmosis I to the Death of Amenophis III," in *The Cambridge Ancient History* Vol.2 part 2 (3rd ed), p.330

whilst the governor is described as a "tall, well-shaped man" with "flaxen" hair; his nose "aquiline, his beard long and pointed." We are told that "The Puntites are painted red, but not so dark as the Egyptians."[109] It will, I think, be admitted that this hardly sounds like a description of the natives of Eritrea or even southern Arabia. Particularly striking is the "flaxen" (light blond) hair of the governor. At this point I would like to draw attention to the fact that at least one of Thutmose III's portrayals of Syrian/Asiatic captives show several of them with blue eyes and fair hair.[110] How is this to be explained? I would suggest two possibilities: Either the Phoenicians, whose voyages to western Europe (Spain and Britain) are well known, had by this time acquired, through intermarriage, a European genetic element; or more probably, the Indo-European features may have derived from the military ruling caste of the region, the Indo-Iranian *mariyanna*, who were prominent in Syria/Palestine during this epoch.

Fig. 6. Perehu, the "Chief of Punt" and his obese wife Ati present themselves to the Egyptian ambassadors. These people look Asiatic, though the Puntite men wear the long pointed beard typical of Egyptian deities and pharaohs.

These then were the typical Puntites. Nevertheless, people of clearly negro physiognomy are indeed portrayed on the reliefs. Velikovsky suggested that they may have been slaves, presented to the Egyptians along with the other gifts. This may or may not be the case, but their presence in Punt is not difficult to explain, though perhaps somewhat dramatic in its own right.

The entire story of Solomon is intimately connected with Africa. The Bible emphasizes that Solomon owed his great wealth to the "gold of Ophir." The latter region has been generally connected with Africa, and over the

---

[109] E. Naville, *The Temple of Deir el-Bahari: Part III* (London, 1907), pp.12-3

[110] See G. Rawlinson, *History of Ancient Egypt* Vol.2 (London, 1881), p.244. Rawlinson notes that many had recognized "in this remarkable picture an actual representation of the oppressed Hebrews." However, he goes on to say that though the countenances "have a Semitic cast," they "are certainly not markedly Jewish ... They have light hair and in several instances blue eyes."

years various attempts have been made to find "King Solomon's Mines" in the southern half of the continent, which to this day is a gold-rich region. These attempts are not mistaken. The Africans on the Deir el-Bahri reliefs are quite possibly neither Nubians nor Somalians, but from much further south. Over the years, various scholars have noted a peculiar physical feature of some of those portrayed on the monument. One or two have protruding buttocks of a type particularly associated with the Khoisan (Hottentot) natives of southern Africa (on the strength of which fact alone some writers have suggested placing Punt on the coastlands of Mozambique or even further south). But such drastic measures are unnecessary. The Africans apparently occupy such a significant position in the reliefs because they were one of the wonders of the Divine Land: People from the 'ends of the earth' had been brought back to Punt/Israel by the Phoenician seamen in Solomon's employ.

So, not only do the Africans on the Deir el-Bahri reliefs fail to present any real problems for the Hatshepsut = Queen of Sheba identification, they may actually cast further dramatic light on the biblical description of Solomon and his fabulously opulent kingdom.

Was the King of Israel Shown on the Punt Reliefs?

Before finishing, I would like to emphasize that it constitutes a profound mistake for a historian to ignore the wider context within which events take place. What David Lorton and John Bimson — as well as the entire Egyptological establishment — require us to believe, when viewed in context, is astonishingly improbable. We are asked by them to accept that Hatshepsut, the ruler of Egypt, devoted her funerary monument to an expedition (in which she did not even take part) to deliver trinkets to the natives of a semi-primitive region somewhere along the African coast of the Red Sea; a region by the way so close and so unremarkable that Thutmose III could claim to have conquered and annexed it in his first regnal year. Most readers, I think, will agree that such a scenario is vanishingly implausible. The whole logic of the expedition and its reporting suggests that Punt, though close to Egypt, was indeed a remarkable and powerful kingdom, and that furthermore the Egyptian queen herself led the expedition to its shores. Logic further insists that the Egyptian travelers must have been granted an audience with the Puntite ruler.

That is the logic of the situation. But Lorton and Bimson, in all fairness to them, can point out that no portrayal of the Puntite king is preserved; nor is there, according to Bimson, any space on the walls of the Deir el-Bahri temple where a meeting between Hatshepsut and the Puntite monarch could have been illustrated. What then is the solution? Why is the meeting not shown?

The answer is glaringly obvious, though like much else relating to this monument, it has been overlooked. Deir el-Bahri was a funerary monument and as such was concerned purely with religious themes. Hatshepsut's journey to Punt, the Divine Land, was above all a pilgrimage. She herself was perhaps the most devoted of all Egyptian rulers to the goddess Hathor, and Punt was the land sacred to Hathor, the "Lady of Punt." In fact, the latter region's close association with Hathor amply explains Hatshepsut's almost mystical love for it.4 At Deir el-Bahri there was a special shrine devoted to Hathor. Naville, who excavated it, believed "the shrine of Hathor to have been originally a cave where, according to tradition the queen was suckled by the goddess and where, at the end of her life, she 'joined' her divine nurse." Hatshepsut identified herself with the goddess, "thus deifying herself and claiming the same worship."5 The murals in the hypostyle hall at Deir el-Bahri show a festive procession on the Nile in honor of Hathor's "sacred birth." The text reads: "Hathor, she reneweth her birth. Thebes is in joy/ Ma-ka-re, while endures ... the sky, thou endures." According to Naville, "we see clearly the confusion which exists between the goddess and the queen, a confusion which is intentional."[III]

The Punt reliefs at Deir el-Bahri are part of a pair located in the middle colonnade of the temple. The other part of the pair, the "matching" part, shows Hatshepsut's divine birth and her being suckled by Hathor. Thus the two sections celebrate events of the queen's life specifically connected with her tutelary goddess. As such, it should come as no surprise that the reliefs make no mention of any meetings with local kings or potentates. It has a purely and completely religious purpose. One side displays her birth and infanthood, overseen by Hathor; the other displays her journey to Hathor's own homeland, Punt/Lebanon. It is, for the queen, a journey home.

It would appear that the journey to Punt constituted a masterful piece of religious propaganda, necessitated, to some extent, by the fact that a woman had assumed the titles of pharaoh. In order to justify this unheard-of situation, Hatshepsut went out of her way to identify herself with Hathor and also, as Lewis Greenberg observed, with Hathor's alter-ego Isis.[112] Thus in journeying to Punt/God's Land, the Queen was retracing the steps of Isis as she sought her divine spouse Osiris. And sure enough, Hatshepsut claimed that the pilgrimage to Punt was undertaken in response to a heavenly

---

[III] Ibid., p. 2.

[112] L. M. Greenberg, "A Linguistic Note on the Land of Punt," Society for Interdisciplinary Studies, *Review* No. 1 (2018) and "The Land of Punt Redux," Society for Interdisciplinary Studies, *Review* No. 2 (2018).

command. Velikovsky's critics were misled by their overly Bible-centered outlook. The Queen of Sheba's visit to Palestine must, they assumed, have been prompted by her desire to meet Solomon. No one imagined that that may have been of little importance to a foreigner; that it was the country itself which the Queen wished to see. When she said she had "built a Punt" in Thebes, it may well have been inspired, as Velikovsky said, by Solomon's temple, but it was also a copy of the terraced hillsides of "God's Land.

As a matter of fact, as Velikovsky himself said, it would have violated all royal protocol for the Queen to have been portrayed at the court of an Asiatic. It would certainly have been seen as demeaning. Traditionally, if a foreign ruler wished an audience with a pharaoh, they had to go to Egypt. It is possible (though not probable) that other monuments, now lost, illustrated the meeting between Hatshepsut and the ruler of Israel/Punt. But it would be unrealistic to suppose that any such illustrations could have survived. Upon Hatshepsut's death Israel became the target of Thutmose III's aggression, an aggression at least partly explainable by reason of Hatshepsut's friendship. Any depictions of Hatshepsut and the Israelite king would certainly have aroused an especially destructive zeal on the part of Thutmose's henchmen. It is of course a great pity that no image of the meeting between Hatshepsut and Solomon has survived, but bearing in mind the politics of the time, such a survival would have been almost miraculous.

Eritrea and Somalia in Hatshepsut's Time: A Primitive Land

The Egyptological establishment is nowadays fairly unanimous in placing Punt at the southern end of the Red Sea, either in Eritrea or Somalia, or a combination of these two places. The reasons for this have been examined above. Yet such a location, we have seen, immediately raises the enormous problem of accounting for the fact that Thutmose III claimed to have conquered Punt — all of Punt — in his first year. No one in his right mind would suggest that any pharaoh ever ruled these territories; aside from the logistical problems of a military expedition to such remote regions, there is no archaeological justification for such a supposition. Not a trace of anything that could be construed as implying Egyptian rule, or even substantial contact with Egypt, has ever appeared.

Yet the first year of Thutmose III's reign did see major military activity; the conquest of Israel/Canaan. He could, and did, claim to have conquered all of that territory.

But locating Punt in Eritrea/Somalia raises an even greater problem. Actually, it is an insurmountable one. The earliest Egyptian contacts with

Punt occurred during the Old Kingdom, in the time of the Fourth Dynasty, as a matter of fact; though there is a suggestion of even earlier connections. The Old Kingdom references make it clear that Punt was a territory well-known to the Egyptians, and there is strong suggestion that it was a country which had attained a level of civilization comparable to that of the Egyptians themselves. Certainly by the time of the New Kingdom Punt was a trading partner of Egypt, and the record of Hatshepsut's expedition suggests a cultured region inhabited by people of mixed Hamitic/Semitic stock who cultivated exotic plants like incense and mined for gold and other precious materials. As such, the archaeologist would expect to find, in Punt, the remains of a thriving Bronze Age culture. Indeed, if the reports of Punt emanating from Old Kingdom inscriptions are anything to go by, he would expect to find plentiful remains even of an Early or at least Middle Bronze Age civilization. Now, we ask ourselves the crucial question: Can Eritrea/Somalia produce the required remains?

The answer, sadly for Velikovsky's critics, is a resounding no!

Neither Eritrea nor Somalia has received the type of intense archaeological attention accorded to Egypt or Syria/Palestine. Nevertheless, a substantial amount of work has been done in both territories; and from this a fairly detailed picture of the region's cultural and ethnic history has emerged. We now know, for example, that the area was colonized by groups of Arabs from across the Red Sea at various times during the first millennium BC. From the intermixing of these newcomers and natives there developed the great and venerable civilization we now call "Ethiopia." But this Ethiopia had nothing whatsoever to do with the Ethiopia of the Bible, which was Nubia.

The Arab incomers were literate metal-workers who introduced high civilization into what had previously been a Neolithic territory. The crucial question for us is: When did they arrive? Ironically enough, John Bimson devotes considerable space to this topic in his critique of Velikovsky. He sought to show that these Arab immigrants were the "Puntites" with whom Hatshepsut and the other Egyptians traded. For all that, he has to admit that the main Arab settlement took place only in the 8th century BC! (though according to Velikovsky's chronology Hatshepsut's expedition would have occurred in the 10th century). In order to get round this difficulty he quotes a number of sources which claim Arab settlement from the early Iron Age. The problem is (and Bimson himself is well aware of this) that Solomon's early Iron Age, of the 10th century, is an Iron Age that exists only on paper. It has no archaeological confirmation. That is precisely why Velikovsky was compelled to identify Late Bronze Age Palestine with the Palestine of David and Solomon. In short, the Arab settlements in Eritrea would have needed to commence in the archaeological Bronze Age for Hatshepsut and Thut-mose III to have found any high culture there. But no such settlements have ever been found. And of course the problem becomes even more acute when we remember that there was frequent intercourse between Egypt and Punt during the Old Kingdom. Eritrea/Somalia should therefore, if it was Punt, have had an Early Bronze civilization. The non-existence of any Bronze Age culture in this area should, in itself, be sufficient to bury once and for all the notion of an African location. The only southern region that could qualify would be Yemen, but this only exacerbates the problem of Thutmose III's conquest of the territory. (Some of the sources quoted by Bimson confirming an Iron Age civilization in Eritrea are as follows: J. Doresse *Ethiopia* (London, 1959); A.H.M. Jones and E. Munroe *A History of Ethiopia* (Oxford, 1935); R. Greenfield *Ethiopia: A New Political History* (London, 1965).

Recapitulation

Thus the evidence of Punt, regarded by Velikovsky's critics as crucial in refuting the Hatshepsut = Queen of Sheba equation, in no way says what they affirmed. Indeed, as I went further into the question of Punt's identity, I became more and more astonished that anyone could locate it anywhere other than Palestine. As we saw, before the discovery of the Hatshepsut reliefs in the middle of the 19th century, it was universally assumed that Punt should be located in Asia. The Deir el-Bahri reliefs, however, with their "African" elements, caused a rethink. Everything that had previously identi-fied Punt with Asia was then either reinterpreted or simply ignored. But the supporters of the African Punt theory, as well as those who deny the Egyp-tian origin of the Queen of Sheba, are now involved in a truly epic amount of ignoring.

Regarding the identity of the Queen of Sheba:
- They need to ignore the fact that "ruler of the South" was a recognized biblical term for the Egyptian monarch.
- They must ignore the fact that "Sheba" was almost certainly the orig-inal pronunciation of the Egyptian Wa.Shet/Thebes.
- They must ignore the evidence which suggests the Queen of Sheba was ruler of a powerful kingdom, not a desert principality.
- They must ignore the fact that Josephus specifically identified her as the "Queen of Egypt and Ethiopia," as did the Abyssinians.

Regarding the identity of Punt:

- They must ignore the evidence which suggests it was a mighty kingdom; otherwise the queen of Egypt would not have decorated an extremely important part of her funerary monument with a visit to it.
- They must ignore the evidence which suggests Punt was very close to Egypt; otherwise Thutmose III could not have conquered it in his first year (this alone absolutely excludes Eritrea and Somalia).
- They must ignore the fact that Byblos is always associated with *Ta Netjer*, the "Land of the God," and that Punt too is always associated with *Ta Netjer*.
- They must ignore the fact that Byblos was specifically linked to the god Osiris, and that "netjer" was a word used specifically for Osiris — indicating that the land of *Ta Netjer* was a region sacred to Osiris.
- They must ignore or "reinterpret" the further evidence specifically linking Punt with Byblos and with other territories in the Lebanon/Palestine region.
- They must ignore or "reinterpret" the fact that the goddess Hathor was specifically linked to Byblos and named the "Lady of Byblos," and that she was also specifically linked to Punt and named the "Lady of Punt."
- They must ignore or "reinterpret" the obvious similarity between the names Punt (*Pwene*) and Phoenicia.
- They must ignore the fact that whilst Punt was described as a land of "myrrh terraces," the Jordan Valley was anciently covered in terraces which were famous for the production of myrrh and other exotic plants.
- They must ignore the fact that communication between Punt and Egypt was apparently halted in the Hyksos age (as hinted at Deir el Bahri). Yet the Hyksos (in Avaris/Sinai) could scarcely have prevented communication between the southern Egyptians in Thebes and the people of Eritrea or Somalia.
- They must ignore the fact that at least one of the animals displayed on the Deir el Bahri reliefs, the rhinoceros, has only ever been attested in Asia, whilst the other supposedly "African" animals have all been attested in Asia, and that in the time of Hatshepsut large numbers of elephants, lions and other supposedly typical African animals roamed throughout Syria/Palestine.
- Perhaps most crucially of all, they must ignore the fact that during the time of the Eighteenth Dynasty (never mind in the period of the Old Kingdom), there was no high civilization in Eritrea or Somalia (or southern Arabia for that matter) that the Egyptians could have traded with or conquered.

CHAPTER 3: IMPERIAL EGYPT

Thutmose III and Shishak

We have seen that reducing the age of the Eighteenth Dynasty by five centuries makes Hatshepsut a contemporary of Solomon, and her successor on the Egyptian throne, Thutmose III, identical to Pharaoh Shishak, whom the Book of Kings claims plundered the temple in Jerusalem. If anything, the evidence linking Thutmose III with Shishak is even more compelling than that linking Hatshepsut to the Queen of Sheba.

Once again, however, as with Hatshepsut = Sheba, I do not intend simply to reiterate the evidence already garnered by Velikovsky. What I hope to do, again, is bring forward new material, material either unknown to Velikovsky's critics or ignored by them. Having said that, it would be useful, at this stage, to look briefly at some of the main points raised by Velikovsky in *Ages in Chaos* 1. These were as follows: (a) Archaeology demanded that Thutmose III be contemporary with Solomon's sons Rehoboam and Jeroboam I. (b) Thutmose III was the greatest of all Egyptian conquerors, and his earliest campaigns involved the subjugation of the Palestine/Canaan region. (c) This territory was known as Retjenu, or Rezenu, a name which is etymologically identical to one of the Hebrew names for Israel, Arzenu "our land." (d) The capital of Retjenu was known as Kadesh, the "holy place," and Jerusalem too was called Kadesh, "the holy mountain," in biblical times. Even today it is still known as Al Kuds "the holy" in Arabic. (e) Thutmose plundered the great temple of Kadesh and showed the material he took from it in

Karnak. (f) This was identical to the plunder taken from Solomon's temple by pharaoh Shishak.

Of all these statements only (a), i.e., the demand for a dramatic reduction in the date of Thutmose III's life, is really objectionable to orthodoxy. Of course, having rejected proposition (a), they then naturally also reject proposition (f), that the temple plundered by Thutmose III was the temple of Solomon. One rejection predicates the other. Nevertheless, no one denies that Thutmose III was the greatest warrior of all the pharaohs, that his first campaigns were directed against the natives of Canaan/Palestine, natives who spoke a dialect virtually identical to biblical Hebrew, and that the capital of this region, whose temple he plundered — Kadesh — has a name which was frequently used for Jerusalem.

Other important issues were raised by Velikovsky in the chapter on Thutmose III: One of the most significant is the fact that the Canaanite/Phoenician captives displayed on his victory stele at Karnak look exactly like Puntites, whilst his inscriptions showed that Retjenu (Palestine) was a source of incense (*anti*), as was Punt. But it was the things that Velikovsky left out that are of most interest to us here, and there were several of these.

Thutmose III Destroys Hatshepsut's Legacy

Thutmose III was the greatest warrior of all the pharaohs. In a series of seventeen campaigns, beginning in his first year and continuing throughout his reign, he extended Egypt's borders from the Euphrates in the north of Syria to the 4th cataract in Nubia. By the end of his life Egypt had reached the zenith of her power and prosperity, a peak she was never to see again. Egyptians of later epochs never tired of honoring the great soldier and there seems little doubt that the mighty king known to Herodotus as Sesostris, the conqueror of Asia, was one and the same as Thutmose III.[113] Echoing ancient tradition, modern historians dubbed him the "Napoleon of Egypt," and his exploits have been compared to those of Caesar or Alexander.[114]

The military achievements of Thutmose III represented a new departure for Egypt. Prior to his time, the Egyptians had been remarkably unconcerned with foreign conquest. It is true that several pharaohs, at various times in history, had made brief expeditions into southern Palestine and the

---

[113] Rawlinson, op cit., p.226 "Thothmes III is the nearest to the ideal Sesostris, the only Pharaoh who really penetrated with a hostile force deep into the heart of Assyria ..." The identity of Sesostris is examined more fully below.

[114] Breasted, *A History of Egypt*, p.320 "The genius which rose from an obscure priestly office to accomplish this [conquest] for the first time in history reminds us of an Alexander or a Napoleon."

coastal regions of Philistia; yet these were minor operations, not in any way to be compared, either in concept or scale, with Thutmose III's program of conquest. What, historians have asked, could have been the driving force behind this aggression? What was it turned the previously inward-looking Egyptians into a nation of imperialists?

The answer is not difficult to find, though, having said that, it has hitherto been missed by all the professional Egyptologists. The clue to Thutmose's character lies in his relationship with his stepmother Hatshepsut and in the true location of her "Holy Land," Punt. Scholars have long known that Thutmose III had very personal reasons for his aggression; they came close to the truth but never took things to their logical conclusion.

For many years of his young life Thutmose III lived under the shadow of his stepmother Hatshepsut, the woman who acted as regent in his minority but who then, in defiance of all tradition and protocol, had the effrontery to mount the throne as a "pharaoh" — even going to the extent of having herself portrayed as a man, complete with royal beard![115] This was an altogether unprecedented humiliation for any crown prince. It must have been doubly galling for a youth as vigorous and virile as Thutmose III. He must have burned with a desire simultaneously to prove himself a man and to exact vengeance against the woman who had so humiliated him. Both these desires were in fact satiated to the full. In the words of Breasted: "Thutmose III was not chivalrous in his treatment of her [Hatshepsut] when she was gone. He had suffered too much. Burning to lead his forces into Asia, he had been assigned to such puerile functions as offering incense to Amon on the return of the queen's expedition to Punt; and his restless energies had been allowed to expend themselves on building his mortuary temple of the western plain of Thebes."[116] With the queen's death or departure, Thutmose wasted no time in exacting revenge. "Everywhere he had her name erased and in the terraced temple on all the walls both her figure and her name have been hacked out. Her partisans doubtless all fled. If not they must have met short shrift."[117]

The above was the view until comparatively recently, and when Breasted wrote these words just quoted, egyptologists assumed, naturally enough, that Thutmose III had defaced Hatshepsut's monuments immediately after he assumed power. We now know, however, that this was not the case; in fact, the destruction of her works — and those of her allies and confidants — appears to have been carried out only after the twentieth year of Thutmose

---

[115] As Velikovsky and others have pointed out, this may explain several Jewish traditions which — inexplicably — described the Queen of Sheba as "masculine" and "hairy."

[116] Ibid., pp. 282-3

[117] Ibid., p. 283

III's sole rule. Why this should be so has proved a major puzzle to egyptologists and has led to all sorts of theorizing and speculating. In the words of Joyce Tyldesley: "… while it is possible to imagine and even empathize with Tuthmosis indulging in a sudden whim of hatred against his stepmother immediately after her death, it is far harder to imagine him overcome by such a whim some twenty years later. Indeed, if we can no longer be certain that Tuthmosis hated his stepmother as she lay on her deathbed, can we be certain that he ever hated her during her lifetime?"[118]

In search of an explanation Tyldesley notes that, "Tuthmosis III was clearly an intelligent and rational monarch. All that we know of his character suggests that he was not given to rash, impetuous acts and it seems logical to assume that throughout his life Tuthmosis was motivated less by uncontrollable urges than by calculated political expediency. We must therefore divorce his private emotions from his political actions, just as we must separate the person of Hatshepsut the woman from her role as Egypt's female pharaoh. Whatever his personal feelings towards his stepmother, Tuthmosis may well have found it advisable to remove all traces of the unconventional female king whose reign might possibly be interpreted by future generations as a grave offence against *maat* [divinely ordained order or truth], and whose unorthodox co-regency might well have cast serious doubt upon the legitimacy of his own right to rule."[119] This hardly sounds convincing reasoning, and Tyldesley herself seems to suspect it; for immediately afterwards she notes: "Wounded male pride may also have played a part in his [Thutmose III's] decision to act; the mighty warrior king may have balked at being recorded for posterity as the man who ruled for twenty years under the thumb of a mere woman."[120]

But the latter is merely a return to the traditional view — that Thutmose III felt humiliated by Hatshepsut's usurpation of the throne and destroyed her monuments out of sheer hatred. It also brings us back to the original problem: If he destroyed her monuments out of hatred, why wait twenty years to do so?

Notwithstanding the amount of ink spilt discussing this supposed enigma, I would contend that even a rudimentary understanding of human psychology would provide an easy answer. Let's consider again Thutmose III's situation: He had lived under the shadow of his aunt and stepmother for many years. He had been well treated and promised the crown in due course; and, in due course, when Hatshepsut died, he received it. At this stage, to begin a campaign against his predecessor's memory would have consti-

---

[118] Joyce Tyldesley, *Hatchepsut: The Female Pharaoh* (Penguin Books, 1998), pp. 224-5
[119] Ibid., p. 225
[120] Ibid.

tuted an admission both to his contemporaries and to himself that he had been humiliated and that he had been too weak to remove his aunt. In such circumstances the only option open to him — from a psychological view-point — was to continue the fiction that all had been well and that Hatshepsut's situation had been normal. But living a lie like this has a price: The young pharaoh would have burned with a suppressed rage — a rage he could safely divert against his stepmother's foreign allies and friends. Many years later, having proved his own manhood repeatedly on the field of battle, he could, perhaps unobtrusively to begin with, commence the destruction of his hated aunt's monuments. And that, of course, is precisely what we do find.[121]

We recall at this point that the identification of Hatshepsut with the Queen of Sheba means that she must have formed a particularly close and even intimate friendship with the ruler of Israel. If this were the case, then we would naturally expect the newly-crowned Thutmose III to have directed a great deal of his pent-up fury against the land of Israel, the ally of his hated stepmother.

Did this happen?

The facts speak for themselves: In his very first year on the throne, no more than a few months after he became sole ruler, Thutmose III led his armies against the land of Israel and reduced it to vassalage. That the campaign of this year was directed against the king of Kadesh and his Canaanite/Palestinian allies is not in doubt, though it is generally assumed that the Kadesh in question was the city of that name on the Orontes.[122] Yet this begs the question: Why would a king of northern Syria surround himself with Palestinian allies? As Velikovsky pointed out, the region of Israel (actually southern Israel, or Judah) was Thutmose III's prime target during his first campaign, and indeed a great number of cities and towns of Israel/Canaan can be identified on the list carved at Karnak: Gaza was taken; Joppa (Jaffa) was besieged; Megiddo was attacked; and Thutmose's list of towns conquered in his first year is full of the names of the towns of southern Palestine: Etam (Itmm) appears at number 36; Socoh (Sk) at 67, and Beth-Zur (Bt sir) at 110. And although not all settlements on the list can be positively identified as yet, it is clear that Thutmose claims to have either conquered or received the submission of everything between southern Palestine and Baalbek (Dan) and Byblos in the Lebanon. Indeed, the latter towns mark the northernmost limits of his conquests, though none of these settlements had to be taken by storm. No actual military action north of Megiddo is recorded, and it is presumed that all towns further north simply submitted.

---

[121] Breasted, *History of Egypt*, p. 283
[122] See e.g. Tyldesley, op cit., p. 214

Dozens of villages and towns to the south of Byblos and Baalbek, on both sides of the Jordan, figure in the pharaoh's catalogue. Many of these are small and can hardly have been more than hamlets. Towns in the Judaean and Samarian uplands are mentioned, as are settlements on the eastern side of the Jordan; yet Jerusalem is absent. Why?

Even before the conquest of Jerusalem by David, biblical sources imply that it was an important city, commanding the very center of Canaan. Why then is it not mentioned along with all the other (very often tiny settlements) that are listed? The answer, the only logical answer, is that Kadesh itself is Jerusalem. Once again, it is Velikovsky who has logic on his side, and his critics who defy it.

It should be remarked that the area covered by Thutmose III's catalogue corresponds very precisely with the combined territories of Judah and Israel as they would have been shortly after the breakup of Solomon's empire. The latter polity stretched from Edom in the south to Dan (Baalbek) in Lebanon and as far as Tadmor (Palmyra) in north-east Syria. Damascus was firmly within Solomon's kingdom. All of these, with the exception of Tadmor, figure on Thutmose III's register; and indeed the northern limit of his conquests corresponds exactly (if we omit Tadmor) with the northern limit of the kingdom of Israel.

Yet Jerusalem, we are told, is not mentioned!

The People of Palestine Fall into Disagreement

Chapter 4 of *Ages in Chaos* contains a section entitled "Thutmose III prepares the disintegration of the empire of Solomon." In these pages Velikovsky argued that the division of Solomon's kingdom into two warring factions had been the direct result of the pharaoh's own actions. He quotes a well-known line in Thutmose's annals,

> Now at that time the Asiatics had fallen into disagreement each man fighting against his neighbor.

This sentence, usually regarded as Thutmose's statement of justification for his invasion, elicits this comment from Velikovsky: "A victory over a foe weakened by internal discord is a diluted triumph. Why, then, do the annals mention this discord in the land of Pharaoh's foes? It was the work of Thutmose III himself to prepare the disunity by setting one part of the population against the other; hence this record does not detract from his right to laurels."[123]

---

[123] Velikovsky, *Ages in Chaos*, p.141

There is no doubt that the biblical account of events leading up to the division of the kingdom lends itself to this interpretation. We are told that Pharaoh Shishak sheltered Jeroboam after he had plotted against Solomon. "And Jeroboam arose, and fled into Egypt, unto Shishak king of Egypt, and was in Egypt until the death of Solomon." (I Kings 11:40). Upon Solomon's death, Jeroboam returned to Israel with the obvious intention of fighting for the throne. Egypt, under Shishak, appears to have been deeply involved.

Fig. 7. Thutmose III, also known as Menkheperre, stepson of Hatshepsut and conqueror of Palestine. Was he the same man as Menerik/Menelik, the son of the Queen of Sheba, who plundered the Temple of Solomon, according to Ethiopian tradition?

Yet here we encounter a problem not mentioned by Velikovsky. If Thutmose III is the same person as Shishak, he cannot have been the ruler of Egypt who sheltered the fugitive Jeroboam. Thutmose III's attack on Palestine took place in his first year as sole ruler; in other words, as soon as Hatshepsut was dead. Hatshepsut, as a friend of Solomon, would not have sheltered one of his enemies: yet we are told that Jeroboam had fled to Egypt well before Solomon's death and that Shishak's attack on Israel took place five years after that event. (I Kings 14:25) Assuming the biblical record to be accurate, this means that Jeroboam fled to Egypt during the lifetime of Hatshepsut.

One solution to the problem is that Jeroboam's sojourn in Egypt was with the tacit approval of Solomon: his stay in that country may have been more of a banishment than a flight.

Taking everything into account, then, it seems that Thutmose's statement about the Asiatics falling into disagreement is not particularly significant. For us, it probably does refer to the ongoing strife between Rehoboam and Jeroboam which, by that time, was already about five years old. But it was not put there as a boast, as Velikovsky believed. Rather, it represents the standard, stock-in-trade excuse of the conqueror throughout history. He came there to "restore order." Nevertheless, it would seem that the northern kingdom under Jeroboam did become a close ally of Egypt and was to remain such for the entire period of the state's existence.

The Road to Kadesh

Thutmose III's records leave us in no doubt that the main foe against whom he waged war was the king of Kadesh. He is described repeatedly as the "wretched foe of Kadesh." All of the action against this enemy took place in Palestine. In actual fact, only two military engagements are mentioned. One was the taking of Joppa (Jaffa), which fell after a long siege; the other was an engagement at the fortress of *Mykty* (normally interpreted as Megiddo), which was followed by the siege and eventual surrender of that city.

The approach to Mykty and the battle that followed is described in great detail by the Egyptian chroniclers. Thutmose's generals feared to approach Mykty by the most direct route, the Aruna road. It was narrow and dangerous and their line would be dangerously drawn out. The pharaoh replied that he would go by the Aruna road even if he went alone. Gaining courage from such decisive leadership, the army advanced by the direct route, approached Mykty and won a decisive victory;

> ... When they saw his majesty prevailing against them they fled headlong to Megiddo, in fear, abandoning their horses and their chariots of gold and silver.

> ... Now, if only the army of his majesty had not given their heart to plundering the things of the enemy, they would have [captured] Megiddo at this moment, when the wretched foe of Kadesh and the

wretched foe of this city were hauled up in haste to bring them into this city. The fear of his majesty had entered their hearts.[124]

A short time later the city surrendered. "Behold, the chiefs of this country came to render their portions." The description of the end of the campaign has not been preserved, but it can be reconstructed. The campaign ended with the submission of the entire land of Retjenu, with its one hundred and nineteen walled cities. The city or country of Kadesh appears first on the list.

It is generally believed that, notwithstanding the earlier mention of Gaza and Joppa, which point to central/southern Palestine, the above events took place in the vicinity of the biblical Megiddo, located to the north of the Carmel Ridge in the Jezreel Valley. Yet such a location causes immense problems, both for the conventional view and for Velikovsky's.

Let's deal first with the problem for Velikovsky.

To begin with, Velikovsky claimed that this campaign of Thutmose III was directed primarily against the kingdom of Judah. Rehoboam was the "wretched foe of Kadesh." Yet Megiddo in the Jezreel Valley is far to the north of Rehoboam's kingdom. The Jezreel Valley and Plain of Esdraelon lay right in the middle of the kingdom of Israel, ruled at that time by Rehoboam's arch enemy Jeroboam I. It is extremely unlikely that Jeroboam, as a long-time friend of Egypt, would have allowed his territory to be used as a rallying-point against the pharaoh.

But locating Thutmose III's Mykty in the Jezreel Valley causes great problems also for convention.

The description of the campaign preserved at Karnak makes it perfectly clear that Thutmose's officers were in great fear of approaching the fortress of Mykty by the most direct route, the road of Aruna. This highway is described by them as a narrow and dangerous passageway; "Will the vanguard of us be fighting while the [rear guard] is waiting here in Aruna, unable to fight[?]" Two other roads, they say, offer a safer alternative; one goes by way of Taanach; the other to the north of Djefti, or Zefti. This latter comes out "to the north of Megiddo." Clearly Thutmose III's battle-hardened officers were terrified of traversing this route; so afraid indeed that they seemed almost on the point of mutiny. Yet according to accepted ideas the "Aruna Road" was the gently-inclining and broad road through the Wadi Ara, which to this day climbs from the Plain of Sharon northwards over Carmel to the Plain of Esdraelon.

Why would the Egyptian strategists have been afraid of passing such a barrier?

---

[124] Breasted, *Records* Vol.2, Sec. 430

The answer, I believe, was provided by Eva Danelius, who possessed a great knowledge of the region's topography. According to Danelius, the Aruna Road was not the path of the Wadi Ara but the steep and treacherous path of Araunah (or Beth Horon) which led from Joppa to Jerusalem. (We remember at this point that immediately before setting out for Mykty and the Aruna Road, Thutmose III besieged and took the city of Joppa). Before its conquest by David, the hill upon which Jerusalem stood was known as the threshing floor of Araun or Horon the Jebusite.[125] Evidently the region, said Danelius, kept this name well after its incorporation into the kingdom of Israel. The road between Lower and Upper Beth Horon is a treacherous defile, rising 225 meters over a distance of 2.8 kilometers. "Due to its special topography, the Beth Horon Ascent ... was always a focal point of battles and attempts to stop troops trying to reach Jerusalem or to descend from the Judaean Hills to the coastal plain," according to the opinion of a modern historian.[126] Danelius quotes, as one example of many, the experience of the Roman general Gaius Cestius Gallus, during the Jewish War in 66 AD. The Roman troops suffered many casualties on their way up the Beth Horon ascent, but on their retreat they suffered disaster;

> While even the infantry were hard put to it to defend themselves, the cavalry were in still greater jeopardy; to advance in order down the road under the hail of darts was impossible, to charge up the slopes was impracticable for horses; on either side were precipices and ravines, down which they slipped and were hurled to destruction; there was no room for flight, no conceivable means of defense; in their utter helplessness the troops were reduced to groans and the wailings of despair.[127]

Only night prevented the complete destruction of the Roman army.

It will be agreed, I think, that the Beth Horon or Araunah road, leading to Jerusalem, seems a far better candidate for the Aruna road of Thutmose III than the thoroughly safe and unremarkable road that passes through the Wadi Ara; and there is other evidence pointing in the same direction.

It will be remembered, for example, that Thutmose III's annals at Karnak refer to two other roads, safer than the Aruna passageway, by which the Egyptian army could reach the stronghold of Mykyty. One of these was to the north of Djefty, or Zefty. Commentators throughout the years have

---

[125] 2 Samuel 24:16
[126] B. Bar-Kochva, quoted by Eva Danelius, "Did Thutmose III Despoil the Temple in Jerusalem?" *Society for Interdisciplinary Studies Review* Vol.2 (1977), p. 71
[127] Josephus, *Jewish War* II, xix, 1-9. Josephus gives the number of killed Roman soldiers as 5,300 infantry and 480 cavalry.

wondered about the latter's location. According to Danelius, it is identical to Zephathah, the spot near Mareshah where Asa met and defeated the Ethiopian invader Zerah (2 Chronicles 14:10). There is no linguistic objection to this identification, but, if it is correct, it means without question that the Road of Aruna must be precisely where Danelius said it was. The site of Mareshah has never been lost. It was the Judean border-fortress guarding against Philistia, located just to the east of Lachish.

The eastern opening of the Beth-Horon road lies in a district called Jebel el Kuds, or in Hebrew, Har Kodsho, "the Holy Mountain." In other words, as Danelius puts it, *Kd-sw* of the Egyptian inscriptions "was not the name of a city, but of a land." And indeed throughout the Scriptures the region around Jerusalem, the territory of the Tribe of Benjamin, is named the "Holy Mountain." This is a crucial point, and it explains why "Kadesh" always heads the Egyptian lists referring to campaigns in the region. But if Kadesh was a country and not a city, we are also presented with an explanation as to why the king of Kadesh was in Mykty rather than a city of Kadesh. Evidently Mykty, a name related to the Semitic *migdol* or "fortress," was the name of the actual capital of the country Kadesh. We ask ourselves: Was the city of Jerusalem ever known as Mykty or any name equivalent to it?

The answer is provided by Danelius: "Among the names enumerated as designating Jerusalem is Bait-al-Makdis, or in brief, Makdis, corresponding to Beith-ha-Miqdash in modern Hebrew pronunciation. The 10th century Arab writer who mentions this name calls himself Mukadassi = the Jerusalemite. The name Makdes was still used by the Samaritans (a Jewish sect who never left the country, who trace their ancestors to three of the northern tribes of Israel) at the beginning of this century, when discussing with Rabbi Moshe Gaster their attitude towards Jerusalem, and a local shop outside Damascus Gate still bears the inscription: Baith el-Makdis."[128]

According to Danelius, the name Miqdash was originally confined to the holy precinct north of the Jebusite city, the area which had originally been the threshing-floor of Araunah the Jebusite. In the time of Rohoboam, this region contained the temple and its precincts as well as the royal palace. It was these which had to be taken, the Jebusite city down the hill apparently having been of no interest to the pharaoh. "Thus it was," says Danelius, "that his officers laid special stress on the fact that the Zaphata defile, too, reached the ridge north of the Temple mount, and that there was no necessity to use the Aruna road for an approach from the north."[129]

---

[128] Danelius, "Did Thutmose III Despoil the Temple in Jerusalem?" loc. cit., pp.73-4
[129] Ibid. p.74

Danelius also stresses the fact that, according to the pharaoh, Mykty could be reached by way of *Ta-'a-na-ka* (interpreted as Taanach). There is of course a well-known fortress by this name on the Plain of Esdraelon, but, as Danelius notes, there is also a ridge on the western approaches to Jerusalem known as the Tahhunah Ridge; and there is a wadi Tahhunah in the same district. The name appears a third time in that of Khirbet at-Tahuna, which overlooks the exit of the defile from the mountains, opposite Zorah, one of the border-fortresses against the Philistines strengthened by Rehoboam (2 Chronicles 11:10).

Jerusalem in the Time of Thutmose III: A Mighty Citadel

Historians have long assumed that Thutmose III neglected to mention Jerusalem in his reports for the simple reason that the town was of little importance at the time (though he did mention numerous other Palestinian settlements that can have been little more than villages). Certainly, a couple of generations after Thutmose III, during the reigns of Amenhotep III and Akhnaton, Jerusalem is mentioned (as Urusalim) in the Amarna royal correspondences; and there it is clearly a rather impoverished center of limited significance. But was that the case in Thutmose III's time?

Archaeologists at Jerusalem face the enormous problem of excavating in a densely populated environment. As such, progress has been slow and rather piecemeal. Nonetheless, we can say that given Velikovsky's thesis, we would expect the Jerusalem of Hatshepsut's and Thutmose III's era to have been a large and extremely important metropolis. And excavations in the city over the past few decades have fully confirmed this supposition: As recently as 2009 archaeologists reported the discovery of an enormous fortification wall close to the Temple Mount. An article from that year on CNN's website spoke of a "'Massive' ancient wall" uncovered at the city and reported the following:

> "An archaeological dig in Jerusalem has turned up a 3,700-year-old wall that is the largest and oldest of its kind found in the region, experts say.Standing 8 meters (26 feet) high, the wall of huge cut stones is a marvel to archaeologists."[130]

All of the boulders comprising this structure weigh between four and five tons, and the section uncovered was 24 meters (79 feet) long. "However, it is thought the fortification is much longer because it continues west beyond the part that was exposed," the Israel Antiquities Authority reported. A joint

---

[130] "Massive' ancient wall uncovered in Jerusalem," CNN News, September 4, 2009 www. cnn.com

statement by the leaders of the dig announced that, "This is the most massive wall that has ever been uncovered in the City of David," and marks the first time that "such massive construction that predates the Herodian period has been discovered in Jerusalem." They also stated that "Despite the fact that so many have excavated on this hill, there is a very good chance that extremely large and well-preserved architectural elements are still hidden in it and waiting to be uncovered."

These latest discoveries only confirmed what archaeologists have known for some time: Namely that the latter part of the Middle Bronze Age marked a peak of power and prosperity at Jerusalem never again attained until the eighth century BC. In the words of Israel Finkelstein: "If one needs to summarize over a century of exploration in Jerusalem, the proper statement regarding the Bronze and Iron Ages would be that archaeology revealed evidence for major building activity in two periods only: The Middle Bronze II-III and the Late Iron II (the eighth-seventh centuries BCE). ... The interval between these periods, which covers the Late Bronze Age, the Iron I, and the Early Iron II (c. 1550-750 BCE) provides indication of habitation but almost no signs of monumental building operations."[131]

Middle Bronze III is right at the end of the Middle Bronze Age in Palestine and historians are in no doubt that this was the epoch contemporary with the early part of Egypt's Eighteenth Dynasty. Archaeologist Aaron Burke confirms that it was the Middle Bronze settlements of the region that Thutmose III overwhelmed. This being the case, it is clear that Jerusalem suffered a serious decline immediately after the time of Hatshepsut.[132] This is precisely what we would expect in Velikovsky's scheme, since it was just then that Solomon's kingdom was divided and Jerusalem was reduced to being the capital of a small and relatively impoverished kingdom of Judah.

Nothing between the Nile and the Euphrates has yet been found to match the mighty defensive walls of Jerusalem in the late Middle Bronze Age.[133] How then, we need to ask, could a conqueror marching through Palestine and Syria leave behind him, unsecured, the most important stronghold in

---

[131] Israel Finkelstein, "The Rise of Jerusalem and Judah: The Missing Link," in Andrew G. Vaughan and Ann E. Killebrew (eds.), *Jerusalem in Bible and Archaeology: The First Temple Period* (Atlanta, Georgia, 2003), p. 81

[132] Aaron Burke has admitted that Jerusalem was probably one of Thutmose III's targets. Burke, "Canaan Under Siege: The History and Archaeology of Egypt's War in Canaan during the Early Eighteenth Dynasty," in (J. D. Schloen, ed.) *Exploring the Longue Dureé: Essays in Honor of Lawrence E. Stager* (Eisenbrauns, Winona Lake, IN, 2009), p. 44

[133] It is highly likely that the great Middle Bronze walls were constructed by Solomon and no one else. We are told (2 Samuel 5:9-12) that David built at Jerusalem after taking the city from the Jebusites, but the Scriptures make it clear that the great defensive walls were the work of Solomon. See (1 Kings 3:1).

the region? And how could he fail, apparently, even to notice the existence of such a citadel? Yet this is precisely what conventional scholarship would have the reading public believe.

In March 2012 I put the following question to two professors of archaeology specializing in the Bronze Age of Palestine. The first of these was the above-mentioned Aaron A. Burke, Professor of Middle Eastern archaeology at University of California, Los Angeles. Burke has written numerous articles on the decline and fall of Canaan's Middle Bronze Age strongholds,[134] and has stressed the role of Thutmose III in that process. I wrote:

"I understand that during the final phases of the Middle Bronze Age many settlements in Palestine were heavily fortified, and this seems also to have been the case with Jerusalem, which has now revealed massive 'cyclopean' walls dating from Middle Bronze III. In view of the apparent importance of the city at this time, is it possible that Thutmose III did not mention it on his register of conquered Palestinian cities? I am aware that this list displays the names of 119 Palestinian and south Syrian sites, some of them rather insignificant, to put it mildly. My question is: Do Egyptologists currently consider Jerusalem to be present?"

I received no response from Professor Burke, so then put the same question to Professor Gabriel Barkay, of Bar-Ilan University in Tel Aviv, another authority on the archaeology of the region and Jerusalem in particular. He too failed to respond.

According to conventional ideas, which presumably Burke and Barkay subscribe to, Kadesh, which leads Thutmose III's register, stood on the Orontes, perhaps 100 miles to the north of the other cities mentioned. This Kadesh of the Orontes has never been identified. Kenneth Kitchen has attempted to link it with Tell Nebi Mend, about 15 miles southwest of Homs in central Syria, but offers no convincing proof.[135] A great city of Kadesh was the scene of the famous battle fought by Ramses II against the Hittites, around a century after the death of Thutmose III, and he clearly locates the stronghold in the vicinity of Tunip, in northern Syria. Whether Kadesh be located at Tell Nebi Mend, however, or further north, it is agreed that Thutmose III *did not actually conquer it* in his first year. This is apparently illustrated by the fact that Thutmose claims to have conquered this northern Kadesh much later in his career. Yet here the subjugation of this supposedly powerful and prestigious city is passed over in a single sentence. We

---

[134] Articles include, "Canaan Under Siege" and "More Light on Old Reliefs: new Kingdom Egyptian Siege Tactics and Asiatic Resistance," in (J. D. Schloen, ed.) *Exploring the Longue Dureé: Essays in Honor of Lawrence E. Stager* (Eisenbrauns, Winona Lake, IN, 2009).

[135] Kenneth Kitchen, *Ramesside Inscriptions*, Vol. 2 (Blackwell Publishing Limited, 1996), pp. 16-7

read: "His majesty arrived at the city of Kadesh, overthrew it, cut down its groves, harvested its grain." (Breasted, *Records* 2, 465). Breasted notes that "it is with peculiar regret" that the taking of such an immensely important city is recorded in these "laconic words."[136]

Let's consider this carefully: The Kadesh which Thutmose III claims to have conquered in his first year (but did not!) stood at the head of a mighty coalition, a coalition which included everything between Edom in the south and Damascus in the north. After defeating this coalition and falsely claiming to have conquered it, the city diminishes in importance. The king of an Orontes Kadesh, at the head of a coalition of warlike states, should still have posed a threat to Thutmose III's conquests in Palestine, yet in the campaigns waged by Thutmose III to the north in subsequent years, Kadesh hardly figures at all. And when he finally takes the city, the event merits no more than a line in his annals.

None of this — the scenario accepted in all textbooks — makes any sense at all.

If, however Jerusalem occurs in Thutmose III's lists as Kadesh — its alternative name throughout the Scriptures — then all is explained. Kadesh is the great power of the region, the stronghold which commands a host of lesser Canaanite cities and towns: it is Jerusalem.

The Conquest of God's Land

Although in later years Thutmose III campaigned as far north as the Euphrates and scored some astonishing military successes — against the Mitannians, for example — none of these later achievements were ever commemorated in anything like the fashion of his first-year conquest of Palestine. Yet it is doubtful if this campaign saw even a single pitched battle. After advancing towards Mykty and Kadesh along the Aruna Road, the Egyptian army lined up against the Asiatics, who simply melted away, apparently. Certainly no record, either at Karnak or anywhere else, mentions a real battle outside the walls of Mykty. The king of Kadesh had to be hauled up the walls of the fortress by the defenders, who had locked the city gates in fear.

Why the extraordinary prominence given to such a victory? As we have seen, the pharaoh ordered a list of the 119 "cities" of Palestine taken during the campaign to be copied three times upon the walls of his temple at Karnak. Most of these, it should be remembered, were not cities, but small walled settlements. In addition to this, he devoted an enormous bas-relief at

---

[136] Breasted, *A History of Egypt*, p. 301

Karnak to an illustration of the treasures he took in that campaign. These certainly came from Kadesh and were seen by Velikovsky as the plunder taken from Solomon's temple by Shishak, a proposition entirely supported by the present writer.

For those not convinced by Velikovsky's arguments however, the question remains, why would such an apparently small success be so commemorated?

The answer, the only possible one, has already been provided. Thutmose III revelled in his conquest of Palestine because this was formerly the greatest power in the region and moreover the kingdom beloved by his hated stepmother Hatshepsut. We recall that the list of conquered Palestinian cities is positioned directly opposite Hatshepsut's obelisk in Karnak.

The actual defeat and capitulation of the king of Kadesh, Rehoboam, is best described by Eva Danelius: "Though Rehoboam had fortified the cities guarding the roads to Jerusalem, he lacked any war experience, and so did his subjects, who like himself were thoroughly demoralized, according to Josephus. These soldiers were in no way prepared to stand up against the sudden attack of the Egyptians, led by the Pharaoh who stood "in a chariot of electrum, arrayed in his weapons of war, like Horus, the Smiter, lord of power; like Montu of Thebes...." In an instant, the country was covered with Egyptian chariots and infantry. Panic seized the Asiatics. Officers and men threw away their weapons and fled, be it in the direction of Jerusalem (Makdis), or down the valley and across the fords of the Jordan. From the walls of the Holy City, the watchmen saw the wild chase: Rehoboam and the princes galloping for their lives, closely followed by the Egyptian chariots. The capital hastily closed its gates before the approaching foe; as to the fugitives: "The people hauled them [up] pulling by their clothing ... (and lowered) clothing to pull them up into the city," as so vividly described in the Annals. And the long siege of Jerusalem began.

"Then came Shemaiah the prophet to Rehoboam, and to the princes of Judah, that were gathered together in Jerusalem because of Shishak, and said unto them, Thus saith the Lord, Ye have forsaken me, and therefore have I also left you in the hand of Shishak. Whereupon the princes of Israel and the king humbled themselves...." Therefore "they shall be his [the Pharaoh's] servants; that they may know my service, and the service of the kingdoms of the countries," reports the Chronicler (II Chron. 12:5-6,8). They opened the gates of the city: "The chiefs of this country came to render their portions, to smell the earth (do obeisance) to the fame of his majesty, to crave breath for their nostrils," writes the Pharaoh. And he "took away the treasures of the house of the Lord, and the treasures of the king's house; he took all: he carried away also the shields of gold which Solomon had made" (II Chron. 12:9).[137]

Danelius ends by quoting Velikovsky, who said: "In the bas-reliefs of Karnak we have a very excellent and detailed account of the vessels and furniture of the Temple of Solomon." "It seems," says Danelius, "that Velikovsky is right. There is nothing in the *Annals* to contradict his statement."

Before moving on, we should note a tradition from Abyssinia which tells how Menelik, the son of Solomon and the Queen of Sheba, returned to Jerusalem after his mother's death and plundered the Temple, taking, among other things, the Ark of the Covenant. From this account, it is clear that the Abyssinians equated Menelik with Sesostris, and therefore regarded him as a king of Egypt. It is perhaps significant too that Menelik, or Menerik, sounds like an abbreviated version of Thutmose III's throne-name Menkheperre.

The People, Flora and Fauna of God's Land

The towns and cities conquered by Thutmose III were shown by him at Karnak. Each town was represented by a kneeling and bound prisoner, in front of whom was shown a shield with the name of the city. These apparently are accurate representations of the inhabitants of Palestine and Syria at the time. The prisoners of Palestine and southern Syria (Lebanon) look exactly like the inhabitants of Punt, portrayed on the Deir el-Bahri temple. There we see the same long hair tied with a headband, and, most importantly, the same peculiar long and pointed beard; the beard which, in Egypt, was the symbol of royalty and divinity.

Fig. 8. People of Retjenu (Palestine) and Syria bringing tribute to Thutmose III. They sport the same pointed beards as the Puntites, and bring with them a baby elephant and a bear – two creatures native to the region.

During Thutmose III's reign Egyptian contacts with Asia opened up as never before. Almost every year of the first half of his reign, Thutmose under-

---

[137] Danelius, "Did Thutmose III Despoil the Temple in Jerusalem?" loc cit., pp.76-7

took a campaign in Asia. Mostly this was concerned simply with collecting tribute, though occasionally there was real military action. These campaigns were extensively reported and depicted throughout the pharaoh's lifetime: and what they tell us about Syria/Palestine at the time is revealing.

In his third year, "year 25," Thutmose III returned to Palestine for inspection. In Upper Retjenu (the central uplands) he found gardens rich in color, form and fragrance. Many of the plants, great quantities in fact, were transplanted to Egypt.

> All the plants that grow, all flowers that are in God's Land which were found by his majesty, when his majesty proceeded to Upper Retenu.

The transplanted collections were reproduced on the walls of the Karnak temple, showing the peculiar and exotic shapes of the Palestinian flora. A zoological collection was also taken along. No inscription mentions it, but the figures of animals appear among the plants on the bas-relief. Many were decidedly exotic, and not what is normally, nowadays, regarded as typical of Palestine. Some of them, particularly the birds, could not even be identified, and seemed to one eminent zoologist to be fantastic inventions of the sculptor.[138] Among the plants, botanists recognized various rare species, such as the blue lotus, the vine date tree, the pomegranate, the dragon plant, the arum, the iris, the chrysanthemum, as well as the cornflower and the mandragora, along with a variety of pine tree and some sort of "melon tree." Many of the plants too, however, just like the birds, could not be identified at all. It seemed clear that several of the various specimens of flora were not indigenous to Palestine. How then was their presence to be explained among those brought by Thutmose III from Palestine? In the words of one commentator, "Possibly, the twofold geographical designation, Palestine and God's Land, could be explained by the fact that a number of plants actually came from God's Land. Still another conjecture to explain the presence of these plants may be made, namely that princes of distant countries sent messengers with gifts to the pharaoh while on his war expedition."[139]

The second surmise, as Velikovsky notes, is strange; given the fact that it is unusual for remote countries to send plants and birds to warriors on a march of conquest. The first surmise, he notes, "merely illustrates the type of conjecture necessary in order to evade the identification of Palestine with God's Land."

---

[138] M. Hilzheimer, quoted by Wreszinski, *Atlas* Pt. II text to Plate 33
[139] Wreszinski, *Atlas* Pt. II text to Plate 33

There seems little doubt, as Velikovsky believed, that many of the exotic plants and animals depicted at Karnak were indeed from the famous collections of Solomon, whose interest in such things is celebrated in the Scriptures:

> And he spake of trees, from the cedar tree that is in the Lebanon even unto the hyssop that springeth out of the wall: he spake also of beasts, and of fowl, and of creeping things, and of fishes. (1 Kings 4:33)

Yet we must also bear in mind what we discovered in the previous chapter: Palestine/Syria in the days of Hatshepsut and Thutmose III was a very different land from the one we now know. Species of animals and plants found nowadays only in Africa or southern Arabia roamed freely throughout the region. Perhaps the most spectacular illustration of this comes from the tomb of an official under Thutmose III named Rekhmire. This is a wall-painting depicting Syrians bringing tribute, amongst which is a young elephant and a bear. The Syrian leading the bear carries large tusks of elephant ivory.[140] It was of course the ivory, as well as the ebony and incense, products of Punt, which helped to convince many experts that this region be located in Africa. Yet the monuments of Thutmose III show that they all occurred in Palestine/Syria. Another official of the time, one Amenemhab, writes in his biography;

> Again [I saw] another successful deed which the Lord of the Two Lands accomplished in Ni. He hunted 120 elephants at their mudhole. Then the biggest elephant which was among them began to fight before the face of his majesty.[141]

This encounter with the elephant herd, enormous by modern standards, took place in northern Syria.

Shishak and Sesostris

During his stay in Egypt, the historian Herodotus was told about a mighty king named Sesostris who had conquered most of Asia and whose military exploits, the Egyptians boasted, were unparalleled in history.[142] Identifying this man from the hieroglyphic records has always been problematic, since neither this name nor anything closely resembling it, has been found in the king-lists and monuments. Nevertheless, it is now generally assumed that Sesostris is a corrupted form of the hieroglyphic Senwosret (a name actually

---

[140] See Maspero, *History of Egypt* Vol.V, p.34
[141] Pritchard, op. cit., p.240
[142] Herodotus, ii, 102-110

written as *Wsr.t.sn* or Usertasen); and indeed kings of the latter name are now routinely called "Sesostris" in the textbooks. Nevertheless, none of these pharaohs were military men of any stature and it is admitted that whilst the *name* Sesostris is derived from them, the *character* of the great conqueror owes much more to the imperialist pharaohs of the New Kingdom — most especially to Thutmose III. Thus in the words of George Rawlinson, "The name Sesostris no doubt comes from Sesortosis, a Grecised form of Usurtasen," but "the figure [of Sesostris] was composed by uniting in one the actions of all the chief Egyptian conquerors. As the greatest of these Thothmes III furnished the most traits."[143]

But why, it may reasonably be asked, should the non-military Senwosret/ Usertasen kings furnish the name of a great conqueror at all? The implausibility of such a circumstance, especially in view of the fact that the Egyptians had other, real military men, whose name or names they could have used instead, makes us wonder whether the word "Sesostris" has anything to do with the Senwosret/Usertasen kings at all.

If the outline of history proposed by Velikovsky is right, then Thutmose III (the admitted model for the character of Sesostris) was also called Shishak, or Sesak. This word of course shares its first syllable with Sesostris, which would naturally lead us to suspect a connection. But this then begs the question: Is Thutmose III actually called Shishak or anything like it, on the monuments?

He is indeed.

Thutmose III, like all New Kingdom pharaohs, possessed a multitude of royal titles. In documents of the time he is in fact more commonly known by the so-called prenomen ("Suten Bat") name Menkheperre (also transcribed into cuneiform as Manikhibiria or something like it). He was also known by the Golden Horus name of Djeser-kau. As early as 1987, Kenneth Birch of South Africa suggested this as the origin of Shishak. The name now transcribed as Djeser-kau was previously rendered variously as Cheser-kau, Tscheser-kau etc, and was probably pronounced something like Djesey-ka or Sheshy-ka (the best guess is that the consonant *dj* was pronounced something like the French *j*).[144]

Admitting that Djeser-kau could quite easily be transliterated into Shishak in Hebrew ears, it may however be argued that the Golden Horus name of a pharaoh was not one commonly used, especially by foreigners. Nevertheless, there is abundant evidence to suggest that pharaohs were

---

[143] Rawlinson, *History of Egypt* Vol.2, p.226n.
[144] K. Birch, *Society for Interdisciplinary Studies: Catastrophism and Chronology Workshop* No.2 (1987), p. 35

often known by nicknames and abbreviations. So for example David Rohl has shown that Ramses II at least was sometimes called "Sheshy" — derived from the *ses* part of his son of Ra title. In addition, it has been pointed out that Shishak sounds very much like the Hebrew *shashak*, (variously "attacker," "assaulter," or "the one who crushes"), so that this at least may have been a nickname given to the pharaoh by his Hebrew victims. I would suggest that Djeser-kau/Sheshy-ka reminded the Hebrews of their own word for attacker, *shashak*, which name was then accorded him in the Book of Kings.

Before moving on, we should note the Abyssinian as recorded in the *Kebra Nagast*, which tells how Menelik, son of Solomon and the Queen of Sheba, returned to Jerusalem after Solomon's death and plundered the Temple, taking with him, among other things, the Ark of the Covenant. It is evident from this that Menelik was, in the eyes of the Ethiopians at least, the same person as Shishak, which means equally that the Queen of Sheba was an Egyptian. Furthermore, the similarities between Menelik, or Menerik, and Menkheperre should not be overlooked.

CHAPTER 4: THE AMARNA LETTERS

Historical Setting

Velikovsky devoted no less than three chapters (out of eight) in *Ages in Chaos* I to a series of documents popularly known as the Amarna Letters. These texts, of which over 380 survive, are a collection of letters written by Syrian and Palestinian vassal as well as rival powers further to the north during the reigns of Amenhotep III (named Nimmuria on the documents) and Akhnaton (named Naphuria). Also included were copies of letters written by the pharaoh in reply.

All of the letters, even those written by Egyptian scribes in Egypt, were composed in the Akkadian language, which proved that Akkadian was then the *lingua franca* of the entire Near East at the time. Those written in Palestine and Syria often contained, to varying degrees, an admixture of Canaanite vocabulary and syntax. This demonstrated that Akkadian was not the first language of the scribes and that obviously they had learned the language in some form of scribal schools or colleges.

The Canaanite elements in the texts proved to be interesting. Scholars were surprised to find precise parallels with biblical Hebrew. Even Hebrew expressions and popular sayings, found throughout the Old Testament, occurred. Thus in one letter to the pharaoh, Labayu, the ruler of the central hill country around Shechem, wrote, in good Hebrew; "If ants are smitten, they do not accept [the smiting] quietly, but they bite the hand of the man who smites them."[145] Albright recognized in this a close parallel with two biblical Proverbs mentioning ants (6:6 and 30:2).[146]

Orientalists were particularly struck by the parallels between the Letters and many expressions in the books of the biblical Prophets. Thus loyalty is expressed by the metaphor, "to lay the neck to the yoke and bear it," found in the letters of Baal-miir and Yakhtiri.[147] Precisely the same expression is found in Jeremiah 27:11.

The submission of an enemy is expressed as "to eat dust" in the letter of the men of Irqata as well as in Isaiah 49:23.

The king's "face" is set against his enemy, or the king "casts down" an enemy's face, or he throws the enemy out of his hand — identical in the letters of Rib-Addi and in Genesis 19:21 and I Samuel 25:29. Rib-Addi's "face is friendly towards the king"; "he has directed his face towards the glory of the king, and would see his gracious face." In the words of S. A. Cook, "Biblical ideas of 'face' and 'presence' will at once be recalled."

The same writer noted that, "Just as Ikhnaton's hymn reminds us of Psalm 104, so Psalm 139:7f is suggested by the words of Tagi (Letter 264): 'As for us, consider! My two eyes are upon thee. If we go up into heaven (*shamema*), or if we descend into the earth, yet is our head (*rushunu*) in thine hands.'"

"The footstool of his feet" is an expression found in both a letter and in Psalm 110. Akhi-Yawi writes, "A brother art thou and love is in thy bowels and in thy heart," very similar to Jeremiah 4:19. "The city weeps and its tears run down, and there is none taking hold of our hand" (i.e., there is no helper). These words, written by the people of Tunip, call to mind Lamentations 1:2 and Isaiah 42:6.

Rib-Addi's appeals to the pharaoh's good name contain turns of speech used also in Deuteronomy 9:27f and in Joshua 7:9. When he says he has confessed his sins, he uses the words "opened his sins," an expression also found in Proverbs 28:13. When he writes that he will die "if there is not another heart" in the king, he uses an expression also found in I Samuel 10:9 and Ezekiel 11:19.

The king of Jerusalem wrote to pharaoh that "because he has his name upon Jerusalem for ever, the city cannot be neglected," words reminiscent of a passage in Jeremiah 14:9. He also wrote, "See! The king, my lord, has set his name at the rising of the sun and at the setting of the sun," almost identical to an expression found in Malachi 1:11.

---

[145] Letter 252
[146] W. F. Albright, "An Archaic Hebrew Proverb in an Amarna Letter from Central Palestine" *Journal of Near Eastern Studies* 89 (1943), pp. 29-32
[147] These examples and quotations are from S. A. Cook, "Style and Ideas," in *The Cambridge Ancient History* Vol.2 (2nd ed). Also mentioned by Velikovsky in *Ages in Chaos* I

These and numerous other parallels moved Cook to write: "the repeated lyrical utterances of Rib-Addi and Abdi-Khiba are early examples of the unrestrained laments of the later Israelites who appeal, not to a divine king of Egypt, their overlord, but to Yahweh."[148] Yet it was the chronology alone that prompted this statement. Believing the correspondences to predate the period of the Israelite kings by about five centuries, historians were amazed at the parallels, both in the language used and in the various expressions and idioms employed. Indeed, were it not for the chronology, they would simply have termed the language of the letters "Hebrew."

Jerusalem and Botrys

If scholars were surprised to find the Canaanites of the 15th and 14th centuries BC using Hebrew of the 8th and 7th centuries, they were perhaps even more nonplussed to find mentioned towns and settlements which should not, according to everything that was known about the history of the region, have existed until the time of the biblical kings.

This was particularly so with regard to the city of Jerusalem, which appeared in the letters as Urusalim. Until the discovery of the archive, it was widely believed that Jerusalem was not known by this name until after its conquest by David, right at the start of the Kings period. It had generally been accepted that prior to this the city had been called Jebus, or Salem.

The ruler of Jerusalem at the time of the letters was named Abdi-Hiba or Abdi-Tibbi, and it immediately became clear that his fiefdom was an important regional power. This again seemed very strange, given the fact that the pre-Davidic city of the Jebusites was an isolated fortress, completely surrounded by the territories of the Twelve Tribes: And this was a situation that had pertained for many generations, ever since the days, in fact, of Joshua. But to admit that the letters predated the time of Joshua caused problems of its own, for such an admission implied that the Exodus had occurred much later than scholars imagined.

The king of Jerusalem who corresponded with pharaohs Amenhotep III and Akhnaton seemed to rule over a territory comparable to that of Judah, the southern of the two divided monarchy kingdoms; and to the north of Jerusalem there existed another regional power, apparently centered on Shechem, which controlled a territory roughly corresponding to the northern kingdom of Israel. We shall have more to say on this northern kingdom presently.

---

[148] Ibid., p.338

As well as carrying a name it was not expected to have had for another four centuries, Jerusalem also, it seems, possessed a temple it should not have: A temple by the name of "Shulman" or "Solomon."

Letter 290, from the king of Jerusalem, referred to a place read as Bet-NIN. IB. Originally, this was believed to be a reference to Assyria (House of Nineveh). However, in 1940, the eminent Assyriologist Professor Jules Lewy suggested that Bet-NIN.IB be translated as "Temple of Shulman" and that this was an alternative name for Jerusalem itself at the time.[149] In the letter in question, Abdi-Hiba complained that the land was falling to the invading bands (habiru), "and now, in addition, the capital of the country of Jerusalem — its name is Bit Sulmani — the king's city, has broken away." Beth Sulman in Hebrew, as Professor Lewy correctly translated, is Temple of Sulman. Believing the Amarna Letters to date from the 14th century BC, Lewy could not, of course, surmise that the edifice was the Temple of Solomon and therefore supposed it to be a Canaanite place of worship of a god found in Akkadian sources as Shelmi, Shulmanu, or Salamu. He wrote; "Aside from proving the existence of a Sulman temple in Jerusalem in the first part of the 14th century BC, this statement of the ruler of the region leaves us in no doubt that the city was then known not only as Jerusalem, but also as Bet Sulman." He saw it as "significant" that it was only the name Jerusalem that "reappears after the end of the occupation of the city by the Jebusites, which the Sulman temple, in all probability, did not survive."

Another unexpected discovery amongst the correspondences was the mention of a city named Batruna. This was immediately recognized as ancient Botrys (modern Batroun),[150] which Menander of Ephesus had claimed was built by king Ithobalos (Ethbaal), the father-in-law of the Israelite king Ahab.[151]

If scholars were surprised to find cities of the first millennium mentioned in texts of the second, they were also surprised to find the political situation in the region during the period of the letters to be remarkably similar to that of the Kings period in the Bible.

The letters reveal, above all, a powerful and ascendant kingdom, named Amurru, located just to the north of Palestine. There is no question in the minds of scholars that Amurru is identical to Syria. During the time of the letters, the kings of Amurru/Syria are involved in conflicts throughout the region; and the two Amurru rulers of the period, Abdi-Ashirta and his son

---

[149] Jules Lewy, "The Sulman Temple in Jerusalem," *The Journal of Biblical Archaeology* 59 (1940), 519ff.

[150] Paul Dhorme, *Revue biblique* (1908) 509f; Weber, in Knudtzon, *Die El-Amarna-Tafeln*, p.1165

[151] Josephus, *Against Apion* i,116; *Jewish Antiquities*, viii,1

Aziru, are both notorious for their violence and treachery. This situation would seem to recall the political makeup of the region during the epoch of the divided Hebrew kingdoms, specifically from the period of Asa in Judah through perhaps to the time of Jehoshaphat, when the Syrian kings Ben-Hadad I, Hazael, and Ben-Hadad II, waged continual war against their neighbors before being finally reduced to impotence at the end of Ben-Hadad II's reign.

The political situation within Palestine itself during the time of the letters also displayed close parallels with Palestine in the epoch of Asa through to Jehoshaphat, when the kings of Judah were in continual conflict with the kings of Israel. The letters reveal prolonged warfare between the king of Jerusalem and another king based in Shechem, one of the capitals of historical Israel.

The kings of the cities who wrote to the pharaoh were hereditary princes. In the letters they call themselves *rabiti sari* (princes, or regents). But next to these princes were attached governors, direct representatives of the Egyptian crown. This of course was to be expected in the letters, but, as Velikovsky remarked, it was a situation that bore a strange resemblance to that of the period of the divided monarchy, during which time the kings of Palestine and Syria are not normally regarded as living under the aegis of Egypt. Thus, for example, in the Book of Chronicles we find reference to a "governor" named Amon, apparently resident in Samaria, whose power was seemingly even greater than that of the Israelite king. In 2 Chronicles 18:25, we are told that the king of Israel ordered the prophet Micaiah to be taken back to Amon "the governor of the city" and to Joash the king's son (the king's son here named only after that of the governor). This Amon, as Velikovsky noted, bore an Egyptian name. Even more to the point, in the passage quoted above he is described as a *sar*, identical to the name given to the regents and governors in the Amarna documents.

Could it be then that the letters in the archive dated from so late a period? Everything we have seen in the present study has, it will be admitted, pointed in this direction. The only real question remaining for us is: To precisely which point in the histories of the biblical peoples do the letters belong? Do they really date from the period between Asa and Jehoshaphat?

The Time of the Letters

In *Ages in Chaos* Vol.1, Velikovsky argued in great detail that the Amarna correspondences were in fact written during the lifetimes of Ahab of Israel and Jehoshaphat of Judah. These, according to Velikovsky, were identical to the Amarna-period potentates Rib-Addi of Sumur and Abdi-Heba of Jerusalem.

The present writer was, for a time, inclined to accept these identifications, though there were always problems with them, notwithstanding the ingenious arguments advanced by Velikovsky. Above all, and most obviously, I could not "fit" Shalmaneser III into the picture. Velikovsky had suggested that this king, who indubitably campaigned deep into Syria during the reigns of Ahab and Jehoshaphat, was the same man as the "king of Hatti" who threatened the cities of Syria during the time the tablets were written. But this "king of Hatti" was unquestionably Suppiluliumas I, as a plethora of evidence made clear. Where then did Shalmaneser III come in? Not even Velikovsky tried to suggest Shalmaneser III as an alter ego of Suppiluliumas I — a proposal which would, in any case, have been easy to refute. Eventually, I became convinced that Velikovsky had — in this part of his Eighteenth Dynasty revision at least — made a fundamental error. Whilst it was for me beyond reasonable doubt that the time of Ahab and Jehoshaphat belonged *roughly* to the same period as the Amarna Letters, it was equally clear that he had been mistaken with regard to the details.

This may be demonstrated by a brief consideration of the facts.

During the time of Jehoshaphat, the Kingdom of Judah was allied to that of Israel; and indeed the two Hebrew powers combined to wage war against the King of Syria, Ben-Hadad II, whom they defeated in battle. Both the Books of Kings and Chronicles make it perfectly clear that Jehoshaphat's reign was one marked by stability and prosperity. Nowhere is there any hint of conflct with the Northern Kingdom and its ruler, Ahab. This is in marked contrast to the situation during the Amarna epoch, where Jerusalem is threatened continuously by another power in central Canaan, a power whose capital or center of worship seems to have been Shechem. The ruler of Shechem is named as Labayu, a lawless character widely regarded as a menace to the peace. He wages relentless war against the King of Jerusalem, Abdi-Hiba, and is reported on at least one occasion to have actually captured the city.

It is significant that Velikovsky makes no mention of any of these events in *Ages in Chaos*, though even a fleeting glance at them should convince that they could not possibly have occurred during the reigns of Jehoshaphat and Ahab.

The records of Egypt state that Amenhotep III, from whose time most of the Amarna Letters date, was the great-grandson of Thutmose III, the plunderer of Solomon's Temple and therefore a contemporary of Rehoboam of Judah. The great-grandson of Rehoboam was indeed Jehoshaphat; thus Velikovsky should, by all accounts, have been correct in placing him at this time. Yet the Amarna documents seem to fit far better the situation in Palestine a generation before Jehoshaphat, in the time of Asa, Rehoboam's grandson. During Asa's reign, particularly in his latter years, the Kingdom of Judah was weak and Jerusalem was continually threatened by Baasha, King of Israel, who built a fortress nearby: It's a situation remarkably similar to that revealed in the Amarna documents. At this point, then, the synchonization of biblical and Egyptian chronologies seems to fail. By Velikovsky's own measuring-rod, Asa (who reigned 41 years) would have been a contemporary of Thutmose III, Amenhotep II, and possibly Thutmose IV — but certainly not Amenhotep III and Akhnaton. And I am in agreement, incidentally, with Velikovsky in identifying Asa as the king who defeated Amenhotep II (biblical Zerah) at Mareshah. Yet even this latter synchronism presents problems if we accept the veracity of the Egyptian and Hebrew royal chronologies. Put simply, if Thutmose III is identical to Shishak, the plunderer of Solomon's Temple, this would mean that Asa, the grandson of Rehoboam, would have begun to reign in year 15 of Thutmose III's sole rule, which would in turn imply that Asa was already in his 18th year as king when Amenhotep II ascended the throne. Yet according to the Bible, Asa routed "Zerah the Ethiopian" sometime in the Hebrew king's eighth year.

So, was Asa on the throne eight years or eighteen when he defeated Amenhotep II? And there exists an even worse problem than that.

If Amenhotep II really was the biblical Zerah, this means that Asa would have been long dead by the time of the Amarna Letters, since Amenhotep II is reckoned to have reigned 26 years and his successor Thutmose IV at least 8, even before the accession of Amenhotep III, during whose time the first of the Amarna Letters were written. In short, if both Egyptian and biblical chronologies are correct, Asa would have been dead 11 years before Amenhotep III became pharaoh. So, Asa — far less Baasha of Israel — cannot possibly have figured in Amenhotep III's Amarna correspondences. On the contrary, accepted royal reign-lengths, transferred onto the matrix of Velikovsky's reconstruction, would demand that most of the Amarna Letters were written neither before the time of Jehoshaphat, nor in his time, as Velikovsky believed, but *after* his time.

Yet there is absolutely nothing in the Amarna documents that would support their positioning at such a late period. On the contrary, as we shall see, all of the evidence points insistently to a time-frame somewhere between the end of the reign of Asa and the beginning of the reign of Jehoshaphat as the correct chronological position.

How can this be explained?

As discussed in Chapter 1, a major discrepancy exists between the chro-nology of Egypt vis à vis that of Israel when we compare the epoch between the reigns of Thutmose III and Akhnaton. Whilst Thutmose III's plunder of the Kadesh (Jerusalem) Temple is placed almost exactly 555 years before the plunder of Solomon's Temple by Shishak, by the time we reach the age of Amenhotep III and Akhnaton, the gap between the Egyptian and Hebrew histories is reduced to roughly 490 years. This means that, somehow or other, over 60 years have been subtracted from Hebrew history in the interim. How could such a thing have occurred?

When we read the histories of the kings of Israel and Judah, as recounted for example in the Books of Kings and Chronicles, we need to remember that everything we are told comes in documents collated and in some cases written many centuries after the events and people they speak of. There are no contemporary written sources, such as we possess for the pharaohs. And, as we noted in Chapter 1, the reigns of David and Solomon seem to have been inflated by later biblical chroniclers, whilst the reigns of their immediate successors correspondingly deflated. Clearly something is very wrong with the overall chronology of the Hebrew kings in this epoch. And the complete unreliability of such can be observed from the fact that neither the Books of Kings and Chronicles nor the comparative reign-lengths of the kings of Judah and Israel can be made to agree, notwithstanding the gargantuan effort by biblical fundamentalists to make them do so.

But even a rudimentary examination of some of the claims made throughout the Books of Kings and Chronicles illustrates their unreli-ability when it comes to dates and numbers. Thus, for example, it is stated in 2 Chronicles 13:4 that when Abijam of Judah fought against Jeroboam he advanced against his opponent with 400,000 men, whilst his enemy had a force of 800,000. This represents an exaggeration by a factor of about one hundred. If a king of Palestine at the time could muster 4,000 men, this would have been considered a very large army. Again, Chronicles tells us that Zerah the Ethiopian advanced against Asa of Judah with a force of "a thou-sand thousand" men (i.e., a million). This of course is absurd. When Ramses II fought the Battle of Kadesh he counted around 20,000 men in his force, and this was regarded as the greatest army ever mustered by the Egyptians.

The chronological objections to placing the Amarna Letters sometime between the end of the reign of Asa and the beginning of that of Jehoshaphat are therefore more apparent than real. We can say, with a fair degree of certainty, that the reigns of Rehoboam and Abijam were unnaturally short-ened by later biblical compilers and editors. Thus Abijam probably sat on the throne of Judah during the last years of Thutmose III and the first decade of Amenhotep II. Asa, we may surmise, became King of Judah sometime near the middle of Amenhotep II's reign, and he defeated the latter at the Battle of Mareshah in his (Asa's) eighth year. Asa was therefore alive during the reign of Thutmose IV and the first half of the reign of Amenhotep III. He *may* thus be identifiable as Abdi-Hiba, the King of Jerusalem of the Amarna Letters, though this is unlikely. More probably, Abdi-Hiba is an otherwise unknown son of Asa who occupied the throne of Judah for about 20 years before the accession of Jehoshaphat. Jehoshaphat himself would have been either Abdi-Hiba's brother or, more likely, son.

As regards the Northern Kingdom of Israel, we may reasonably conclude that Labayu was not Baasha but his equally lawless son Elah. According to the Scriptures, Elah reigned only two years before being assassinated, whilst Labayu definitely ruled the territories of the North Kingdom for several years, perhaps more than a decade. This, however, as has been shown, should not be seen as an insurmountable barrier to the proposed identification since dates and numbers were often arbitrarily altered — sometimes for propaganda or didactic purposes — by later editors.

Abdi-Ashirta, Grandson of Hiram

One of the most important and controversial figures of the Amarna correspondences is Abdi-Ashirta (also written Abdi-Astarte), king of Amurru. The double-dealing, scheming and aggression of this man made him a real menace to the security of the region. He was eventually put to death, perhaps on the orders of the pharaoh — an event which happened, apparently, just immediately prior to the death of Amenhotep III. He was replaced as king of Amurru by his son Aziru, a man who proved as treacherous and violent as his father. If the chronology outlined in the present volume is correct, Abdi-Ashirta, who is described as a ruler of greater Syria, including the coastal regions,[152] must have been alive during the third generation after the time of Solomon.

Does the history of Palestine/Syria in the days of king Asa provide us with any character who could be identified with Abdi-Ashirta?

In fact, Abdi-Ashirta apparently needs no introduction or alter ego explanation; he seems to be Abd'Astartus (Abdastartus) of Tyre, whom Menander of Ephesus names as the grandson of Solomon's great ally, King Hiram. The

---

[152] See Margaret S. Drower, "Syria, c.1550-1400 BC," loc cit., p.427

identification is strengthened by the fact that both the Amarna correspon-
dent and Menander's Tyrian king were removed violently from the throne.[153]
    The list of Tyrian kings provided by Menander is as follows;

>   Abibaal (no length of reign)
>
>   Hiram (34 years) (Ally of Solomon)
>
>   Baalbazer (7 years)
>
>   Abdastartus (9 years)
>
>   Methusastartus (12 years)
>
>   Astharymus (9 years)
>
>   Phales (8 months)
>
>   Ethbaal (32 years)
>
>   Baalazor (8 years)
>
>   Mattan-Baal (29 years)
>
>   Pygmalion (47 years)

    The above list apparently provides us not only with a precise historical
location of the Amarna Letters and, by extension, the latter Eighteenth
Dynasty, but also with the gap separating this epoch from the other, equally
well-known time, of Shalmaneser III. Ethbaal, the fourth king removed
from Abdastartus, was said by Menander to have been the father-in-law
of Ahab of Israel, who was also a contemporary of Shalmaneser III. Since
Abdastartus/Abdi-Ashirta died near the end of the reign of Amenhotep III,
and the 21 years of the combined reigns of Methusastartus and Astharymus
take us roughly into the fourth year of Tutankhamun, this would make
Ethbaal, Ahab's father-in-law, begin to reign in about the fifth year of the
latter pharaoh.
    We may conclude that Shalmaneser III was roughly contemporary with
Tutankhamun, Ay, Horemheb, and Seti I.
    There is, however, one major objection to the equation of Abdi-Ashirta
of the Letters with Abdastartus of Menander. The Amarna Letters were all
written at least four to five generations after the lifetime of Hatshepsut, in
whom we see Solomon's contemporary the Queen of Sheba. Menander's
Abdastartus, by contrast, flourished just two generations after Solomon's
contemporary Hiram. No matter how long a life Abdastartus enjoyed, he

---

[153] Josephus, *Against Apion* i, 122

could certainly not have been around and active two to three generations later.

Where then does this leave us?

We have to remember that Menander, like the biblical compilers, lived many centuries after the events and people he describes. It is highly likely that his king-list, like the king-lists employed by Manetho in Egypt — and indeed like the king-lists employed by the biblical scholars — is corrupt, and that characters and events of some significance have been omitted. Thus I would suggest that Abdi-Ashirta of the Letters is indeed one and the same as Menander's Abdastartus, though he did not belong precisely to the position assigned him by Menander.

One other possible objection exists. Abdi-Ashirta of the Letters is described as the king of Amurru, a region which, though not specifically identified as incorporating Tyre and the other Phoenician cities, nevertheless is at least recognized as taking in much of Syria, including the coastal regions. Following Abdi-Ashirta's death, his son Aziru became ruler of Amurru. Yet now, contemporary with Aziru, another, quite separate person, Abimilki (Abimelech), is named as king of Tyre. This latter character is not regarded as a son of Abdi-Ashirta. How is this to be explained?

To begin with, Menander does not state that the successor to Abdastartus on the throne of Tyre was his son. Methusastartus was the next king, but not necessarily the son of his predecessor. Considering the widespread fear and hatred of Abdi-Ashirta during his lifetime, we should not be surprised to find the Tyrians appointing someone not related to him as his successor. Thus there is no objection to seeing Methusastartus as identical to Abimilki.

Labayu of Shechem

The earlier Amarna letters, dating from the time of Amenhotep III, are full of the activities of a king named Labayu. This ruler waged continual warfare against his neighbors — especially against Abdi-Hiba, the king of Jerusalem, and was widely viewed by the correspondents as a real menace to the region's stability. It is strange, and significant, that Velikovsky makes no mention of Labayu, save for a passing reference in a footnote. Yet any reading of the Amarna documents makes it very clear that this man, whose operations center seems to have been Shechem — right in the middle of historical Samaria — was a figure of central importance at the time; and that he must figure prominently in any attempt to reconstruct the history of the period. The political situation is described thus by Aharoni:

"In the hill country there were only a few political centers, and each of these ruled over a fairly extensive area. In all the hill country of Judah and Ephraim we hear of Jerusalem and Shechem with possible allusions to Beth-horon and Manahath, towns within the realm of the Jerusalem king.... Apparently the kings of Jerusalem and Shechem dominated, to all practical purposes, the entire central hill country at that time.

"The territory controlled by Lab'ayu, King of Shechem, was especially large in contrast to the small Canaanite principalities round about. Only one letter refers to Shechem itself, and we get the impression that this is not simply a royal Canaanite city but rather an extensive kingdom with Shechem as its capital."[154]

Labayu's territory in fact takes in most of what was the ancient Northern Kingdom of Israel. It is somewhat surprising that this fact has not been taken into consideration by historians, for Shechem was the new capital of the Northern Kingdom built by Jeroboam I immediately after the division of the kingdom upon the death of Solomon. Thus in the Book of Kings we read: "And Jeroboam built Shechem in mount Ephraim, and dwelt there ..." (1 Kings 12:25) This, from the point of view of the present reconstruction, is a crucial clue. Shechem remained Israel's capital — more or less — for only two generations, until after the death of Baasha, when Omri built Samaria (1 Kings 16:24-25).[155]

All the evidence examined so far suggests that the Amarna Letters were composed sometime between the end of the reign of Asa and the beginning of the reign of Jehoshaphat in Judah and between the end of the reign of Baasha and the beginning of the reign of Omri in Israel. Now this pivotal piece of evidence points us in the same direction. The facts lead us to only one or two persons who could be identified with Labayu: He can only be Baasha's son Elah, the immediate predecessors of Omri on the throne of Israel: And everything fits. Labayu, we know, waged continual war against the king of Jerusalem (Urusalim), whom we must identify either as Asa (impossible chronologically) or as some unrecorded king of Judah who came between Asa and Jehoshaphat. Of Baasha we read: "And there was war between Asa and Baasha king of Israel all their days." (1 Kings 15:32) Baasha's son Elah was equally belligerent towards Judah.

Labayu of the letters was a daring and reckless character. His neighbors in central Palestine complain continuously of his activities. Even Biridia, the

---

[154] Y. Aharoni, *The Land of the Bible* (London, 1966), pp.162-3
[155] Shechem was however only one of the Israelite king's residences during this time. Tirzah was another, of equal importance: And it is surely significant that Labayu is not exclusively linked to Shechem in the Letters. See e.g. R. de Vaux, *The Early History of Israel* Vol.2 (London, 1978), p.801

commander of the Egyptian royal stronghold of Megiddo, is moved to warn the pharaoh of his aggression, and he declares that unless reinforcements are sent quickly, Megiddo may be lost. But Labayu, whom the king of Jerusalem says had thrown in his lot with the nomad SA.GAZ, finally overstretched himself. A letter written by Biridia informs us that he and his brother had captured the outlaw and handed him to Zurata of Acco, who took him to his home city in bonds, apparently with the intention of putting him aboard a ship for Egypt. But Labayu succeeded in bribing his jailer to release him, at which point Biridia, along with his brother, set out personally to recapture him. But the fugitive was killed by other foes, people of the town of Gina (modern Jenin) before he could be apprehended.

Strange to relate, Elah was also victim of assassination. I Kings 16 tells us that Elah, along with his entire family, was murdered at Tirzah by his chariot commander Zimri. Tirzah, it should be noted, stands no more than five miles as the crow flies from Jenin, the spot where Labayu was killed.

Labayu's long-suffering opponent, the king of Jerusalem, is commonly named Abdi-Hiba. The latter however is a hybrid title, combining the Semitic "Abdi" with the Hurrian "Hiba." An alternate and more probable reading is the purely Semitic (Hebrew) Abdi-Tibi, or Ebed-Tov, which in Hebrew denotes "the Good Servant." Abdi-Hiba's (Abdi-Tibi's) reign was disastrous for the people of Judah, and his very existence, as we shall see, was effaced from the history books by later biblical compilers.[156]

Aziru: Hadadezer I of Syria

One of the most satisfying aspects of the present reconstruction, I believe, is that it relies very little upon alter ego identifications. We saw, for example, how Abdi-Ashirta has the same name in the Letters as in the literary tradition of Menander. And just as there was no need to find an alter ego for Abdi-Ashirta, neither is there any for his equally ruthless son Aziru.

We have argued that the Letters seem to belong in the time of kings Asa and Baasha or shortly thereafter. During this period the ruler of Syria, according to the Scriptures, was named Ben-Hadad I. It was to this man that Asa turned when Baasha built the fortress of Ramah to threaten Jerusalem. A prophet admonished Asa for this lack of faith in the Lord, placing his trust instead in the arms of the notorious Syrian leader. A curse, the prophet said, would fall upon Asa's house because of this. We know that Ben-Hadad I was succeeded by a son and namesake known as Ben-Hadad II. He too waged

---

[156] During Abdi-Hiba's reign Jerusalem itself was, for a brief period, actually lost, as we learn in the Amarna correspondences.

war against the Kingdom of Israel, in the time of Ahab, two generations after the death of Baasha. This aggressive and powerful Syrian monarch also occurs in the records of Shalmaneser III, and his death, as well as the usurpation of Hazael, is noted in year 14 or perhaps 15 of the Mesopotamian ruler. In Shalmaneser III's records, however, the Syrian king is not called Ben-Hadad, but Hadad-idri (Hadad-ezer). The Assyrian records how,

> I defeated Hadadezer of Damascus together with twelve princes, his allies. I stretched upon the ground 20,900 of his strong warriors like su-bi, the remnants of his troops I pushed into the Orontes river and they dispersed to save their lives; Hadadezer (himself) perished. Hazael, a commoner, seized the throne, called up a numerous army and rose against me.[157]

Apparently the Syrian autocrat was known both as Ben-Hadad and Hadadezer, each of which names reflected his devotion to the storm-god Hadad. If Ben-Hadad II was known as Hadadezer, it is highly likely that his father Ben-Hadad I went by the same name.

If the reconstruction of history proposed in these pages is correct, Ben-Hadad I must appear in the Amarna Letters. Indeed, as a personality of major importance at the time, he must occupy a prominent position in the correspondences. Now we ask ourselves: Where is he?

As a matter of fact, given the geopolitical situation at the time of the Letters, there is only one person who could be identified with Ben-Hadad I; and that is Aziru, the notorious son of Abdi-Ashirta. Aziru's kingdom of Amurru is recognised as basically identical to Syria: it included Damascus (Letter 107 notes how, "Aziru, a son of Abdi-Ashirta, is with his brothers in Dumasqa") and a treaty concluded with Suppiluliumas of Hatti lists Karaduniash (Babylonia) and Astata (the Middle Euphrates below Carchemish) as kingdoms bordering on that of Amurru. Clearly then Aziru must be the same person as Ben-Hadad I: And here we remember that the latter's son was known in the records of Shalmaneser III as Hadad-ezer. Evidently the name Aziru, which on its own is meaningless (i.e., "([divine name] is) he who helps"), is but a hypocoristicon (accepted shortening) of Hadad-ezer, the latter meaning "Hadad is he who helps."[158] Ezer, or Ezra, would be the precise Aramaic and Hebrew equivalent of Akkadian Aziru.

Another piece of the jigsaw fits into place.

---

[157] Pritchard, op. cit., p.280

[158] Having made this equation, I now find that David Rohl came to the same conclusion, though the Hadadezer he equates with Aziru is a much earlier ruler of Syria who lived at the time of David. See David Rohl and Bernard Newgrosh, "The el-Amarna Letters and the New Chronology," *Society for Interdisciplinary Studies; Chronology and Catastrophism Review* Vol. X (1988), pp. 39-40

Fig. 9. One of Aziru's letters to the pharaoh. Aziru seems to be an abbreviated version of Hadadezer, one of the names apparently used by Ben-Hadad I.

The Captains of the King of Jerusalem

The Amarna documents make it clear that Abdi-Hiba remained on the throne of Judah until late in the reign of Akhnaton. His great foe Labayu (almost certainly Elah), however, was killed near the end of the reign of Amenhotep III.

The Book of Kings asserts that Elah sat on the throne of Israel only two years, a claim that must be contested, as we have already seen. Irrespective of how long he reigned, however, we know that he was succeeded (after a reign of just a few days by his killer) by Omri, one of Israel's best-known monarchs. If we are on the right track, these events must have occurred early in the reign of Akhnaton. Omri is said to have reigned twelve years, which, if correct, would suggest that some of the final letters in the Amarna correspondences were composed during his time. However, as most of the documents dating from the second half of Akhnaton's reign seem to have been removed when the royal court returned to Thebes, it is unlikely that any mention of Omri would be found therein. Omri was the father of Ahab, and it was of course to the latter's lifetime that Velikovsky dated the Amarna Letters — though we now see that his epoch actually begins just at the end of the Amarna age. Nevertheless, since only a couple of years separate the end of the Amarna epoch from the time of Ahab and Jehoshaphat, it is clear that many of the characters named in the correspondences must still have been alive in the time of the latter Hebrew kings.

It is probable, therefore, that some of the character identifications proposed by Velikovsky for this period are valid. In actual fact, he identifies something like a score of individuals from the Letters who share the same names as persons from the time of Jehoshaphat and Ahab. Most of these, however, could not have been the same persons. Random chance alone dictates that in a collection of hundreds of letters from Palestine/Syria containing hundreds of names, some of these will be the same as names occurring in the Old Testament — from almost any era we might wish to choose. Characters must share not only the same name; they must also be associated with the same region and have personality traits in common, before we can hazard an identification. Bearing this in mind, we find that of the score or so names singled out by Velikovsky, a handful are significant.

Right at the start of his section on the Amarna Letters, Velikovsky lists six men who are described in the Book of Chronicles (17:14-19) as the captains of Jehoshaphat; these are: "Adnah the chief," "Jehohanan the captain," "Amasiah the son of Zichri," "Eliada a mighty man of valor," and "Jehozabad," another captain. Three of these names occur in the Letters. Thus a man named Addudani (or Addadani) is mentioned in Letters 292 and 294. In Letter 294 the pharaoh calls upon him to "protect the cities of the king," whilst in Letter 292 Addudani replies:

> Thus saith Addudani, thy servant ... I have heard the words, which the king, my lord, has written to his servant: 'Protect thy deputy and protect the cities of the king, thy lord.' Behold, I protect, and, behold, I hearken day and night to the words of the king, my lord. And let the king, my lord, pay attention to his servant.

This Addudani, like Adnah, was stationed in central-southern Palestine. After the above introduction he reported on various affairs in his locality, including a garrison he had placed in Jaffa.

In view of the fact that the above letter was written in the time of King Abdi-Hiba, probably no more than a decade before the accession of Jehoshaphat, it is highly likely that Addudani of the Letters was the same as Jehoshaphat's captain Adnah.

Similar words are written by the pharaoh to a man "of Zuchru," who is enjoined to "Protect the cities of the king which are in thy care." In the words of Velikovsky, "The first name of the writer is not preserved, only his second name, 'of Zuchru.' In the scriptural list of the five chiefs of Jehoshaphat, only one is called by the name of his father; Amaziah, son of Zichri. It is interesting to note that in the el-Amarna letters also, only in the case of the son of Zuchru is the name of the father attached. The scriptural text explains the distinction: Zichri sacrificed himself willingly to God; his descendants were honored by the name 'sons of Zichri'."[159]

Here Velikovsky jumps a little bit ahead of himself. The man of the Amarna Letter is not called "son of Zuchru"; he is simply someone whose name is missing, "of Zuchru." Nevertheless, since Zuchru is not the name of a town or a country, the missing words must, as Velikovsky assumes, be "son of." So, the identification is absolutely valid; and this is surely one of the strongest pieces of evidence in the whole of *Ages in Chaos!*

There was another military commander from southern Palestine who wrote regularly to the pharaoh. This was Iahzibada, a man identified by Velikovsky with Jehoshaphat's captain Jehozabad (Iehozabad). The names, indeed, are identical, and, given the fact that the biblical Jehozabad was a chief in the land of Benjamin, which is southern Palestine (2 Chronicles 17:17-18), the identification of the two men seems virtually certain.

It should be noted, before going on, that Knudtzon placed the letters of Addadani, the son of Zuchru and Iahzibada next to the letters of the king of Jerusalem.

Aftermath

As noted, Shalmaneser III of Assyria must have begun to reign near the end of Akhnaton's life, and his thirty-five years on the throne corresponds almost precisely with the reigns of Tutankhamun, Ay, Horemheb and Seti I. If archaeologists were ever to discover the royal archives of these latter pharaohs, they would find the kings of Palestine and Syria still complaining about an invader from the north; but now it would not be Suppuliliumas of Hatti whom they feared, it would be the king of Assyria.

Two of the later Amarna Letters, from the time of Akhnaton, were composed by a king of Assyria named Ashuruballit. The first of these documents is polite in tone, even humble. A later missive, however, displays a degree of confidence, even arrogance: The Assyrian is now asking from the

---

[159] Velikovsky, *Ages in Chaos*, pp. 229-30

pharaoh gold to the value sent to the previous king of Hanigalbat.[160] It is clear, as we shall argue later, that Ashuruballit can be nothing other than an alter ego of Ashurnasirpal II, the father of Shalmaneser III. In his nineth year Ashuruballit/Ashurnasirpal became seriously ill with a debilitating disease, as a consequence of which he seems to have associated his son, Shalmaneser III, with himself on the throne. The young co-regent Shalmaneser III was determined to win glory on the battlefield, and in his first two years we find him engaging the Hittites in northern Syria. His enemy is named: It is Suppiluiumas.

> From the mountain Amanus I departed, crossed the Orontes river and approached Alimush, the fortress town of Sapalulme from Hattina. To save his life Sapalulme from Hattina [called for] Ahuni, man of Adini, Sangara from Carchemish, Haianu from Sam'al, Kate from Que, Pihirim from Hilukka, Bur-Anate from Iasbuq, Ada ... Assyria ... [their/ his army] I scattered, I stormed and conquered the town ..."[161]

Scholarship holds that the above Suppiluliumas (Sapalulme) merely copied the name of the earlier Great King of the Hittites against whom Ashuruballit waged war. It never occurred to anyone that the two might be identical — though we see from Shalmaneser's inscription that his opponent was a powerful monarch who could call on the support of vast numbers of allies and vassals.

Shalmaneser III's war against the Hittites and their close ally, the Hurri kingdom of Urartu, proved to be devastatingly successful. He wrote: "I swept over Hatti, in its full extent [making it look] like ruin-hills [left] by the flood ... [thus] I spread the terror-inspiring glare of my rule over Hatti."[162] As well as; "The land of Hatti to its farthest border I brought under my sway" and "I received gifts from all the kings of Hatti."[163]

When Suppiluliumas died, in about the tenth year of Shalmaneser III (which must also have been year 20 or 21 of Ashuruballit/Ashurnasipal II), Hittite power was in full retreat, and Suppiluliumas' successor, Mursilis III, has to face "incessant" Assyrian pressure.[164] Adad-Nirari, a great-grandson of Ashuruballit (and of Ashurnasirpal II) boasted how his ancestor had "scat-

---

[160] Letter 16

[161] Pritchard, op. cit., pp.277-8. It is of interest to note that the Orontes river, here mentioned by Shalmaneser III, was reputed by Strabo to have been named for an individual of the same title who had bridged the stream (Strabo, *Geography* 16:2-7). But Orontes was apparently a Medish name, and Strabo mentions various Mede officials of the same appellation.

[162] D. D. Luckenbill, *Ancient Records of Assyria and Babylonia*, (Chicago, 1926), I sec.616ff.

[163] Ibid. I sec.563

[164] Goetze, "Anatolia from Shuppiluliumash to the Egyptian War of Muwatallish," loc cit., p.121

tered the mighty hosts of the far-reaching lands of the Subartians." Subartu was another name for Hatti-Land.[165] From this point onwards it was Assyria, not Hatti, that was the dominant power in the region. In his eighteenth year Shalmaneser relates how he "crossed the Euphrates for the sixteenth time. Hazael of Aram came forth to battle." The Syrian king, he says, made his stand at Senir (Anti-Lebanon). In the battle Shalmaneser captured 1121 chariots. "As far as Damascus, his royal city, I advanced. His orchards I cut down." The Assyrian monarch also records the submission of "Jehu of the house of Omri" and "tribute" sent from Musri, which may (or may not) be Egypt. By our calculations, these events would have taken place in the fifth or sixth year of Horemheb.

Around his thirtieth year, about five years before his death, Shalmaneser faced the greatest crisis of his life, when the Assyrian heartland rebelled against him. The rebel leader, his own son Ashur da'in apla (Sardanapalus), styled himself as an Assyrian freedom-fighter against the oppression of his Mede father (Shalmaneser's Mede name, it can be shown, was Cyaxares). This was the famous Battle of the Nations mentioned by Ctesias of Cnidus: a veritable 6th century BC world war, and of which more shall be said in Chapter 7. Shalmaneser's death, in his thirty-fifth year, with the battle for Assyria still raging, would have coincided roughly with the last year or two of Seti I (i.e., year 15 or 16), a year which saw the pharaoh lead a great army against the Hittites. For Egypt too was drawn into the struggle, and when in his fifth year Ramses II led a mighty army to the Euphrates he was met by Hittite and North Mesopotamian forces and defeated in a great battle near a town called Kadesh. The combined Hittite and Mesopotamian armies were led by a prince Alyattes, who is known to modern scholars also by the name of Hattusilis.

Ugarit

One of the Syrian cities mentioned in the Amarna Letters was Ugarit, a Phoenician port on the north Syrian coast, whose location was discovered at the village of Ras Shamra in 1928. To the delight of scholars, excavations uncovered an enormous archive composed of clay tablets with cuneiform texts. It was found that the archive was part of a great library and documents of every type soon came to light.

Whilst, as expected, many of the documents were written in Akkadian and Sumerian, some proved to be written in an alphabetic script. This was understood even before the texts were translated. Syllabic scripts, such as

---

[165] As I demonstrate in some detail in *Ramessides, Medes and Persians* (2000)

Akkadian and Sumerian, have hundreds of different signs; alphabets usually have no more than thirty or so. The discovery of an alphabet in a context five hundred years before one was expected was sensational enough. But the language in which the alphabetic texts were composed provided perhaps an even greater surprise. It proved to be a Canaanite dialect virtually identical to biblical Hebrew. In *Ages in Chaos* Velikovsky looked at a few of the literally hundreds of precise parallels between the language and culture of Ugarit at this time and Israel of the 7th/8th century BC. Everything he said there is valid and fully supported by some of the greatest linguists and orientalists of our time.

In the alphabetic documents, words are separated by a characteristic stroke — to facilitate reading. As scholars noted, a stroke of identical type was used just across the sea in Cyprus during the 6th/7th century.[166]

The texts revealed the presence of Jm'an at Ugarit as well as the worship of a god Ddms. These were interpreted as the Jaman (Ionian Greeks) and the god Apollo Didymeus, of Ionia.[167] But Ionian Greeks, as well as the cult of Apollo Didymeus, were impossible in 14th century Phoenicia.

The ruler of Ugarit during the time of the Amarna Letters was a king named Nikmed (also written, following French usage, as Niqmaddu). This was recognized as the Greek (Ionian) name Nikomedes.[168] Again, impossible in the 14th century.

Sometime during the reign of Nikmed the city was attacked and briefly occupied by the king of Hatti — Suppiluliumas I. However, at a slightly later date, apparently, the city was attacked again, and an inscription was discovered which proclaimed the expulsion of the Jm'an (Ionians), the Khur (Hurrians) and all foreigners, "together with the king, Nikmed." Who was the king, Velikovsky asked, who drove Nikmed and the other foreigners from the city? For Velikovsky, placing Shalmaneser III at the time of Akhnaton, the answer was obvious. Quoting a text from year 4 of Shalmaneser, which spoke of a battle at a port and a pursuit across the sea, he argued that this was the event described in the inscription from the city. But Shalmaneser's document does not speak of Ugarit. Instead it talks of the cities of two princes named "Nikdem" and "Nikdiera." He argued that "Nikdem" was a variant of Nikmed, and he pointed out that Semitic languages often inverted consonants in the pronunciation of foreign words.

---

[166] Charles Virolleaud, "Les Inscriptions cuneiforms" *Syria* X (1929), 309
[167] Paul Dhorme, "Premiere traduction des textes pheniciens de Ras Sharma," *Revue biblique* Vol. 40, No. 1 (1931)
[168] See M. Hrozny, "Une Inscription de Ras-Shamra en langue Churrite," *Archiv Orientalni* IV (1932), 129, 176

As it happens, Velikovsky was absolutely right here. Any reader of the Gospels will be aware that "Nicodemus" was a normal Semitic rendering of the Greek Nikomedes. We might note too that Nikdiera, the other prince attacked by Shalmaneser, may also bear a Greek name, Nikator.

Although we reject Velikovsky's notion that Shalmaneser III reigned at the time of Akhnaton, it is true that he began his attacks on the cities of northern Syria immediately after Akhnaton's death, and that it was thus he, as Velikovsky believed, who expelled Nikmed from Ugarit.

Yet Ugarit did not cease to exist after this event. Certainly its importance was diminished. Nevertheless, Nikmed's son as well as his grandson reigned in the city in their turn. In fact, the settlement continued to be occupied at least until the reign of Ramses II or perhaps even Merneptah, at the end of the Nineteenth Dynasty. As such, we must expect it to appear, under its own name, in the monuments and inscriptions of those Neo-Assyrian kings whom we claim were contemporary with the latter Eighteenth and Nineteenth Dynasties: namely Ashurnasirpal II through to Tiglath-Pileser III.

Does Ugarit appear in the monuments of these kings?

It does indeed. In his account of an expedition to Carchemish and the Lebanon, Ashurnasirpal II (whom we identify as an alter ego of Ashuruballit of the Amarna Letters) records this:

> The tribute of the seacoast — from the inhabitants of Tyre, Sidon, Byblos, Mahallata, Maiza, Kaiza, Amurru, and (of) Arvad which is (an island) in the sea ..."[169]

Here the chroniclers appear to list the Phoenician cities in a south-to-orth sequence. Thus Tyre is the southernmost of the cities mentioned; Sidon comes next, with Byblos to the north of Sidon. The location of the next town, Mahallata, is unknown, though it occupies the position, to the north of Byblos, where we might expect Ugarit to be mentioned. Could Mahallata be Ugarit?

We need to consider the following. Vowels in cuneiform are conjectural. Thus, it would be perfectly valid to write Mahallata as Muhallit; and, given the interchangeability of "l" and "r," the name could even be written as Muharrit. Finally, pronunciation of the aspirant "h" is by no means clear and is often given a harder tone: thus Hatti can also be written Khatti or even Katti. In the same way it would be perfectly valid to write Muharrit as Mukarrit.

Still not identical to the cuneiform word normally given as "Ugarit," but not far removed, it must be admitted.

---

[169] Pritchard, op. cit., p.276

Scholars did not expect to find Ugarit (a city which supposedly ceased to exist in the 13th century BC) in the records of Neo-Assyrian kings. Thus the connection between Ugarit and Mukarrit was never made. But for the chronology, it would have been made automatically.[170]

The City of Samaria

Velikovsky believed that a city named Sumur, mentioned frequently in the Amarna Letters, was identical to Samaria, the capital built by Omri as his new residence in his sixth or seventh year. Yet Sumur of the letters was a port closely affiliated to Gubla (Byblos) and so its identification with ancient Simyra, which stood a short distance along the coast from Byblos, is hardly open to question.

The Israelite city of Samaria is not mentioned prominently in the letters because it had not yet been built when they were written; or at least it was only under construction when the last series of them were written. According to the reconstruction proposed here, Omri would have become king of Israel sometime near the beginning of Akhnaton's reign, and he would not, therefore have begun construction of Samaria until roughly the last decade of Akhnaton's life. Most likely, a lot of the major building work would have been carried out during the early years of Tutankhamun.

Now the site of Samaria has been reliably identified and extensively excavated. This provides us with a fairly rigorous test of our chronology. The settlement, it seems, was built upon virgin ground; and so we would expect the earliest levels of occupation to coincide fairly precisely with the end of the Eighteenth Dynasty and the start of the Nineteenth. In the terms employed by archaeologists this is the beginning of Late Bronze IIB, an epoch usually defined by the type of pottery on location.

Before however going into the question of the archaeological epoch during which the earliest structures at Samaria were raised, I would like to draw the reader's attention to certain aspects of the material culture found there.

First and foremost, it was discovered, much to the surprise of the excavators, that the predominant cultural influence was Egyptian. This was not expected, since, in conventional terms, Egypt of the (supposedly) 9th century BC was ruled by the weak and uninfluential "Libyan" Dynasty, whose military power could scarcely have been expected to extend into Palestine. But

---

[170] It would be foolish to expect everyone in the ancient world to write the name Ugarit in exactly the same way. Towns and cities have slightly different names in different countries. Thus the English call the capital of Denmark Copenhagen; the Danes themselves write Kobnahven. The French name for London is Londres.

the Egyptian-style artwork discovered at Samaria looked as if it belonged to the New Kingdom rather than the Libyan period. In particular, scholars were impressed by the great quantities of carved ivory from the site, which seemed to recall biblical passages about a "house of ivory" built by Ahab (I Kings 22:39) and the "beds of ivory" mentioned by Amos (Amos 6:4-5). But the ivories were of Egyptian design. The Egyptian double crown, clearly cut, was found on several ivory plates.[171] There were plaques which represented Egyptian gods, and the subjects in furniture "are all Egyptian."[172] Winged figures in human form were found in Samaria. "The forms of winged figures on the ivories ... are derived from Egyptian models. Tutelary goddesses of this type stood at the four corners of the shrine of Tutankhamun."[173] Three human-headed and winged sphinxes were found at the site. These too were recognized as similar to a human-headed lion from the tomb of Tutnakha-mun.[174]

The excavators, observing the close similarities between the artwork of Samaria and that of late-Eighteenth Dynasty Egypt, believed that the ivory workers of Samaria had revived the forms of the "Egypt of yesterday." Ivories almost identical to those of Samaria were found in a number of different places, often with Egyptian objects of the Eighteenth Dynasty. One such place was Megiddo. But although the ivories of Samaria and Megiddo display the same patterns and workmanship, they were assigned to two different epochs.[175] This happened in numerous other cases: either the ivories were assigned to the latter Eighteenth Dynasty or to the period of the kings of Samaria (9th and 8th centuries BC).[176]

As well as New Kingdom Egyptian-style artwork, the excavators found two tablets in cuneiform. These are very similar to the Amarna Letters, though they have a Hebrew seal.[177] One of them contains the words: "Abiahi to the governor of the cities to deliver six oxen, twelve sheep." Since the Hebrew/Phoenician alphabet was already well attested from the time of Omri and Ahab (as for example on the Mesha stele), the use of cuneiform in business and diplomatic documents was not expected and seemed to hark back to an older Palestine, the Palestine of the Amarna Letters.

---

[171] J. W. Crowfoot and Grace M. Crowfoot, *Early Ivories from Samaria*, (London, 1938), p.23

[172] Ibid., p.9

[173] Ibid., p.18

[174] H. Carter, *The Tomb of Tut.ankh.Amen* (London, 1923-33), Vol.II Plate XIX

[175] See G. Loud, *The Megiddo Ivories* (Chicago, 1939)

[176] Ibid.

[177] G. A. Reisner, O. S. Fisher, and D. G. Lyon, *Harvard Excavations at Samaria* (1908-1910), I, 247

All of the above suggests very strongly that we are on the right track; that Samaria was built by Omri during the last decade of Akhnaton's reign. It could even be that Omri's move to a new capital was inspired by the "new era" inaugurated by Akhnaton, who moved his capital from Thebes to Akhet-Aton. The striking parallels between the ivories of Samaria and the artwork of Tutankhamun's period agrees precisely with this scheme, since Ahab, who built the ivory palace, would have begun to reign just about two or three years before Tutankhamun ascended the throne.

Yet here we encounter a problem, one that has been made much of by Velikovsky's critics. Archaeologists claimed that the earliest pottery on the site (aside from a tiny amount of Early Bronze material) was early Iron Age, or Iron I.[178] We, and Velikovsky, would expect material from the Late Bronze IIA/IIB interchange, which corresponds to the final years of the Eighteenth Dynasty and the early years of the Nineteenth, so that the fact of the earliest remains dating from Iron I seems to be decisive proof against our thesis.

A cultural designation is dependent upon a number of features — one of the most important of which is pottery types. Other characteristics, such as technological level and artistic styles, are also significant. The reader will note how one of these, artistic styles, which should have placed early Samaria at the end of the Eighteenth Dynasty (end of Late Bronze IIA) was ignored because it clashed so decisively with accepted chronology.

Still, the excavators claimed the earliest pottery was of Iron I type, which, from the accepted chronological viewpoint, was still about 300 years too early. After all, Iron I is normally dated to the 12th century BC, whereas the beginning of Samaria should be dated to the 9th century — Iron IIB in conventional terms. As a solution to the problem, Kathleen Kenyon simply down-dated the end of Iron IIA slightly and suggested an overlap with Iron I pottery types. Others, including Albright and Wright, would not accept any down-dating of the pottery sequence and postulated an earlier undocumented settlement as the source of the pottery. And this is the view normally accepted amongst archaeologists today.

Yet the ease with which the experts were able to reassign the clearly late Eighteenth Dynasty ivory-work should make us very suspicious about their pronouncements regarding pottery. As a matter of fact, the evidence suggests that a lot of such judgments are dependent upon individual interpretation: Thus, for example, in nearby Shechem an American team was bitterly divided over where to place the pottery found in stratum 13. One of them, Campbell, put it in the 10th century, Iron IIA, whereas his colleague Toombs

---

[178] Ibid.

put the same stratum in LB IIB.[179] In the words of Bob Porter, "this surprising confusion extended over all the Field VII strata from ten to sixteen." He continues, "Both Campbell and Toombs were experts who had participated in the Shechem excavations and should have been able to identify pottery at a glance. Clearly there is an element of art rather than science in pottery identification and/or an overlap between LB and Iron Ages!"[180]

In fact, pottery and culture in general changed very little, if at all, between the Late Bronze and Iron Ages. The Iron Age settlements are regarded as little more than slightly poorer versions of the Bronze Age settlements. Clearly, as Porter said, it's all a question of interpretation.

Samaria was founded at the end of the Eighteenth Dynasty. The pottery used at the time, normally described as Late Bronze IIA/B, was indistinguishable, in all its essentials, from Iron I. It was however designated Iron I because that was closer to where it "should" have been in terms of accepted chronology. To have designated it Late Bronze Age would have been even more problematic. The designation "Iron I" was a compromise, still not entirely acceptable, but at least not as outrageous as Late Bronze II.

The King of Israel Becomes a Vassal of Syria

We have stated that Samaria was built in the latter years of Akhnaton's reign. As such, we should not expect the city to figure prominently in the correspondences, though we might expect its erection to be mentioned in some of the later ones.

As noted earlier, a city named "Sumur" does appear prominently throughout the Amarna Letters; though the context within which it is mentioned makes it clear (in spite of Velikovsky) that it is the Phoenician port of Simyra that is being alluded to. But if Samaria were to be mentioned in the documents, its name would, in all probability, have been spelled identically to that of Simyra — thus "Sumur." Now it so happens that the building of a fortress-city called "Sumur" does appear in a number of the later correspondences. Here the builder, or prospective builder, is none other than Aziru (Hadad-ezer) of Syria. Three letters in all from Aziru to the pharaoh refer to the erection of this place and all offer excuses as to why the construction work has not begun. Thus letter 159 says:

> And in respect to the regents I say: "They are all enemies of my lord — they." My lord, I will now build Sumur in haste. Now let him appoint me when I have built Sumur.

---

[179] I am indebted for this information to R. M. Porter. See his "The Stratigraphy of Israel," *Society for Interdisciplinary Studies: Chronology and Catastrophism Workshop* No.1 (1992), p. 19
[180] Ibid.

Letter 160 goes into more detail, offering the hostility of the kings of Nuhasse as an excuse for the failure to begin construction: "and the kings of Nuhasse are hostile to me, and consequently I have not built Sumur. (But) in one year I will build Zumur." Letter 161 also mentions the hostility of the kings of Nuhasse as the reason for the delay.

These three texts date from sometime near the middle of Akhnaton's reign and are therefore in exactly the right place to refer to the construction of Samaria, if the chronology outlined in these pages is correct. But if this "Sumur" or "Zumur" is Samaria, two questions immediately arise: First and foremost, why would the king of Syria be responsible for the building of an Israelite city; and second, why would the hostility of the kings of Nuhasse, in northern Syria, have prevented its construction?

The second question has the most obvious answer. If the Syrian monarch had been ordered by the pharaoh to finance the erection of a fortress-city in Israel, he could reasonably offer as an excuse for his failure to begin that he had more important priorities on his northern border, namely the hostile actions of the kings of Nuhasse.

But this then brings up the other, more difficult, question: Why would the king of Syria, of all places, be charged with building a new capital for Israel? To attempt to answer this question I think we need to briefly cast our minds back to earlier events. We remember that Asa, whom we identify as the immediate predecessor of Abdi-Hiba of the Letters, hired the king of Syria to help him against Baasha of Israel, whom we identify as the father of Labayu (Elah) of the letters. The Bible does not make it clear, but it appears that the intervention of the Syrian king was decisive in bringing Baasha's reign to an end. His son Elah, who can only have been Labayu of the Letters, sat on the throne aferwards. Elah/Labayu ceratinly reigned longer than the two years accorded him in the Scriptures, but his end was nonetheless violent. Omri, who seized the throne thereafter, had to fight four years before securing his position. Clearly this was a period of profound political disturbance in Israel. Nowhere does it say that Omri won his battle for the throne with Syrian help, yet the context within which his accession took place would suggest Syrian involvement. The previous king had been torn from power by the Syrians; it is highly likely that the new king would have ascended the throne with assistance from the same quarter. And this view is confirmed by the fact that nowhere is there any mention of war between Omri (recognized as an able soldier) and the Syrians.

It would appear that Omri's dynasty was a client line established in power by the Syrian king.

When Omri's son Ahab began his long war against Ben-Hadad II it was, in its essential character, a war of liberation. The Book of Kings describes how this conflict began. The Syrian ruler arrived outside Samaria with this demand:

> Thy silver and thy gold is mine; thy wives also and thy children, even the goodliest, are mine.

> And the king of Israel answered and said, "My lord, O king, according to thy saying, I am thine, and all that I have." (I Kings 20:2-4)

But Ben-Hadad was not satisfied:

> And the messengers came again, and said, "Thus speaketh Benhadad, saying. Although I have sent unto thee, saying, Thou shalt deliver me thy silver, and thy gold, and thy wives, and thy children;

> "Yet will I send my servants unto thee tomorrow about this time, and they shall search thine house, and the houses of thy servants; and it shall be, that whatsoever is pleasing to thine eyes, they shall put it in their hand, and take it away." (I Kings 20:5-6)

This humiliation was too much for Ahab, and he replied thus to his master:

> "Tell my lord the king [Ben-Hadad]. All that thou didst send for to thy servant at the first I will do: but this thing I may not do."

In this way, the war of liberation began. It went well for Israel. After defeating Ben-Hadad twice, Ahab captured him, then allowed him to go free. At that point the Syrian made a very significant announcement:

> And Benhadad said unto him, "The cities, which my father took from thy father, I will restore; and thou shalt make streets for thee in Damascus, as my father made in Samaria." (I Kings 20:34)

Apparently the building of a city, or part of it, was a symbolic act of ownership. The biblical scribe makes it very clear that the father of Ben-Hadad (Hadadezer) II, namely Hadadezer I, either built the whole of Samaria or at least a large part of it. This is precisely in agreement with the testimony of the Amarna Letters, which leaves us in no doubt that the king of Syria, Aziru, played a major part in the construction.

CHAPTER 5: THE FALL OF THEBES

Egypt and the Zoroastrian Fire Cult

Whilst the founders of Egypt's Eighteenth Dynasty fought for their country's independence against the hated Hyksos, a great conflict simultaneously took place in Mesopotamia: The Old Assyrian Empire, that of Sargon and Naram-Sin, battled for survival against a new people, the Mitanni, a nation whose rulers bore Old Persian names and who worshipped Indo-Iranian gods. One of those deities was represented as a winged solar disc. Centuries later, the Achaemenid Persians would employ precisely the same symbol to represent their supreme god, Ahura Mazda. The worship of Ahura Mazda is widely regarded as signalling the first appearance of true monotheism on the world stage. The monotheism of the Hebrews was not really comparable: The early Israelites did not deny the existence of gods other than Yahweh; they merely insisted that their god was the greatest.

The Greek authors had much to say about the Persian religion. From them we learn that it was Zoroastres or Zoroaster (Persian Zarathustra), a wise man of the Medes, who first preached the faith of Ahura Mazda. According to Zoroaster, God was fire, pure and simple, and was represented by earthly fire. He, the one and only god, was worshipped upon "fire altars," in which burnt a sacred flame. He was invariably shown in pictorial illustrations as a winged disc.

Modern historians can say little with certainty about Zoroaster. Outside the Greek historians and a few fragmentary Persian inscriptions, facts are hard to come by. Estimates of the date of his lifetime are wildly contradictory. We should, however, probably give most credence to Persian sources. In Chapter 36 of the *Bundahishn*, one of the Pahlavi historical texts, there occurs a detailed list of Persian rulers, in which Alexander the Great is mentioned as ruling Iran 258 years after the death of Zoroaster. Since Alexander conquered Persia in 331 BC, this means that Zoroaster would have died around 589 BC. If this is correct, then we might expect monotheism to have been preached by Zarathustra around Iran in the latter years of the 7th century BC.

Strange to relate, however, the Egyptians seem to have pre-empted the Iranians by the now-familiar span of seven hundred years: For we are told that Amenhotep IV, later known as Akhnaton, one of the last pharaohs of the Eighteenth Dynasty, introduced his own monotheistic and solar cult around the middle of the 14th century BC, and died sometime near 1335 BC. If, however, as we have argued in the present volume, the Mitannians were identical to the Medes, then the adoption by Akhnaton of a Zoroastrian-type religion is no longer incomprehensible, but something that we might even expect.

The cult of the Aton, the Solar Disc, was not a new one. Nor indeed was that of the winged solar disc, known in Egypt as Behdety and originally identified with Horus. In Iran of course the winged disc came to be the symbol of Ahura Mazda. But it was not Behdety that Akhnaton chose as his Supreme God; it was the Aton, another old deity, a fiery god of the solar disc, whose life-giving energy was portrayed as descending upon the earth in rays terminating in hands. Aton is first encountered in the Story of Sinuhe, dating from the Twelfth Dynasty. His name is mentioned occasionally thereafter, but always as one god among many. What was remarkable about Akhnaton's innovation is that he raised the Aton to the position of the sole god.

When scholars first began reading the hieroglyphs and recovering the story of Akhnaton's life, they were amazed at the personality that emerged. In recognition of his suppression of polytheism, he was soon hailed as the world's "first monotheist." To his beloved god he composed a series of hymns, some of them quite beautiful, which were more than a little reminiscent of the Hebrew Psalms — hymns not dated by any scholar before the 6th or 7th century BC.[181] As if to underline his break with the past, Akhnaton constructed a new capital city, miles to the north of Thebes, which he named Akhet-Aton in honor of his god. The remains of Akhet-Aton were discovered at a site named Tell el-Amarna, and archaeologists gradually began to piece together the picture of a marvellously-planned metropolis where the

---

[181] According to Breasted, the 104th Psalm shows a "notable similarity" to one of the Aton hymns. *History of Egypt*, p.371. The relationship of these hymns to Hebrew literature in general has been the subject of much debate over the years.

ecstatic religion of the strange pharaoh was practiced to the full. In the bas-reliefs of Akhnaton's palace and other monuments, scenes from the daily life of the king emerged. He was portrayed with his wife, his mother and his children. Sometimes he was shown showering gifts on the populace. He was frequently shown displaying affection to his relatives. Never, however, was he shown hunting or taking part in warfare, in virtue of which the heretic king was extolled all the more: Not only was he the first monotheist, he was also the first pacifist.

As if all this was not enough, Akhnaton had also instituted a new age of artistic freedom. He ordered his craftsmen to portray him as he really was — not the aesthetic ideal that had always been mandatory in portraits of the pharaoh. Since Akhnaton was physically deformed, this meant that his deformities were openly displayed; indeed, they may even have been exaggerated. His stooped posture, his long emaciated-looking face, and above all his enormously swollen hips and thighs, now began to appear on royal and commoner portraits, the pharaoh's appearance assuming the aspect of a new orthodoxy. An age of naturalism and realism ensued, producing some of the finest art ever to emerge from Egypt.

But in spite of all this, scholarly opinion was not unanimous in its praise for the apostate ruler. Some historians noted with suspicion his callous and indifferent treatment of Egypt's Syrian and Palestinian vassals, as revealed in the Amarna diplomatic correspondences. Others regarded him as a religious fanatic.[182] Furthermore, and perhaps even more alarming, there were suggestions of sexual deviancy on the king's part. He was, for example, portrayed in an apparently erotic pose with his son Smenkhare.[183] Again, his relationship with his daughters and his mother Tiy were not above suspicion. On top of this, his thoroughly unfilial treatment of his father's name and monuments could not be overlooked. This factor alone was sufficient grounds for Karl Abraham, a disciple and close associate of Freud's, to draw parallels between the pharaoh and the legendary Oedipus of Greece, who slew his father.

Where, it was asked, did Akhnaton acquire his revolutionary ideas? To this question, Egyptologists have supplied no convincing argument. In view of the revision proposed in these pages, however, we might wonder whether the pharaoh had been influenced by ideas currently in vogue in Iran?

It is a matter of record that there existed very strong ties between the Theban dynasty and the rulers of Mitanni. Thutmose IV, grandfather of Akhnaton, married a daughter of the Mitannian king Artatama, whilst

---

[182] S. R. K. Glanville for example believed Akhnaton to be worthy of nothing but censure, whilst A. H. Gardiner and J. Pendlebury criticised his religious extremism.

[183] Velikovsky, *Oedipus and Akhnaton* (London, 1960), pp.108-9

a generation later Amenhotep III married another Mitannian princess, Gilukhipa (or Gilukhepa), sister of Tushratta. Upon her marriage to the pharaoh, Gilukhipa was escorted to Egypt by 317 ladies-in-waiting, women from the Mitannian king's royal palace. Twenty-six years later, Gilukhipa's niece Tadukhipa also became Amenhotep's wife. Amenhotep III died shortly after Tadukhipa arrived in Egypt and she is believed then to have married Akhnaton. Some scholars tentatively identify Tadukhipa with Kiya, one of Akhnaton's queens, whilst other have even suggested that she might be an alter ego of Nefertiti — though this seems unlikely.

Fig. 10. Fig. . Ahura Mazda, the One God of the Iranians, as he normally appeared in Persian monuments; an anthropomorphic figure inside a winged solar disc. Such portrayals first appeared during the reign of the "Assyrian" king Ashurnasirpal II, though faith in the One God, as preached by Zoroaster, only appeared in the latter years of the seventh century. (See Chapter 6 for correct date of Ashurnasirpal II and Shalmaneser III).

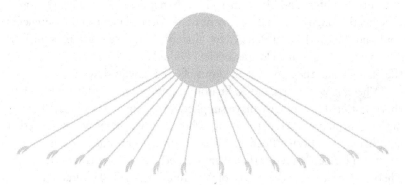

Fig. 11. The Aten, the One God of Akhnaton; a solar disc with hands reaching toward the Earth. Akhnaton's faith shows striking parallels with Zoroastrianism.

One thing however is clear: Akhnaton and his court had intimate links with the land of Mitanni, and it has even been suggested that the heretic pharaoh spent a part of his childhood and adolescence there.[184] If this is the case, and if Mitanni Land is the land of the Medes, then Akhnaton would have been there during the lifetime of Zarathustra. He may even have met him.

The Heretic Pharaoh in Ancient Legend

If Akhnaton really lived in the latter years of the 7th century BC, then we might expect something of his story, so strange and outrageous in many ways, to have survived in the memory of the peoples of the eastern Mediterranean. Indeed, this would almost be a requirement. Dying perhaps around 610 BC, the heretic pharaoh lived just over a century before the Battle of Marathon (490 BC). The Greeks were familiar with Egypt long before that time and would scarcely have ignored the life-story of such a unique character.

In his *Oedipus and Akhnaton* (1960), Velikovsky argued that the Greeks did not ignore the incredible tale of Akhnaton: On the contrary, his legend was incorporated into the body of Greek literature and became a central theme of Hellenic drama and theatre for centuries. For Akhnaton, said Velikovsky, did not just have an "Oedipus Complex," as Karl Abraham had suggested, he was the very source of the Oedipus legend itself. The entire "Theban cycle" of stories surrounding Oedipus and his children, said Velikovsky, rightfully belonged in Egypt and described the downfall of the Eighteenth Dynasty. Thus Eteocles and Polyneices, the two sons of Oedipus who battled for the throne of Thebes after the exile of Oedipus, were identified by Velikovsky with Tutankhamun and Smenkhare, who also apparently were in contention for the throne of Egypt. According to Velikovsky, the aged politician Ay fomented conflict between Smenkhare and Tutankhamun with a view to acquiring the throne for himself. In *Oedipus and Akhnaton*, Velikovsky suggested that after being deposed Smenkhare fled abroad, where he gathered armies in a bid to retake the throne. With these troops he marched on Egypt, where both he and Tutankhamun were slain in battle. These events are apparently recalled in the Greek story of the War of the Seven Champions. The Greek legend suggested that just a few years later another foreign army, led by the descendants or "epigoni" of the Seven Champions, marched on Thebes (i.e., Egypt) and that this invasion succeeded.

---

[184] Ibid., Chapter 5: "A Stranger on the Throne."

Velikovsky argued his case from both perspectives: On the one hand, he showed that Akhnaton's life and character, as revealed in the hieroglyphic documents, bore close comparison with the life and character of Oedipus as revealed in the legends of Greece. On the other hand, he demonstrated that the Oedipus legend contained a number of very obviously Egyptian elements and that the story could only have originated in Egypt.

It is beyond doubt that the Egyptian elements revealed in the Oedipus cycle are too clear to be coincidence. First and foremost, Oedipus was famous for slaying the sphinx, an Egyptian creature otherwise unknown in Hellenic mythology.[185] It was said that upon his return to Thebes, Oedipus encountered the man-eating monster in the hills outside the city. After the creature's mysterious riddle was successfully answered by the young prince, it jumped to its death from a high precipice. The role of the sphinx in the story has always been puzzling. It does not form an essential element in the drama. Indeed, its presence is totally superfluous. However, according to Velikovsky, the cult of the sphinx in Egypt, closely connected to that of the god Amon, required human sacrifice.[186] Akhnaton abolished the cult of the sphinx, as well as that of Amon, and put an end to human sacrifice. This was probably one of his first acts as king.

As we know, Oedipus became king of Thebes; but, as Velikovsky rightly emphasized, there were two cities named Thebes in the ancient world. The Egyptian city was of far greater importance than the Greek, and it was Egypt's capital during (or at least at the beginning of) Akhnaton's reign, the great period of the Empire.

In the Oedipus story the dead are interred in tombs carved from rock, and great importance is attached to proper burial. All this tends to contradict the customs of Greece, where burial in rock-cut tombs was extremely uncommon (in archaic times at least), but accords very closely with the practice and tradition of Egypt.

Thus the Oedipus legend contains a number of very clear clues which point to Egypt. Equally important however was the fact that Akhnaton's life and character matched that of Oedipus in a number of striking ways. The most outstanding facts about Oedipus of course were that he killed his father and married his mother. Now Velikovsky could not show that

---

[185] Strikingly, during the Amarna Age a number of portrayals of a female, winged sphinx, identical to the one bested by Oedipus in Greek legend, were produced in Egypt. Furthermore, the Greeks themselves admitted that the sphinx which terrorised Thebes had flown to Greece from Nubia (southern Egypt).

[186] In my *Genesis of Israel and Egypt* (2nd ed 2001), I discuss the origin of the sphinx in some detail. There the monster is shown to represent the fearsome lioness-goddess Sekhmet, who symbolised the forces of cosmic destruction at the termination of World Ages.

Akhnaton had actually killed his father, Amenhotep III, but he could show that he was possessed of an intense hatred of him. Akhnaton defaced his father's name wherever he found it (a common misconception, it should be noted here, is that Akhnaton attacked all the gods of Egypt; he did not. His ire was reserved for Amon alone, his father's tutelary god). It is quite possible that he actually desecrated his tomb. To the Egyptians, that would have been the equivalent of murder.

Even more outrageous than the pharaoh's well-attested hatred of his father was his relationship with his mother. Sometime around year 12 of his reign, his beautiful young wife Nefertiti disappears from the scene; her place now apparently being filled, for a time at least, by his own mother Queen Tiy, who, on one occasion, is described as the "great royal wife." Velikovsky argued very convincingly that this proved Akhnaton had actually married Tiy and that in addition she bore him a daughter, whose name was Beketaten.[187] Whether Velikovsky was correct or not, it is not disputed that around the same time the pharaoh appointed one of his wives as co-regent. This woman, named Neferneferuaten ("Beauty of beauties of the Aten"), has caused heated debate amongst historians. For a while, it was believed that Neferneferuaten was another name for Nefertiti, though it is now certain that Nefertiti had neither died nor taken another name, for an inscription of hers dated to year 16 of Akhnaton has recently been discovered. This has simply deepened the mystery of Neferneferuaten. Everything about Neferneferuaten is strange: First and foremost, it was quite unprecedented for a pharaoh to name a wife as co-regent. Sons were made co-regents, not wives. Second, this female co-regent appears wearing a pharaoh's crown. No woman since Hatshepsut had dared do such a thing. Third, and perhaps strangest of all, Neferneferuaten is portrayed naked along with Akhnaton in an affectionate embrace.

At one time it was suggested by some that Akhnaton's mysterious new queen, who had usurped the beautiful Nefertiti, might have been a man — Smenkhare, one of Akhnaton's sons, was suggested — a man with whom Akhnaton was having a homosexual relationship. However, it was later discovered that Neferneferuaten was unquestionably a woman and unquestionably not the same person as Smenkhare. But this only further deepened the mystery of her identity. Was Neferneferuaten an alter ego of the pharaoh's own mother? If such was the case, then it was scarcely a fact which would have been ignored and would unquestionably have won Akhnaton an enduring reputation.

---

[187] Velikovsky, *Oedipus and Akhnaton*, Chapter 6: "The King's Mother and Wife," pp.86-95

Fig. 12. A naked Akhnaton is caressed by a naked female, almost certainly Neferneferuaten, who also wears a pharaohnic crown and is clearly a core-gent. Was this woman his own mother?

In addition to all of this, Velikovsky uncovered a whole series of details connecting the wayward king to the legendary hero. Most importantly, perhaps, the name Oedipus in Greek means "swollen leg" or "swollen foot," and Akhnaton famously did indeed suffer from a rare disease characterized by deformed swelling of the thighs. In addition, there was evidence that Akhnaton, like Oedipus, had been exiled at birth. (This in turn incidentally helps to explain his later hatred of his father. Apparently the hedonistic Amenhotep III may have viewed the deformities of his son as an embarrass-ment. Akhnaton's subsequent open display of those deformities in royal art would then have beem a final act of revenge). There is some evidence too that Akhnaton, like Oedipus, had gone blind after being deposed.[188] As in the story of Oedipus, Akhnaton had two heirs who appear to have contended for the throne after his departure. These, according to Velikovsky, were Smenkhare (Polyneices of legend) and Tutankhamun (Eteocles of legend). At the end of *Oedipus and Akhnaton* Velikovsky argued that the contendings of Smenkhare and Tutankhamun led to the famous expedition known from Greek tradi‑ tion as the War of the Seven Champions. Smenkhare (Polyneices), according to Velikovsky, fled the country, raised armies, and marched against Egypt (Thebes). Both brothers were killed in the subsequent war. One of them, said Velikovsky, was declared to be a national hero and accorded a splendid funeral by the new king, Ay (Creon of legend); the other, Smenkhare, in agreement with the legend, was refused burial. According to Velikovsky the cruelty of Ay towards the spirit of Smenkhare and to his young wife Meri‑ taten (Antigone of legend, who was buried alive for disobeying the new king's orders), brought a "tumult of hatred" against the aged pharaoh. This "tumult of hatred" would soon bring the Eighteenth Dynasty, and Egypt's Empire, to a sad end.

The present writer accepts the above identifications, and I have little or no doubt that the Oedipus legend is based squarely on the actual lives of Akhnaton and his progeny. In early times, when Mycenae was the greatest city of Greece, there were important trading contacts between Egypt and the Aegean world. Very probably the story of the Theban king with the swollen legs who married his mother reached Greece very shortly after the events took place. Yet in spite of the strength of the evidence, it may be argued that myth, as such, is an unreliable source when reconstructing history. This of course is true; and it is for this reason that I intend, in the present work, to use it as little as possible. On the contrary, I hope to show that, irrespec‑ tive of how one views the Oedipus story, it is possible to demonstrate, using the hieroglyphic records alone (along with Egyptian traditions recounted in Manetho and other ancient authors) that the fall of the Eighteenth Dynasty was marked by civil war and foreign invasion. It is possible too to identify the source of the foreign armies which marched against Egypt at this time.

Wars of the "Polluted Wretches"

The fall of Akhnaton's dynasty is recounted not only in the Oedipus Cycle but also in at least two or perhaps three other traditions emanating

---

[188] This evidence is somewhat circumstantial, being contained in various legends of a blind king who sought to know the gods and who was exiled in Ethiopia. Some of these accounts will be mentioned as we proceed.

from Egypt and elsewhere in the Near East. Sometimes the story is couched in the language of myth and legend; occasionally it is mixed with related episodes from other events. Always, however, it is possible to untangle the web of facts and to identify the essential elements of the story. What we find again and again is the tradition of an impious king who fled either to or from Ethiopia, and whose country eventually fell to invaders without a battle being fought. These elements are found in both Herodotus and Diodorus,[189] but the most detailed and clear-cut account comes from Manetho.

Josephus Flavius quotes Manetho the Egyptian historian at some length in his polemic *Against Apion*. Manetho, it seems, had associated the Jews with the hated Hyksos, who had reputedly invaded Egypt and imposed a tyran-nical rule upon her for many centuries. But although Manetho begins his account with the Hyksos and their expulsion from Egypt, he soon launches into an entirely different story and an entirely different conquest. Contained in these pages is the story of Egypt's fall at the end of the Eighteenth Dynasty. We hear a strange tale, unknown to any history books, of Egypt's conquest by Asiatic armies in the days of a pharaoh named Amenophis, a pharaoh who sought to "see the gods." Contemporary with this king was a great seer, also named Amenophis, who was the "son of Papis." There seems little doubt whatsoever that these two men were Akhnaton (Amenhotep IV) and the famous seer Amenhotep, son of Hapu. Historians are generally agreed on these two identifications, and there is little dissention on the point.[190]

According to Manetho, the seer Amenophis informed his royal namesake that in order to communicate with the gods, as he desired, he would have to expel certain "polluted wretches" from the country.[191] These "polluted" persons are then rounded up and put to work in quarries. After these events the seer has pangs of conscience, realizing that the cruel treatment of the "polluted" persons would bring retribution from heaven. After preparing a letter in which he warned the king that the country was destined to be invaded and that he would be driven into exile for thirteen years, the seer commits suicide.

All this calls to mind the career of Amenhotep son of Hapu, who, in Velikovsky's reconstruction, played a major role in the events surrounding Akhnaton's life and death. In Greek tradition, according to Velikovsky, this man is known as Tiresias.

[189] Diodorus Siculus has the more complete account in his story of Actisanes (ie Akhnaton) i, 60, 1-6
[190] Some commentators, it is true, regard 'Amenophis' as Akhnaton's father Amenhotep III. Nevertheless, there is little disagreement on the opinion that the story as a whole is concerned with the Amarna epoch and the Atenist heresy.
[191] Josephus, *Against Apion* i, 26

The prophesied invasion comes and is led by one Osarsiph, whom the "polluted" persons had chosen to lead them. These are not the Hebrews, as Manetho apparently believed, but can only be Smenkhare and his associates, who were regarded as tainted by their too close association with Akhnaton. In the immediate aftermath of Akhnaton's reign there was a concerted effort in Egypt to purge the country of all traces of the heresy; and such terms as "criminal," "enemy" and "polluted" were regularly applied to Akhnaton and his beliefs as well as to his entourage. In Manetho's account the invaders, who have received the assistance of the Asiatic "Solymites" (identified by him with the Hyksos who had earlier been expelled from Egypt by Tethmosis), are met either by king Amenophis or by his son at Pelusium. According to Manetho the pharaoh then fled, without even a token fight, and retreated with all his followers into Ethiopia.

This sounds remarkably like the famous War of the Epigoni in Greek legend, when the descendants of the Seven Champions captured Thebes without a fight, after King Creon and his people had fled on the advice of the seer Tiresias.

Thus Manetho appears to have preserved a somewhat garbled account of the story of Akhnaton and the downfall of the Theban dynasty. The sequence of events, as recorded by Manetho, is of course far from clear; and at a later stage we shall see that elements from two entirely different, though closely related events, are present in his version of the story.[192] One very striking difference between Manetho and the Greek accounts as interpreted by Velikovsky is that the Egyptian historian tells us of only one invasion of Thebes/Egypt, whereas the Greeks all agreed that there had been two. In Manetho the "polluted" persons return and capture the country without a fight, whilst the Greek story-tellers insisted that the Theban exile Polyneices and his followers were defeated, and that it was their descendants, the Epigoni, who took the city without a battle. But the version of Manetho preserved in Josephus may not be wholly in line with the original, and there is at least a hint that Manetho knew of two invasions of Egypt at this time. In his description of Osarsiph's rebellion, Manetho/Josephus tells us that king Amenophis met the invaders at Pelusium, only to retreat without risking a battle. However, at a later stage Josephus comments on the fact that the son of Amenophis had met the invaders at Pelusium. Thus it would seem clear

---

[192] It is quite possible that the penal colony of Rhinocolura may have partly inspired the story of the "polluted" ones. This colony, which seems to have been located near Avaris, was established by Horemheb shortly after his accession to the throne. The exiled miscreants, many of whom were probably followers of the aged pharaoh Ay, had their noses cut off (in Assyrian style), and to all intents and purposes resembled lepers. Diodorus confusedly attributes the founding of Rhinocolura to Actisanes (probably Akhnaton).

that two distinct invasions are implied. According to our interpretation, the son of Amenophis who met the invasion would have been Tutankhamun, or Eteocles of Greek tradition.

Thus Manetho's account is by no means clear-cut and presents its own peculiar difficulties. Nevertheless, the essential elements of the story are so evident that it is impossible to miss them, and we are perfectly justified in drawing the above-mentioned conclusions. Manetho's version tells us quite clearly that towards the end of the Eighteenth Dynasty exiles from Egypt enlisted the help of foreigners in an attempt to win the throne. The evidence indicates that the "polluted" exiles were none other than Smenkhare and his supporters.

At this stage one question in particular springs to mind: If Egypt really were attacked at this time, who were the attackers? Who were these invaders who assisted Smenkhare? Which nation or power would have the strength to attempt an invasion of Egypt? Manetho speaks of the involvement of "Solymites" as well as "Hyksos," and commentators throughout the centuries have thereby assumed that Manetho believed the Hyksos to be Hebrews. However, the Hebrews were never known by the name "Solymite," and so the identification is questionable. Still, it could be that if Smenkhare did flee from Egypt, as Velikovsky claimed, then his first port of call could have been Israel. Certainly the pharaohs, as noted in Chapter 3, always had close links with the northern kingdom of Israel, and it is likely that a fugitive Smenkhare would have found succor in the newly-erected fortress of Samaria. Nevertheless, even if the Egyptian prince and his entourage did stop at Samaria, it is unlikely they remained there for long. Their ultimate goal, I aim to demonstrate, lay much further to the north.

It is possible that Manetho derived "Solymite" from a hieroglyphic word written as *slm* or *srm*. The latter of course is not dissimilar from *Assurim*, the Hebrew/Phoenician name for the Assyrians.[193]

Other evidence from ancient tradition points in the same direction. Thus we find that Tydeus, greatest of the Seven Champions who in the Greek story invaded Thebes, has a name which, although meaningless in Greek, is a precise transliteration of the Semitic name Adad.[194] Adad was an extremely common component of names amongst Syrian and Mesopotamian monarchs during the epoch of the Eighteenth Dynasty.

We are told by the Greeks that both invasions of Thebes were launched at the behest of a queen, a woman named Eriphyle. Eriphyle was the sister

---

[193] The normal Egyptian word for the Assyrians was Assuru, a name first appearing in the annals of Thutmose III. Assuru may have been used interchangeably with Assurim, the word used throughout Palestine and Syria.

[194] Thaddeus is likewise a Greek version of Adad.

of Adrastus, king of Argos, and it was she who persuaded her brother to organize the expedition of the Seven.[195] Strikingly, this woman was clearly identified with the region of Syria in Greek tradition. According to Pausanias, the dress of Eriphyle was preserved in a sanctuary in Gabala, a town of the Syrian coast which may well have been Byblos.[196] Another tradition claimed that Eriphyle's necklace was dedicated in a sanctuary of Adonis (a Syrian god) in the Cypriot city of Amathous.[197] Thus a major player in the whole Theban cycle is clearly identified by two separate traditions with the Near East.

It is clear then that the legends both of Greece and Egypt seem to suggest that Asia, particularly the region of Syria, may have been the source of the forces which advanced against the kingdom of the Nile at this time. We shall presently attempt a much more precise identification of these armies and their leaders.

A Pharaoh Deposed and Exiled

Egyptologists profess to know nothing of Akhnaton's fate, though there is continual debate about certain bodies and remains found in the Valley of the Kings and elsewhere. If Velikovsky is correct, however, Akhnaton did not die in Egypt but, upon going blind and being deposed, was driven into exile. This is certainly the impression one would gain from a reading of the Greek traditions, and it is reinforced by the various Egyptian accounts as recorded in Manetho and elsewhere. We saw, for example, that in the story of the "Polluted Wretches," the seer Amenophis, son of Papis, warns his royal master that he will be driven into exile in Ethiopia. In another tradition, recorded by Herodotus, we hear of a blind king named Anysis who dwelt in a city of the same name. This, remarked Velikovsky, sounds very much like Akhnaton and his almost identically-named capital of Akhet-Aton. Anysis, we are informed, was driven into exile by the Ethiopian king Sabakos.

Thus three separate traditions, one from Greece and two from Egypt, speak of a pharaoh who can reasonably be identified with Akhnaton, who was driven from the throne after (in two of the traditions) going blind and exiled either in Ethiopia or by an Ethiopian king. Drawing on the evidence of all three traditions we can say the following: Towards the end of his reign, Akhnaton went blind; this affliction being attributed by the seer Amenhotep son of Hapu to the pharaoh's impious actions. After this, a *coup d'état* was

---

[195] Apollodorus, iii,62-3. Sophocles actually composed a play, now lost, named *Eriphyle*.
[196] Pausanias, ii, 1 ,7
[197] Ibid., ix, 41, 2

organized against him, and he fled, with a substantial portion of his court, to Ethiopia (Nubia).

The above conclusion is strikingly confirmed by the survival of the Aton cult in Nubia until the time of Shabaka and Tirhaka, of the Twenty-Fifth Dynasty. The latter mentions Gem-Aton, Akhnaton's southern-most center of Aton-worship, on several occasions; only now it is redesigned as the temple of "Amon, Lord of Gem-Aton."[198] Early in the 20th century Breasted drew attention to this strange anomaly, remarking that the Nubian city bore the same name as the Aton temple erected by Akhnaton in Thebes: "The name of the Theban temple of Aton therefore furnished the name of the Nubian city, and there can be no doubt that Ikhenaton was its founder, and that he named it after the Theban temple of his god.... We have here the remarkable fact that this Nubian city of Ikhenaton survived and still bore the name he gave it nearly a thousand years [sic] after his death and the destruction of the new city of his god in Egypt (Amarna)."[199] Breasted hypothesized that, though the shrine was founded by Akhnaton, its continued survival suggested the arrival of Atonist refugees from Egypt at the end of Akhnaton's reign and the overthrow of the Atonist heresy.[200]

The survival of the Aton cult in Nubia into the epoch of the Twenty-Fifth Dynasty also, of course, poses immense problems for conventional scholarship, which imagines (as expressed by Breasted) an enormous gap of time between Akhnaton and the Nubian pharaohs. It is regarded as most strange that the cult survived over six centuries in the south and that furthermore it remained unnoticed in contemporary documents during the intervening centuries. Before Tirhaka, who mentions the Gem-Aton in one of the side-chambers of his temple at Gebel-Barkal, "its earlier history is totally unknown."[201] However, from the perspective of the revised chronology proposed in these pages, we are not at all surprised by the survival; for only a century and a quarter separates the two epochs. Akhnaton was driven from the throne around 610 BC and Tirhakah (as I demonstrate in some detail in *Ramessides and Persians*) mounted the Nubian throne around 480 BC and thereafter launched his military excursions to the north in support of his ally Seti II (Inaros), who was involved in a war of liberation against the Persians.

The eventual fate of Akhnaton therefore seems fairly clear. Sometime in the latter part of his reign, perhaps in his fourteenth or fifteenth year, the king went blind, which affliction was attributed by the populace to his

---

[198] Breasted, "A City of Ikhenaton in Nubia," *Zeitschrift für Aegyptische Sprache* 40 (1902/1903), p. 107.
[199] Ibid.
[200] Ibid.
[201] Ibid. p. 106.

impiety and perverse relations with his mother. Driven from the throne, the heretic and his entourage made their way to Nubia, where the younger members of the household intermarried with local potentates, who, about a century later, as the Twenty-Fifth Dynasty, claimed to be the legitimate rulers of Egypt.

Tutankhamun's Reign

Fig. 13. The desecrated sarcophagus found in tomb KV55. The body inside is believed to be that of Smenkhare, brother of Tutankhamun.

It is generally agreed that after the reign of Akhnaton his son Smenkhare briefly occupied the throne. Whether or not Smenkhare actually shared a co-regency with Akhnaton is unclear, but it seems certain that he was regarded as too closely linked to the heretic. In any event, after an extremely short reign — perhaps no more than a year — Smenkhare too was deposed.

We know he was not murdered, for a mummified body almost certainly belonging to him was discovered by Davis in a rubble-filled tomb in the Valley of the Kings.[202] Had he been murdered, it is likely that his body would either have been completely destroyed or that his murderers, attempting to conceal their deed, would have accorded hi
m all the normal funerary rituals of a dead pharaoh.

The discovery of Smenkhare's mummified corpse in a wrecked tomb suggests very unusual circumstances indeed.

In any event, Smenkhare's reign was followed by that of the young Tutankhamun — a boy of no more than nine or ten years at the time of his coronation. The exact relationship of Tutankhamun with Smenkhare is uncertain. Tutankhamun was clearly a close member of the royal family. Medical examination of his corpse suggests that he too was probably a son of Akhnaton — though a son by one of the lesser wives. Thus Smenkhare and Tutankhamun were in all probability half-brothers.

The very youth of Tutankhamun upon his ascent of the throne suggests that right from the start he was a pawn in a political game over which he had little control or understanding. Always, behind these events, behind the removal first of Akhnaton and then of Smenkhare, we may discern the hand of the wily old Ay.[203] This man had been a major player during the time of Akhnaton and his eventual elevation to the kingship after the death of Tutankhamun suggests that he had a pivotal role in everything that went before.

If Smenkhare was not killed when he lost the crown, we may well wonder what became of him. According to Velikovsky he fled abroad, there to gather armies in an attempt to win back the royal diadem. Leaving aside for one minute the truth or otherwise of this claim, we need to look at the circumstances surrounding the end of Tutankhamun's reign. For whether or not Smenkhare led foreign armies against Egypt there seems little doubt that Tutankhamun faced a foreign invasion, and that after little more than seven or eight years on the throne the young pharaoh met a violent death on the battlefield. This can be demonstrated by a number of key pieces of evidence:

---

[202] The tomb, found in 1907, was numbered 55. It contained a "decayed mummy in an elaborate coffin of the royal type and the remains of funerary furniture ... The burial had been desecrated and the names on the coffin excised before the tomb was re-sealed in antiquity." Recent scientific investigation on the mummy has left "little room for doubt that it is of Smenkhare." Cyril Aldred, "Egypt: The Amarna Period and the end of the Eighteenth Dynasty," in The Cambridge Ancient History Vol.2 part 2 (3rd ed.), pp.67-8

[203] According to Aldred; "Since the king [Tutankhamun] was still a minor when these decrees [restoring traditional worship etc] were promulgated, it is clear that they were made at the suggestion of his advisers, the most prominent of whom was the vizier and regent Ay..." Ibid., p.67

- Detailed examination of Tutankhamun's body has revealed that death was probably caused by a leg injury which became infected. It has been argued very convincingly that, given the immense panoply of military equipment with which the young pharaoh was interred, this injury was inflicted during a battle.
- The splendid funeral accorded the young pharaoh is perhaps sugges-tive that he died a hero's death.
- A decorated chest found in his tomb shows him in battle against foreign enemies.
- Inscriptions of various characters who served under Tutankhamun and Ay speak graphically of major military action at the time and appar-ently of an attempted invasion of Egypt.

Points (a), (b) and (c) are so well-known and accepted that there seems little need to say much more about them here. On the subject of Tutankha-mun's death, for example, a BBC documentary in 2014 subjected the body to an extensive detailed post-mortem which suggested that he had died of a thigh injury which may have resulted from a chariot accident. The makers of the program went so far as to postulate that the injury was inflicted during a battle.[204]

Where the young pharaoh could have received such a wound may well be displayed on the decorated chest, where he is shown riding his chariot into the serried ranks of his enemies. These include Asiatics (apparently either Syrians or Assyrians) and Ethiopians, and the accompanying inscription reads: "The good god, son of Amon, valiant and without his peer; a lord of might trampling down hundreds of thousands and laying them prostrate." This certainly sounds like the description of a heroic warrior-king: but whether or not the chest describes a real event has been debated for years.

Other artefacts from the young pharaoh's tomb also display defeated foreign enemies; but it is the written testimonies of high officials of the time which form by far the most crucial evidence. In the tomb of Huy, viceroy of Ethiopia under Tutankhamun, the following is inscribed:

The chiefs of Retenu the Upper [the uplands of Palestine/Lebanon], who knew not Egypt since the days of the gods, are craving peace from His Majesty. They say "'Give us the breath which thou givest, O Lord! Tell us thy victories; there shall be no revolters in thy time, but every land shall be in peace.'"[205]

---

[204] See. https://www.history.com/news/king-tut-death-mystery See also Brian Handwerk, "King Tut's New Face: Behind the Forensic Reconstruction," *National Geographic* (June, 2005)

[205] Cited from J. Baikie, *A History of Egypt* Vol.2 (London, 1929), p.327

Why, we might ask, would the chiefs of Retjenu (Syria/Palestine) be "craving peace" from Tutankhamun, unless that peace had been broken? And what were Tutankhamun's "victories" about which the Asiatics wanted to hear?

The general Horemheb (whose career will be examined shortly) apparently took part in the same campaign. In his early (pre-royal) tomb he states that he had been:

King's follower on his expeditions in the south and north country [against the Nubians and Asiatics] ... King's messenger at the head of his army to the south and north country ... Companion of the feet of his lord upon the battlefield on that day of slaying the Asiatics.[206]

It really is not possible to be much more explicit than this. A major military encounter, almost certainly during the reign of Tutankhamun, is described. There seems little doubt also that this campaign was identical to the one referred to on Tutankhamun's decorated chest. In the same place Horemheb is shown introducing captive Asiatics to a king. The accompanying inscription reads:

Fig. 14. Tutankhamun's decorated chest, showing him in action against warriors from northern Syria/Assyria.

The princes of all foreign countries come to beg life from him. It is the Hereditary Prince, Sole Companion, and Royal Scribe Hor-em-heb, the triumphant, who will say, when he answers [the king:] "['The countries] which knew not Egypt — they are under thy feet forever and ever, for Amon has decreed them to thee. They mustered [every] foreign country [into a

---

[206] Ibid. pp.326-7

confederacy] unknown since Re. Their battle cry in their hearts was as one. [But] thy name is flaming [against them, and they become] subject to thee. Thou art the Re [who comes] that they [abandon] their towns...."[207]

Any remaining question that important military activity took place in Tutankhamun's latter years should be laid to rest by this passage. Even more to the point, the statement that Egypt's enemies had mustered every foreign country into a confederacy strongly suggests that Egypt herself was being attacked.

The Wily Vizier

By common consent, the hand of the wily courtier Ay, formerly Master of the Horse and later vizier, behind the major political events of the time. According to Velikovsky, Ay is the Creon of legend, the cruel, scheming and unscrupulous general who overthrew Oedipus, engineered the deaths of Oedipus' sons, and eventually had himself raised to the kingship.

With the death of Tutankhamun, Ay now revealed the true extent of his unscrupulousness and his ambition.

At his death, Tutankhamun can have been no older than nineteen or twenty. His wife Ankhesenamun must have been of similar age. This young woman was now effectively the reigning monarch. Yet in Egypt a queen could not be "pharaoh," since the pharaoh was the living incarnation of the god Horus — a male deity. The one exception[208] to the rule was of course Hatshepsut, but Ankhesenamun was young and inexperienced, and the powers that be in the land were certainly unlikely, at this stage, going to allow a repetition of Hatshepsut's example.

Now, in Egypt heredity was carried through the female line. Tutankhamun himself could not have become pharaoh without marrying Ankhesenamun, the crown princess. This meant that whoever married Ankhesenamun would be raised to the kingship. Ankhesenamun herself was well aware of this, and well aware too, no doubt, of who was next in line among her suitors: the aged Ay, the man whom she quite possibly now suspected of engineering Tutankhamun's death.[209] In any event, at this stage she did something quite extraordinary; she sought a husband among the royalty of a foreign land. Ankhesenamun's two letters to the Hittite king Suppiluliumas requesting

---

[207] Prichard, op cit., p.251

[208] It is claimed that Sebeknefru of the so-called Twelfth Dynasty similarly reigned on her own, as did a queen named Nitokris, perhaps of the Sixth. But the evidence is scanty.

[209] Greek legend said that the wily Creon had advised Oedipus' two sons to settle the issue of the kingship by single combat. Velikovsky suggested that Ay may have advised Tutankhamun to assume a dangerous position in the line of battle.

him to send one of his sons are among the most famous of ancient correspondences. For a while, there was debate as to the true authorship, but a
subsequent discovery proved beyond doubt that the letters were those of
Tutankhamun's widow. The first communication reads thus:

My husband has died and I have no son. People say that you have many
sons. If you were to send me one of your sons, he might become my husband.
I am loath to take a servant of mine and make him my husband.[210]

Suppuliumas was initially suspicious of the queen's intentions and
made further enquiries. This prompted a second letter from the queen:

Why do you say: "'They may try to deceive me?'" If I had a son, would I
write to a foreign country in a manner which is humiliating to myself and
my country? You do not trust me and tell me even such a thing. He who was
my husband died and I have no sons. Shall I perhaps take one of my servants
and make him my husband? I have not written to any other country. I have
written [only] to you. People say that you have many sons. Give me one of
your sons and he is my husband and king in the land of Egypt.

Now the Hittite king delayed no longer; he dispatched his son Zannanzash to marry the widowed queen. But, as is reported in another document,
he was murdered on the way.

The identity of the man responsible for the foreign prince's murder is
hardly open to question. Ay was the only person with either the power or
the motive, and his subsequent behavior more or less confirms his guilt. Soon
the hapless Ankhesenamun was compelled to marry the old scoundrel, who
now, as the reigning king, performed the obsequies at Tutankhamun's interment.

If there is any truth in Velikovsky's claims, this was scarcely the last or
even the worst of Ay's crimes. For whilst the aged king decreed an elaborate
funeral for one brother, he refused burial to the other, the hapless Smenkhare,
on the grounds that he was a traitor who had brought foreign armies against
his country. For this, Smenkhare's body was to be cast into the desert to be
devoured by jackals and carrion birds. For Egyptians, this was quite literally
a fate worse than death. It meant eternal damnation for the dead man's spirit.
But just as in the Greek story, where Antigone secretly buried the body of her
dead brother Polyneices, so, said Velikovsky, Meritaten, the wife/sister of
Smenkhare, secretly buried the body of her husband. Tragically, her actions
were discovered by the cruel ruler who, furious that his first decree as king
had been defied, ordered the girl herself to be interred alive in the Valley of
the Kings.

---

[210] From Pritchard, op cit., p.319

According to Velikovsky, the rock-cut chamber wherein the hapless girl was imprisoned was actually discovered. In this small pit was found a collection of small eating and drinking vessels, along with an Egyptian headscarf embroidered with the words; "Long live Smenkhare." Did the tragic girl embroider these words in the long and lonely hours she spent in her terrible tomb?[211] In the end, said Velikovsky, a public outcry forced the elderly autocrat to retract and he ordered the girl's release. But when the soldiers arrived at the tomb to let her out, they found her already dead.

Whether or not Ay was guilty of all he has been accused of, there seems little doubt that he was an experienced and able survivor in the politics of courtly intrigue; and the meteoric rise of this commoner to the kingship, after the deaths of two young members of the royal family, was a circumstance certain to attract the suspicion and opprobrium of the populace.

Horemheb

Ay was an old man when he compelled Tutankhamun's widow to marry him. After making a brief appearance to legitimize the old courtier's position, the young queen disappeared. She may have been murdered. But Ay himself was not to enjoy the throne much longer. His reign lasted no more than four years.

With the death or deposition of Ay, Egypt was ruled by a pharaoh named Horemheb. Some authorities consider this man to be the last king of the Eighteenth Dynasty; others count him as the first of the Nineteenth. It is not known how Horemheb managed to attain the crown: he was not of royal blood, and it is strongly suspected that he organized a coup against Ay.[212] His attitude to his aged predecessor's memory was certainly one of great hostility.

We recall at this point that Greek tradition spoke of Creon (in whom Velikovsky recognized Ay) as an unpopular ruler, and that the seer Tiresias warned of a "tumult of hatred" arising against him. In Sophocles' *Antigone* the blind seer upbraids Creon, prophesying that the "other cities/Whose mangled sons received their obsequies/From dogs and prowling jackals" would turn in fury against his house. As we have noted, the tradition that Thebes (Egypt) fell in the second war (of the Epigoni) without a fight strongly suggests that a substantial element of the Egyptians themselves had rebelled against Ay and had colluded with the invading Epigoni. Further support for this view comes from the *Antigone*, where Sophocles has Haemon,

---

[211] Velikovsky, *Oedipus and Akhnaton* "A Tomb-pit in the Rock," pp.150-160.
[212] See eg James Baikie, *The Story of the Pharaohs* (3rd ed., London, 1926), p.195

Creon's son, warn his father of the anger of the populace over the cruel fate of
Antigone, the girl he had condemned to be buried alive:

As your son, you see, I find myself
Marking every word and act and comment
Of the crowd, to gauge the temper
Of the simple citizen, who dares not risk
Your scowl to freely speak his mind. But I
From the shadows hear them: hear
A whole city's sympathy towards
This girl, because no woman ever faced
So unreasonable, so cruel a death
For such a generous act: She would not leave
Her brother lying on the battlefield
For carrion birds and dogs to maul. "Should not
Her name be writ in gold?" they say. And so
The whisper grows.[213]

This whisper, we hold, grew and grew, swelling into a shout of open
rebellion against the cruel and scheming king. A close look at the life and
career of Horemheb reveals quite clearly the biography of the man who overthrew Creon, the pharaoh Ay.

The major events of Horemheb's times are preserved on a number of
monuments erected at various stages of his life. He seems to have started
his career as a high-ranking officer in Tutankhamun's army. In his pre-
regal tomb at Memphis, the general (or staff officer) Horemheb states that
he was the companion of the king (whose name is defaced) in two great
campaigns; one in the "south country" and one in the "north country."[214]
It is here too that Horemheb speaks of "that day of slaying the Asiatics."
A bas-relief in the tomb shows Horemheb receiving groups of captured
Asiatics, who are being led, shackled, towards the pharaoh. These prisoners are attired precisely like those on the monuments of Tutankhamun,
and are probably prisoners of the war we find illustrated on his decorated
chest. Yet the pharaoh to whom Horemheb leads the prisoners was probably not Tutankhamun but his successor Ay. We know that Horemheb
served under Ay for a time and that he was raised to great honors by him.
Thus during Ay's reign Horemheb could describe himself as "greatest of the
great, mightiest of the mighty, great lord of the people ... presider over the

---

[213] Sophocles, *Antigone* 770-780
[214] Baikie, *The Story of the Pharaohs*, pp.326-7

Two Lands, in order to carry on the administration of the Two Lands."[215] In another place he writes that he had been,

Appointed ... chief of the land, to administer the laws of the Two Lands as hereditary prince of all this land. He was alone without a rival.... The council bowed down to him in obeisance at the front of the palace, the chiefs of the Nine Bows came to him, South as well as North: their hands were spread out in his presence, they offered praise to him as to a god.[216]

The name of the monarch who appointed Horemheb to such an exalted position (without precedent, according to Breasted), is unfortunately effaced, though historians are in no doubt whatsoever that it was Ay. But only two or three years later Horemheb was to reveal himself as a great enemy of Ay, defacing his name and memory wherever he found it. What can explain such a remarkable *volte face*?

Fig. 15. Defeated Asiatics plead for mercy; from the Memphis tomb of Horemheb.

It is widely believed that Ay was childless. This is assumed not only because his children are nowhere mentioned, but because of the way he was apparently grooming Horemheb for power after his death. But something must have happened. We might never be sure, of course, but it seems likely that Ay may have, in his old age, produced a child, probably by one of the numerous secondary wives who were now available to him as pharaoh. In any event Horemheb must have had a very strong reason for turning against him. It is commonly surmised, we have seen, that Horemheb actually orga-

---

[215] Breasted, *Records*, Vol. 3, 20
[216] Ibid., Vol. 3, 25

nized a coup against him. Such a move would have been unnecessary had Horemheb remained the heir apparent he had earlier been.

The logic of the situation therefore demands that Horemheb could only have reached the throne through organizing a *coup d'etat*. Nothing else can explain the wanton destruction by Horemheb of everything his predecessor had built. To have raised the country against Ay would probably not have been difficult, as he was evidently an unpopular ruler from the start and widely viewed as a usurper. If what Velikovsky said is true, about him burying Meritaten alive in the Valley of the Kings, then we might well imagine a country seething with anger against him.

Horemheb's ascent of the throne was legitimized by his marriage to Akhnaton's' sister-in-law Mutnodjmet. Needless to say, he left no explicit reference to a rebellion or coup. His account of how he became king is typically enigmatic:

> Now when many days had passed by, while the eldest son of Horus [Horemheb] was chief and hereditary prince in this whole land, behold, the heart of this august god, Horus, lord of Alabastronpolis, desired to establish his son upon his eternal throne.... Horus proceeded with rejoicing to Thebes ... and with his son in his embrace, to Karnak, to introduce him before Amon, to assign him his office as king.[217]

According to Velikovsky, as well as the various ancient traditions mentioned earlier, it would appear that Horemheb actually called in the assistance of foreign troops against Ay — successors to the warriors who had four years earlier launched an unsuccessful assault on the country in the attempt to reinstate Smenkhare. This, in Velikovsky's interpretation, was the War of the Epigoni in Greek tradition, where the descendants of the earlier Seven captured Thebes without a battle. If there is any truth in this account, it would appear that Ay was so unpopular that he could not muster enough troops to fight his cause. But if Horemheb did call in foreign troops, where, we must ask, did they come from? We have already suggested that they came from Asia. But can we be more precise?

An Asiatic Interlude

The reign of Horemheb marks the end of the Eighteenth Dynasty and the beginning of the Nineteenth. The Nineteenth Dynasty is also known as "Tanite" after the city of Tanis in the Delta, which became Egypt's new capital at this time. Tanis was the cult center of the goddess Neith under her Syrian guise of Tanit. Why a capital of Egypt should receive its name from an

---

[217] Ibid., Vol. 3, 27

Asiatic goddess is a question that few authorities have cared to examine: yet it is only one element in a great body of material which suggests very strong links between the Nineteenth Dynasty rulers and Asia. These links were evident right from the start. Thus a vizier named Seti celebrated a peculiar anniversary during the time of Horemheb. According to Pritchard, "when Hor-em-heb was pharaoh, a vizier named Seti came to the city of Tanis in the Delta to celebrate a four hundredth anniversary. This anniversary took the form of the worship of the Egyptian god Seth, who is represented in the scene carved on the stela as an Asiatic deity in a distinctly Asiatic dress."[218] Pritchard also notes that "the god of the [Asiatic] Hyksos was equated by the Egyptians with Seth," and that "Seth held a high position under the Nineteenth Dynasty, with two pharaohs named Seti, 'Seth's Man'."[219]

Why, it has been asked, would a vizier and then two pharaohs associate themselves so closely with a deity linked to the Hyksos, the hated Asiatic conquerors of Egypt, who had subjected the country to a reign of terror in an earlier age? Could it be that the Nineteenth Dynasty was established in power by forces from the same region as the Hyksos came from?

This impression of Asiatic influence is confirmed in numerous ways, and the preponderance of Asiatic deities during the Nineteenth Dynasty is one of the most striking characteristics of the period. According to Pritchard, "From the end of the Eighteenth Dynasty on [i.e., reign of Horemheb], there is an abundance of evidence of Asiatic gods worshipped in Egypt."[220] Most popular of these was Baal. We find that from the end of the Amarna period Baal even had his own priesthood in Egypt. Lepsius noted a Memphite individual from this period who was a "Prophet of Baal" and a "Prophet of Astarte."[221] Pritchard remarks that "By the Twenty-second Dynasty, a family had several generations in which there had been a 'Prophet of the House of Baal in Memphis'."[222] The devotion to the gods of Asia is demonstrated in the Egyptian royal family itself, where we find Ramses II's daughter bearing the purely Semitic name Bint Anath, "daughter of Anath."

Thus the worship of Asiatic gods was greatly popularized in Egypt during the Nineteenth Dynasty, and this was accompanied by a veritable flood of Asiatic influences. Semitic words in great numbers entered the Egyptian language, and these were often used in preference to the Egyptian equivalent.

---

[218] Pritchard, op cit., p.252
[219] Ibid.
[220] Ibid., p. 249
[221] C. R. Lepsius, *Denkmaeler aus Aegypten und Aethiopien* (ed. E. Naville, Leipzig, 1897), I, 16
[222] Pritchard, op cit., p.250

We have said that the traditions recorded in Manetho (i.e., the legend of the "polluted wretches") and the classical authors suggested that Egypt was invaded by Asiatic forces during or shortly after the time of Akhnaton. Now we see that the new dynasty established after Akhnaton's death brought a pronounced Asiatic influence to the country. This strongly suggests that Horemheb did indeed seize the throne with military help from Asia. But still we have not answered the question: From where did such forces originate? Although the legends from Greece suggest a confederacy of many states going to war against Egypt/Thebes, other evidence suggests that the main forces came from the land of Assyria. This is hinted by the depiction of the enemies against whom Tutankhamun fought on his decorated chest. But it is put beyond reasonable doubt by other information entirely.

When he came to the throne Horemheb issued his famous Edict, a document preserved on the north face of the Ninth Pylon at Karnak. Here he comments upon the state of lawlessness into which the country had sunk, presumably at the end of Ay's reign, and threatens "savage" punishments for transgressors. Amongst these punishments is that of severing parts of the body, including noses. We know that Horemheb carried out his threats and that the unfortunate miscreants were exiled to a penal colony, apparently near Avaris, which the classical authors knew as Rhinocolura ("cut-off noses"). This type of punishment, it has been remarked by several writers,[223] is quite alien to the traditions of Egypt, but very much in accordance with those of Mesopotamia — particularly Assyria. Assyrian influence too is seen in the cavalry units depicted upon Horemheb's monuments.

The king of Assyria during the latter years of Akhnaton was named Ashuruballit; and this monarch wrote several letters to the heretic king requesting gold, among other gifts. Ashuruballit had a long life and it is not doubted that he was still alive during the reigns of Tutankhamun, Ay and Horemheb. He was a king noted for his military exploits. His great-grandson Adad-Nirari said that he had "scattered the mighty hosts of the far-flung land of the Subartians." It is surmised by some scholars that these Subartians may have been Mitannians, but they are more likely to have been Hittites; for other documents of the period confirm that he waged relentless war against this people. Most strikingly of all, however, Ashuruballit was said to have "subdued Musri."[224] Now Musri is the normal Semitic name for Egypt (Hebrew *Mizraim*), and the claim that Ashuruballit subdued this country has caused all sorts of problems for historians: so much so that alternative

---

[223] As for example Velikovsky "The Correct Placement of Haremhab in Egyptian History," *Kronos* IV No.3

[224] C. J. Gadd, "Assyria and Babylon: c.1370-1300 BC," in *The Cambridge Ancient History* Vol.2 part 2 (3rd ed.), p.28

locations for Musri have been sought. But such alternatives are unnecessary. The claim that Ashuruballit had subdued Egypt is fully supported by the evidence from Egypt herself.

Chronological Considerations

At this stage it is necessary once again to say something about chronology. It can be shown, as I mentioned in the previous chapter, that the Assyrian ruler Ashuruballit, who wrote to Akhnaton, is one and the same as Ashurnasirpal II, the father of Shalmaneser III. Ashurnasirpal II reigned altogether twenty-six years, but became seriously ill in his ninth year and thereafter may well have associated his son Shalmaneser III on the throne with him.[225] Thus, by my reckoning, Shalmaneser III's first year was probably Ashurnasirpal's (Ashuruballit's) tenth year. Ashurnasirpal II and Shalmaneser III were, like Ashuruballit and his son Enlil-Nirari, aggressive kings who undertook continuous warfare against the Hittites.

The contemporaneous nature of these early Neo-Assyrians and the kings of the late Eighteenth and early Nineteenth Dynasties is illustrated in many ways, not least by the discovery of countless artefacts belonging to these pharaohs in the ruins of the Neo-Assyrian cities. As noted in Chapter 1, a number of late Eighteenth Dynasty scarabs, most especially from the reign of Amenhotep III, were found in Neo-Assyrian settlements of Ashurnasirpal II's time in the Khabur region. Among a multitude of cultural links between the Assyria of Ashuruballit (of Akhnaton's time) and that of Ashurnasirpal II and Shalmaneser III is the identical dress and military equipment of the two epochs. Thus the Asiatics whom Tutankhamun fought, as illustrated on his decorated chest, carry rectangular wickerwork shields. These are identical to the shields carried by the soldiers of Shalmaneser III on his various monuments. This was the only period in Assyrian history when such shields were used.

The chapter to follow takes a closer look at the lives and careers of these Assyrian and Neo-Assyrian kings, and further evidence will be brought to bear demonstrating, I feel, beyond all reasonable doubt, that Ashurnasirpal II was one and the same as Ashuruballit, the king who was said to have subdued Egypt.

---

[225] This I have argued in great detail in *Ramessides, Medes and Persians*. The Ashurnasirpal who suffered from a prolonged illness is generally believed to have been Ashurnasirpal I, a man held to have lived around four centuries before Ashurnasirpal II. But these two were identical.

Fig. 16. Ashurnasirpal II with royal attendants. In his palaces at Calah and elsewhere, archaeologists found an abundance of Egyptian artefacts of Late-Eighteenth Dynasty manufacture, as well as numerous scarabs of Late-Eighteenth Dynasty pharaohs. As such, he is almost certainly the same man as Ashuruballit I, two of whose letters to Akhnaton were discovered at Amarna. (Note also image of Ahura Mazda above the king.)

During his long reign Shalmaneser III made many forays across the Euphrates into Syria/Palestine. On his famous Black Obelisk he even claims to have received the submission of King Jehu of Israel. In the same place he records "tribute" sent from Musri, or Egypt. That Musri, on this occasion at least, does not mean Egypt, is suggested by the appearance there of an Indian single-horned rhinoceros, a water-buffalo (i.e., "river ox") and a Bactrian camel. Nonetheless, there is other evidence that Shalmaneser III was instrumental in putting Horemheb on the Egyptian throne, and the alliance established at this time would have far-reaching consequences, as we shall see.

We have found how various indicators suggest that Shalmaneser III's accession to the throne of Assyria coincides almost precisely with the end of the reign of Akhnaton in Egypt. Thus the war in which Tutankhamun was slain (after an eight-year reign) must have occurred in Shalmaneser III's eighth or ninth year (corresponding to year 17/18 of Ashuruballit/Ashurna-sirpal). That this expedition is not recorded on the Assyrian monuments is no surprise, as it was a major defeat for the Assyrians. Four years later however, at the end of Ay's reign, the Assyrians were back. This would have been year 12 or 13 of Shalmaneser III. We know in fact that he made numerous expeditions through Syria and probably Palestine at this time. If it was then that his armies entered Egypt (Shalmaneser need not have been personally present), then military action was unnecessary, since the country welcomed the Asiatics as liberators (an event recalled, as we have seen, in Manetho and the Greek sources). I would suggest then that sometime near Shalmaneser III's year 16 or 17 (year 25 or 26 of Ashurnasirpal/Ashuruballit), Assyrian forces entered Egypt peacefully and installed Horemheb as a client king. It was these forces who introduced the pronounced Asiatic elements observed by archaeologists in every sphere of Egyptian life during the Nineteenth Dynasty.[226]

---

[226] It should be remarked here that the Assyrian origin of the forces which came to the aid of Smenkhare and Horemheb helps to explain Manetho's linking of the story of Osarsiph with the Hyksos. These Shepherd Kings, said Manetho, who had earlier been expelled from Egypt by Tethmosis, were now called into the fray by Osarsiph; and the Shepherd Kings responded by sending a mighty army. As we saw in Chapter 1, the Hyksos, who used the Akkadian language, are to be associated with the Imperial Assyrians.

CHAPTER 6: ARCHAEOLOGY AND CHRONOLOGY— THE STRATIGRAPHIC GAP

Mitannians and Neo-Assyrians

If what we have found in the foregoing chapters is correct, it means that the final years of Egypt's Eighteenth Dynasty were contemporary with the rise of the newly-invigorated and mighty Neo-Assyrian Empire, whose first important king, Ashurnasirpal II, extended Assyrian control westwards to the Mediterranean and northwards into Anatolia. Ashurnasirpal II was followed on the throne by his equally vigorous and aggressive son Shalmaneser III, who pushed Assyrian might southward as far as Israel and eastward perhaps even to the borders of India. He also claimed to have conquered the whole of Hatti-Land.

Both Shalmaneser III and his father were tireless builders, and a great deal of the monumental structures they erected has survived. Upon the walls of palaces, temples and forts, these early Neo-Assyrians left a detailed record of their lives and reigns, with vividly carved bas-reliefs of court-life, war, and hunting. These scenes, as well as the smaller objects of art which have survived in abundance in the Neo-Assyrian monuments, show very clear and precise parallels with the art and culture of Egypt during the late-Eighteenth and Nineteenth Dynasties.

Yet the above statement flies in the face of the narrative told in conventional textbooks and encyclopedias. According to this, the Mitannian Empire — contemporary with Egypt's Eighteenth Dynasty — was overthrown by the Hittite Suppiluliumas I sometime early in the reign of Akhnaton, after which a new dynasty of native Assyrians reasserted its independence, forming what has now become known as the Middle Assyrian kingdom. This latter kingdom, it is stated, inaugurated — under its first ruler Ashuruballit — a new era of Assyrian power and prosperity. It was these Middle Assyrians, we are told, who reigned at the time of the Nineteenth Dynasty, and it was they who battled against the Hittites under their great kings Mursilis II and Hattusilis III.

That the Middle Assyrians actually existed is beyond question: We possess numerous inscriptions and artefacts belonging to well-known Middle Assyrian kings — men such as Shalmaneser I, Adad-Nirari I and Tukulti-Ninurta I. Yet archaeology can rarely, if ever, show a clear sequence from Mitanni to Middle Assyria to Neo-Assyria, and indeed the normal stratigraphic sequence places the Mitanni strata immediately under those of the Neo-Assyrians, beginning with Ashurnasirpal II and Shalmaneser III. This of course is precisely the situation we would expect if Velikovsky was correct in placing the latter two monarchs contemporary with the end of the Eighteenth Dynasty. But if the Middle Assyrian kings mentioned above did not come before the Neo-Assyrians, as claimed by Velikovsky and this author, where do they belong; and who were they?

The only possible answer to the above conundrum is that the "Middle Assyrians" are alter egos of the Mitannians themselves: Mitannian kings used royal names significant to their Semitic-speaking Assyrian subjects. Supporting this conclusion is the fact that the art and culture of the Mitannian period is virtually identical to that of the Middle Assyrian. This was dramatically illustrated by the appearance of P. Pfälzner's *Mitannische und Mittelassyrische Keramik* (Berlin, 1995), where it became clear that in all the relevant north Mesopotamian sites, Mitannian pottery is indistinguishable from, and contemporary with, Middle Assyrian pottery. A detailed examination of this evidence was presented by Bob Porter in 2002, and his conclusions fully support those of the present author.[227] In addition to this, it should be noted that Assyria is almost completely devoid of domestic or monumental structures erected during the Mitannian epoch, though the gap could be filled if the Middle Assyrian kings are alter egos of the Mitannians.

Since the Middle Assyrians are believed to be a native dynasty which overthrew the Mitanni conquerors, the enthusiasm of these kings for Indo-Aryan epic poems is regarded as most mysterious.[228]

---

[227] Bob Porter "Recent Developments in Near Eastern Archaeology," *Society for Interdisciplinary Studies Review* 2, (2002), pp. 30-2
[228] See eg. W. Von Soden "Der Aufstieg des Assyrereiches als geschichtliches Problem," in *Der alte Orient* Vol.31 No.12 (1937)

The supposed last of the Mitanni Great Kings, Tushratta, was assassinated in a palace conspiracy by one of his sons. His death closely resembles that of the last important Middle Assyrian Great King, Tukulti-Ninurta I, who was also murdered by a son. Tushratta, it is known, was contemporary with a Hittite king named Suppiluliumas (I). Yet Tukulti-Ninurta I, apparently a century later, was also contemporary with a Hittite ruler called Suppiluliumas (II). The murderer of Tushratta is named variously as Kurtiwaza, Mattiwaza, or Shattiwaza. He fled, half-naked, to the court of Suppiluliumas I, who placed an army at his disposal. With this help, the parricide prince conquered the Mitanni Land and was apparently rewarded for his efforts by his Hittite sponsor by being made ruler of Haniglabat, the Mitannian heartland.

The murderer of Tukulti-Ninurta I is named in the Babylonian Chronicle as Ashurnasirpal. If this man is identical to Ashurnasirpal II, as seems likely (Assurnasirpal II's father was Tukulti-Ninurta II), it seems that this parricide prince also prospered, for with him Assyria entered a great new epoch of power and prosperity. And if Tushratta of Mitanni was the same as Tukulti-Ninurta of Middle Assyria, then the murderer of Tushratta — Shattiwaza — must have been the same person as Ashurnasirpal II.

The Neo-Assyrian kings who followed Ashurnasirpal II all bore typically Middle Assyrian names, titles such as Shalmaneser, Adad-Nirari, Shamshi-Adad, etc. According to A. K. Grayson, "The adoption of Middle Assyrian nomenclature [by the early Neo-Assyrians] is indicative of a feeling that they were recreating an old empire that was still rightfully theirs."[229] But what old empire were they recreating? A clue lies in their enthusiasm, already mentioned, for Indo-Iranian (Old Persian) epic poems. The empire they were recreating was that of the Mitannians, the Medes.

The archaeology of Assyria thus produces the following: Old Assyrians (and Akkadians) equal Empire Assyrians; Middle Assyrians (and Mitannians and early Neo-Assyrians) equal Medes; late Neo-Assyrians equal Persians (a question to be discussed in detail elsewhere). The following identifications suggest themselves:

---

[229] A. K. Grayson, "Assyria: Ashur-dan II to Ashur-Nirari V (934-745 BC.)," in *The Cambridge Ancient History* Vol. 3, part 1 (2nd ed), p. 280

KINGS OF THE MEDES

700 BC (MITANNI)	(MIDDLE ASSYRIANS)	
Parattarna	= Shamshi-Adad I (Phraortes)	
Shaushtatar	= Ishme-Dagan (Cyaxares I)	
Artatama	= Adad-Nirari I	
Shuttarna	= Shalmaneser I	
Tushratta	= Tukulti-Ninurta I	(NEO-ASSYRIANS)
Kurtiwaza	= Ashuruballit I	= Ashurnasirpal II
		Shalmaneser III (Cyaxares II)
		Shamshi-Adad V (Arbaces)
		Adad-Nirari III (Astyages)
		Ashur-Dan III
		Ashur-Nirari V
550 BC PERSIAN AGE		
		Tiglath-Pileser III (Cyrus)
		Shalmaneser V (Cambyses)
		Sargon II (Darius I)

Hittites, Hurrians and Urartians

When Suppiluliumas of Hatti overthrew the Mitannian Empire, he installed Shattiwaza, son of Tushratta, on the latter's throne — even though Shattiwaza was accused of murdering his father. The new Mitannian Empire over which Shattiwaza ruled was, however, smaller than the old. The Mitannians had previously controlled the entire country of the Hurrians, a region in the mountains of Anatolia directly to the north of Assyria. This territory, known as Uruatri or Urartu, had furnished the Mitannians with a large portion of their wealth and learning. Mitannian kings, though evidently Persian-speakers, invariably used the Hurrian language in royal correspondences. This was the case, for example, with Tushratta's letters to Amenhotep III and Akhnaton. For this reason, the Mitannian Empire is commonly known as the Hurrian Empire. However, as we saw in Chapter 1, the evidence indicates that the Hurrians were a subject people ruled by an Indo-Iranian elite, for all the royal names are Iranian, as are the most important gods worshipped. The ruling aristocracy, too, are known by the Old Persian name *mariyanna*.

When Suppiluliumas defeated Mitanni, he therefore seems to have divested the kingdom of its Hurrian component, the region known as Urartu. This latter territory now became an important province of the Hittite Empire. The Hittites had ethnic as well as economic and strategic reasons to do this. The Hurrians had always formed an important element in Hittite society, and Hurrian was one of the languages discovered in the Boghaz-koi documents. The Hittites worshipped gods with Hurrian names, and there is strong evidence to suggest that the Hittite royal family of the Imperial Age was of Hurrian extraction.[230] At Yazilikaya, outside Boghaz-koi, the assembled deities "are arranged in Hurrian order and given names that are linguistically Hurrian."[231]

We know for a fact that Suppiluliumas brought the region of Urartu into the Hittite sphere influence; that he incorporated it into the Hittite confederacy. He records linking the "Hurri-land" to the Land of Hatti by treaty.[232] Even more to the point Hittite royal texts of the period "record alliances, both matrimonial and political" between the ruling families of Hattiland and the region of Urartu.[233] This being the case, it is reasonable to suppose that as soon as becoming master of eastern Anatolia, Suppiluliumas I and his successors could have adopted Urartian throne-names. The present writer regards it as likely that Sarduri I, the earliest Urartian king to leave monumental inscriptions or records of any kind, stands a good chance of being an alter ego of Mursilis II, the son of Suppiluliumas. Conventional scholarship regards Sarduri I as the king of a previously obscure and mountainous region of eastern Anatolia, who united various adjoining territories under his leadership, and who copied the art, architecture and literature of Assyria, which apparently impressed his barbarous tastes. Yet for the ruler of a state supposedly just emerged from obscurity, Sarduri I adopted some rather grandiose airs and graces: He "revives an ancient claim to the former Hurrian [i.e., Mitannian] kingship of Mesopotamia: he is the 'great king, mighty king, king of the lands of Nairi, king without a rival.'"[234] Only a monarch capable of meeting Shalmaneser III on equal terms could adopt such a title; only a Great King of Hatti in fact.

But Shalmaneser III was to launch a series of savage attacks deep into Anatolia, where he scored major triumphs, rocking the Urartian kingdom to its foundations. If we are correct, these campaigns represent the eastern

---

[230] MacQueen, op cit., p.120
[231] Ibid.
[232] Ibid., p.45
[233] R. D. Barnett, "Urartu," in *The Cambridge Ancient History* Vol.3 part 1 (3rd ed.), p.328. The region of Urtartu came to be called the "Upper Land" in Hittite royal texts.
[234] Ibid., p.337

front of the prolonged conflict waged between Assyria/Media and Hatti/ Lydia from the latter years of Suppiluliumas right through to the end of the reign of Mursilis his son, and beyond. In the documents of Shalmaneser III we now meet a character named Aramu or Arame, who "emerges into the limelight of history as the first leader to be singled out as the organizer of Urartian defense and the unifier of the Urartian tribes, whose capital he may be strongly suspected of having founded at Tushpa or Turushpa (Van)."[235]

Shalmaneser waged war against Arame, who is named as the ruler of 100 cities. Many of these are captured and some destroyed. In one campaign, particularly successful, Shalmaneser records the destruction of the great city of Arzashkum: "The destruction of Arzashkum and the campaign in general may have been partly a hollow victory, for Arama survived and returned to Arzashkum; but in Assyrian eyes it was a major event, earning the unusual distinction of being commemorated in poetic form at the hands of the priest-hood of Ishtar or their circle."[236]

Just how formidable a foe Arame was can be gauged from this fact: an epic poem was composed to mark a victory over him. This man Arame was to have a long and eventful life; and we shall meet him again a generation later, in the documents of Boghaz-koi.

Before moving on, we should note that in his fifteenth year Shalmaneser again marched "against Nairi" (i.e., Urartu). During this campaign he records the defeat of Melid (Malatya). Yet Malatya was a thoroughly Hittite state, complete with monumental Hittite sculpture, even as late as the reign of Tiglath-Pileser III. Clearly the term Nairi, which historians assume to be more or less the same as Urartu, actually meant the whole of Anatolia, from east to west. In documents of a slightly later period, during the time of Adad-Nirari III and his immediate successors, all of the Hittite states of northern Syria were clearly part of the Urartian Empire, a circumstance which moved one commentator to write; "The North Syrian Hittite states ... may have felt a certain racial or cultural affinity with Urartu, and first Meld, then Gurgum, Sam'al, Unqi (Hattina), Arpad, Carchemish, Kummukhi, and Que, all became adherents of its kings Argistis I and Sarduris II."[237]

Thus the Great Kings of Hatti are almost certainly identical to the Great Kings of Urartu, who are also identical to the mighty monarchs of Lydia, of whom the classical authors had so much to say. The following three-way identifications are therefore suggested:

---

[235] Ibid., p.334
[236] Ibid., pp.335-6
[237] O. R. Gurney, The Hittites (Pelican Books, 1952), pp.44-5

Hatti-Land	Urartu	Lydia
Mursilis II	Sarduri I	Ardys
Muwatallis	Ishpuini/Menua	Sadyattes
Hattusilis III	Argishti	Alyattes
Tudkhaliyas IV	Sarduri II	Croesus

The Strategic Land of Northern Syria

It is clear that Shalmaneser III, the Assyrian king who flourished in the time of Horemheb and Seti I, was in fact a Mede, and his reign must be fixed in the final decade of the 7th century and the early years of the 6th. Classical sources inform us that the Medes and their neighbors the Lydians were involved in a great war, or rather series of wars, throughout this period.

Now it is obvious that in any conflict between the Lydian kingdom, centered in Anatolia and Asia Minor, and the Mede Empire, centered in Assyria and Iran, the region of northern Syria would play an exceptionally important strategic role. This area, after all, controlled the routes, both military and trading, which linked the civilizations of the south with the great nations of Mesopotamia and Anatolia. Whoever controlled this territory controlled the way to Egypt.

It was Suppiluliumas I, a contemporary of Amenhotep III and Akhnaton, who conquered and annexed the whole of northern Syria in the course of a great campaign against the Mitannians (Medes). From the time of Suppiluliumas onwards, the cities of northern Syria formed an essential element in Hittite strategic policy and are frequently mentioned in documents recovered from Hattusas and other places. Suppiluliumas installed his own sons as rulers of these cities and they remained an integral part of the Hittite Empire for the next four generations.

This much at least is agreed by orthodox scholarship. According to the textbooks however, after four generations, in the time of Tudkhaliyas IV, the Hittite Empire came crashing to destruction, supposedly under the onslaught of the mysterious "Sea Peoples," though a few would suggest the involvement of an Assyrian king named Tukulti-Ninurta. Nevertheless, all are agreed that sometime near the beginning of the 13th century the Hittite culture and nation ceased to exist in its Anatolian heartland. The next few centuries are regarded as a "Dark Age" in the history of Anatolia, from which very few remains have survived. Yet around the middle of the 9th century BC, and contemporary with the rise of the early Neo-Assyrian kingdom, Hittite culture and civilization experienced a spectacular "rebirth" in the city-states of northern Syria. These city-states, whose kings had names familiar from the Imperial Age, are commonly regarded as the inheritors of Hittite culture after its destruction in central Anatolia.

Nevertheless, the centers of power during the Neo-Hittite period were also important during the earlier Imperial age. Carchemish, for example, was a major provincial capital of the Empire from the time of Suppiluliumas I to that of Tudkhaliyas IV. It was, as we saw, Suppiluliumas who made Carchemish, as well as the other cities of the region, part of the Empire and installed its first Hittite king, his own son Sarre-Kushukh, on the throne. But Carchemish was also a major regional power during the Neo-Hittite age, and its name frequently occurs in the annals of Assyrian rulers from the time of Ashurnasirpal II to Tiglath-Pileser III.

Archaeologists were surprised at how faithfully the Neo-Hittites of northern Syria (of the 9th to 8th centuries) had preserved the culture and traditions of the Imperial Age after so many centuries. Their surprise grew as excavation after excavation revealed the astonishing parallels between the two cultures and epochs. How could mere refugees from the depredations of the Sea Peoples preserve traditions of monumental sculpture and other fine arts so well? Furthermore, what had actually happened to the Hittites during the four centuries that separated the fall of the Empire from the rise of the Syrian city-states? It is almost as if they had ceased to exist, and then suddenly burst into new life, like seeds regenerating in spring.

But the Neo-Hittite cities had another surprise in store for archaeologists. Given the supposed history of these settlements scholars had expected to find abundant remains of the Hittite Empire directly underneath strata containing material of the Neo-Hittite epoch. They found nothing of the sort. Invariably they discovered plentiful evidence of Neo-Hittite occupation (9th and 8th centuries) but a strange, indeed incomprehensible, absence of almost all Hittite Empire strata.[238] Where artefacts and other remains of Hittite Empire design and manufacture were discovered, these were usually found in a Neo-Hittite context.

This fact alone should have caused archaeologists to stop and think. Yet it is only a single aspect of a vast body of evidence which tells us very clearly that the Anatolian Dark Age never existed, that the four centuries which reputedly separate the demise of the Hittite Empire from the rise of the Neo-Hittites and Neo-Assyrians is a textbook construct, and that these two epochs are in fact contemporary.

---

[238] This is a question discussed at some length by P. James, "Chronological Problems in the Archaeology of the Hittites," *Society for Interdisciplinary Studies Review* Vol.VI (1982), p. 43

Fig. 17. Fig. King Sulumeli of Malatya offers a libation to the Hittite Storm God. The bas-relief is in Imperial Hittite style, though Sulumeli was a contemporary of Tiglath-Pileser III, who supposedly reigned five centuries after the fall of the Hittite Empire.

Fig. King Tudkhaliyas IV, embraced by the god Sharruma. This portrayal shows the detailed parallels between Empire Hittite art and that of the so-called Neo-Hittite epoch (as above).

An examination of just one aspect of Hittite culture should illustrate the point very clearly.

One of the most characteristic features of Neo-Hittite architecture was the so-called *bit-hilani*, or hilani-house. It is described as "one of the most remarkable architectural inventions of the ancient Near East."[239] The hilani-house was a palace-type structure consisting of a vestibule with one to three supports on the front side, behind which lay a large room with a hearth. Around this room were grouped smaller rooms. These hilani-buildings were a peculiar feature of the Neo-Hittite states, and the earliest example from the latter belonged to a prince named Kilamuwa, of Sam'al, who reigned during the time of Shalmaneser III and his son Shamshi-Adad V. However, it seems that Kilamuwa merely revived an ancient architectural feature, for another hilani house, belonging to Nikmepa (or Niqmepa) of Ugarit, was already known.[240] Nikmepa was a contemporary of Mursilis and Hattusilis, the Hittite Great Kings, and with Horemheb and Seti I of Egypt. This means that, according to conventional chronology, Nikmepa's hilani-house was constructed roughly five centuries before that of Kilamuwa, a situation that defies all reason. The two buildings had to be contemporary. Thus it is clear that Nikmepa, who is indubitably contemporary with the early Nineteenth Dynasty, must be placed alongside Kilamuwa, who is indubitably contemporary with Shalmaneser III and Shamshi-Adad V.

Once more we find Velikovsky's original proposition fully vindicated: the revived Neo-Assyrian kingdom of Ashurnasirpal II and Shalmaneser III was truly contemporary with the final years of the Eighteenth Dynasty, and the five centuries separating these epochs in the textbooks needs to be removed.

The Kings of Carchemish

Throughout his reign, Shalmaneser III waged a series of bitter wars against the Hittites. It was the Hittite states of northern Syria that bore the brunt of Shalmaneser's attacks, and of all these, the city of Carchemish figures very prominently. Again and again we hear how Shalmaneser III compelled the king of the city, who is named Sankara (also written as Sangara), to pay tribute.

Clearly then the "Neo-Hittite" city of Carchemish was an important regional power, and we should expect the king named by Shalmaneser III to have left abundant material remains at the site - and yet, astonishingly

---

[239] Akurgal, op cit., p.69
[240] Ibid., p.71

enough, the monuments of Carchemish are silent: Neither Sankara himself, nor any member of his line, has left so much as a brick or inscription.

Now this is a situation we have come to expect from the Imperial Hittite epoch. As with all the other north Syrian settlements, the dynasty estab-lished in the city by Suppiluliumas I is compelled to get along with almost no remains or inscriptions. From documents unearthed at Boghaz-koi we know that the first of these Hittite kings was a son of Suppiluliumas named Sarre-Kushukh (also read Sarre-sin-akh), an individual who was to have a long and chequered career as ruler of the settlement. Carchemish, we know from the Boghaz-koi texts, was to remain under the dynasty of Sarre-Kushukh for another four generations, until the time of the Hittite Empire's collapse. Yet of these kings, who governed the city at the height of its prosperity and importance, not a trace has been found.

Thus Carchemish is, archaeologically, in an almost uniquely unfortunate situation. It can produce almost nothing attributable either to the Imperial Hittite or to the Neo-Hittite epoch.

Nevertheless, and strange to relate, a line of four kings, covering four generations and beginning with a man named Sukhis, is well attested at the city. These kings, whose names have been reconstructed thus; Sukhis I, Astuwatamanzas, Sukhis II, and Katuwas, are now believed to have directly preceded Sankara (of Neo-Assyrian records) and his family, because none of them is mentioned in the Neo-Assyrian annals. Yet in stratigraphic, palaeographic and artistic terms there is no reason to separate this line of rulers from the early Neo-Assyrian age, and one scholar at least has argued forcefully for placing them just there.[241] On the other hand, and much to the consternation of the scholarly community, a great deal of the material associ-ated with the Sukhis kings looks classically Imperial Hittite.

A Hittite Great King named Ura-tarhundas (or Khar-tarhundas), author of the archaic stele A4b from the Temple of the Storm-god at Carchemish, is regarded as the "probable predecessor" of the Sukhis dynasty.[242]

From what has been said earlier, it will be obvious that the material belonging to the four generations of the Sukhis dynasty can only represent the four missing generations of the Imperial Hittite cadet dynasty, and that Sukhis I, founder of the line, must be an alter ego of Sarre-Kushukh, the son of Suppiluliumas. It should be noted that the cuneiform Sarre-Kushukh could legitimately be reconstructed as Surkis (ukh) since vowels are conjec-

---

[241] Akurgal, op.cit., pp.109-10, argues for identifying the Sukhis dynasty, from Sukhis I through to Katuwas, with the Hittite kings of Carchemish known from the Neo-Assyrian monuments, from Sankara through to Pisiris, the latter being a contemporary of Tiglath-Pileser III.

[242] Hawkins, "The Neo-Hittite States in Syria and Anatolia," loc cit., p.384

tural. Scholars however did not dare equate the hieroglyphic Sukhis with the cuneiform Sarre-Kushukh because it was already obvious that Sukhis and his dynasty belonged to the Neo-Hittite and Neo-Assyrian epoch, whereas Sarre-Kushukh and his father Suppiluliumas had already been placed in the 15th century.

Fig. 18. Stela A4b, dedicated to the Sorm God, erected in Carchemish by the Great King Ura-Tarhundas. Ura-Tarhundas apparently established the Neo-Hittite Sukhis dysnasty at Carchemish, though the stela is in classical Imperial Hittite style. As such, Ura-Tarhundas is to be identified with Suppiluliumas, who established his son Sarre-sin-akh as king of Carchemish.

Having equated Sukhis with Sarre-Kushukh, it will be equally clear that Sankara of the Assyrian inscriptions, who is as absent from the monuments as Sarre-Kushukh, is yet another alter ego of the same man. Admittedly, there is an apparently substantial philological difference between Sankara and Sarre-Kushukh. However, we remember at this point that the latter's name is also reconstructed as Sarre-sin-ah, or Sarre-sin-akh, and it will be immediately evident that Sankara is little more than a shortened variant of this version of the name.

As we have said, virtually all of the surviving Hittite art and architecture of Carchemish is associated with this line of kings, a dynasty which, if we are on the right track, must be contemporary with the pharaohs of the Nineteenth Dynasty. Sure enough, amongst the debris of the Sukhis kings was a stone mace-head, bearing the name of a pharaoh, almost certainly that of Ramses II.[243] Again, an inscription of the same period (the Kelekli stela) refers to preparations made for the marriage of a Great King Tudkhaliyas to the daughter of Sukhis II. That it is Sukhis II is proved by the fact that the inscription names his father as Astuwatamanzas.[244] If we are correct, this document must date to the time of Tudkhaliyas IV and Katuwas, son of Sukhis II, a man also known by the Hurrian name of Ini Teshub, and is therefore to be placed right at the end of the Nineteenth Dynasty (Tudkhaliyas IV was a contemporary of Merneptah). Yet by the same token, since the Sukhis dynasty is identical to that of Sankara (of the Assyrian records), the document also belongs to the age of Tiglath-Pileser III.

The Archaeology of Carchemish

Carchemish could reveal no clearly defined Empire age stratum preceding a Neo-Hittite one. Where artifacts and other artwork of Hittite Empire design and manufacture were discovered, these were always found in a Neo-Hittite context.

One of the great mysteries of Carchemish centered on a series of relief sculptures found on the so-called "Herald's Wall," a structure comprising part of the inner defenses of the fortress. Whilst these buildings clearly dated from "the latest phase of art from Carchemish," in other words, around the 7th century, the style of the reliefs was archaic.[245] The evidence was baffling: "Either the whole wall was a survival from an earlier period incorporated in the late Palace, or the individual reliefs had been from an older building and re-used."[246] The nearby King's Gate showed "unmistakable evidence" that

---

[243] James et al., *Centuries of Darkness*, p.128
[244] Ibid., p.136
[245] L. Woolley, *Carchemish III* (London, 1952), p. 190.
[246] Ibid.

the series was of a late date, though "the Herald's Wall and the King's Gate are continuous, and form part of the same building."[247]

The Temple of the Storm-god was dated by Woolley "on grounds of style" to the Empire, though "the Temple complex as we have it was definitely of the Late Hittite ('Syro-Hittite') period."[248] His report on the northern wall of the Temple states: "In the angle there stood undisturbed the basalt stela A.4b bearing a winged disc and an incised inscription which mentions the 'Great King'. It should therefore go back to the time of the late Empire of the Bogazkoy Hittites," and "must therefore be part of the furniture of the original building."[249] However, because it was found in a Neo-Hittite building Woolley had to add: "It is not, of course, in its original position because the north wall of the angle in which it stands was *ex hypothesi* not built when the stela was dedicated."[250]

A tomb underneath the floor of a room (room E) in the North-West Fort of Carchemish contained a great hoard of priceless gold objects. Some of the objects were damaged by fire, since the remains were cremated, and many of the offerings were thrown into the burial pit whilst the ashes, which had been removed from the funeral pyre, were still hot. Nevertheless, thirty-nine small figures were recovered from the ashes and they attracted much attention. According to Woolley, "These little figurines are the jeweller's reproduction in miniature of the great rock-cut reliefs of Yazilikaya. Not only is the general subject the same — a long array of gods, royalties, and soldiers — but the individual figurines are identical in type, in attitude, in attribute, and in dress."[251]

This, however, presented a problem: "The close relation between the rock carvings [of the Hittite Empire] and the Carchemish jewellery cannot be mistaken. The difficulty is in the first place one of date; the carvings are of the thirteenth century BC and the grave is of the last years of the seventh century. Either then the jewels are themselves much older than the grave in which they were found and had been handed down through very many generations, or they are relatively late in date and of Syrian manufacture (the Hittites of Anatolia having disappeared hundreds of years before) but preserve unbroken the old Hittite tradition. It must be admitted that the 'heirloom' theory is far-fetched in view of the fact that Carchemish is far

---

[247] Ibid., p. 191.
[248] Ibid., p. 170.
[249] Ibid.
[250] Ibid.
[251] Ibid., pp. 250ff.

removed from Hattusas and any family continuity bridging that gulf of space and time is most improbable."[252]

But Woolley's interpretation was countered by others. Güterbock, for example, insisted that the gold objects were indeed of Hittite Empire age, and held that they must, notwithstanding Woolley's objections, have been heirlooms.

But the question: How did carvings of the 13th century get into a tomb of the 7th? is answered by the simple proposition that neither the carvings nor the artwork of Yazilikaya upon which they are modeled date from the 13th century but from the latter 7th and 6th centuries.

The Art of War

Among the ruins of Calah, the new capital erected by Ashurnasirpal II, excavations uncovered a veritable treasure-trove of sculptures and bas-reliefs. These showed the Assyrian kings and their entourages engaged in worship, warfare, and various other royal duties. The dress, equipment, and techniques of warfare employed by the Assyrians during the reigns of Ashurnasirpal II and Shalmaneser III were observed in detail by the Assyrian artists, and these have provided first-class material with which to date the lifetimes of these kings. All of them find their most exact parallels in the weapons, equipment and techniques of Egypt of the late Eighteenth and early Nineteenth Dynasties.

The most striking feature observed by the archaeologists was the first-ever use of cavalry. These are portrayed on the monuments of Ashurnasirpal II, and it is evident from the awkward way in which they are deployed that they were an entirely novel feature. Riders are bareback and the only weapon used is the bow. But the mounted bowmen, having "little confidence" in their own abilities, ride alongside another cavalryman, whose sole job is to guide both his own mount and that of his companion, holding the reins of both.[253] These mounted cavalrymen are deployed as an auxiliary force of the chari-otry. In the words of Maspero: "The army [of Assyria] ... now possessed a new element, whose appearance on the field of battle was to revolutionize the whole method of warfare; this was the cavalry, properly so called, introduced as an adjunct to the chariotry."[254] So, it is not doubted that cavalry was an entirely new element in warfare at the time. As might be expected, however, things evolved rapidly, and by the time of Shalmaneser III the horsemen,

---

[252] Ibid.
[253] Maspero, *History of Egypt* Vol. VII, p. 8
[254] Ibid.

while still bareback, no longer ride in tandem; the mounted archers by now apparently confident enough to guide their horses on their own.

But the Egyptians, supposedly five centuries earlier, portrayed cavalrymen in exactly the same way.

The first ever Egyptian portrayal of a man on horseback comes from the Memphis tomb of Horemheb, first pharaoh of the Nineteenth Dynasty. Here, as in the Assyrian reliefs of supposedly five centuries later, the rider is mounted bareback — and in apparently very Asiatic-looking pose. About a decade or two later cavalrymen are again depicted by the Egyptian artists on the walls of Seti I's Hypostyle Hall at Karnak — and here they are part of a Hittite army and fight exactly like those portrayed on the bas-reliefs of Ashurnasirpal II. These Hittite (or Hittite allies) are mounted archers, like the Assyrians, and operate as an adjunct of the chariotry, also like the Assyrians. However, they do not ride in tandem, like the cavalrymen of Ashurnasirpal II, but singly, each archer apparently confident enough to control the reins of his own steed.[255] This would strongly suggest that the cavalrymen on Seti's monument date from a slightly later period than the cavalrymen of Ashurnasirpal II and belong to the time of Shalmaneser III — though in conventional history the latter king reigned 500 years after Seti I!

I have searched the academic literature in vain for any meaningful discussion of these Egyptian portrayals of cavalry allegedly dating 500 years before the Assyrians introduced the concept into the Near East.[256]

Many of the bas-reliefs of Calah showed Ashurnasirpal II and Shalmaneser III riding their chariots into battle. In all cases these are depicted in detail. Wheels are six-spoked and the cart is designed for two warriors; the king, who is armed with a bow, and his charioteer. The cart itself is richly decorated with crossed quivers for bow and arrows affixed to the side. The design and deployment of these machines matches precisely those of Egypt during the late Eighteenth and Nineteenth Dynasties.

In Egypt and in Mesopotamia the chariot went through a very precise and parallel development. In actual fact, the chariot seems to have been introduced into Egypt from Mesopotamia. It was the Hyksos, the Asiatic invaders, who brought it to the country, and with it they brought the Akkadian or Mesopotamian word: *markabata*. This was a light-weight, fast-moving machine, with four-spoked wheels, a design that remained in use until the

---

[255] See illustration in I. Woldering, *Egypt: The Art of the Pharaohs* (London, 1962). From an illustration by Adolph Erman.

[256] Robert E. Gaebel, (*Cavalry Operations in the Ancient Greek World* (Oklahoma, 1937), p. 45) does mention 'two unarmed Hittite riders fleeing before Seti I,' and notes that they seem to be properly-trained cavalrymen, but fails to remark on the peculiarity of their appearance on the field of battle 500 years before the cavalry of Ashurnasirpal II.

middle of the Eighteenth Dynasty. By the reign of Thutmose IV, however, the wheel is strengthened by the use of six spokes, and this remained the norm in Egypt ever afterward.

The first-ever Assyrian portrayals of chariots come in the palaces of Ashurnasirpal II and, as we have said, they are identical to those deployed in Egypt from the late Eighteenth Dynasty onward. However, this design lasts only another century in Assyria where, during the reign of Tiglath-Pileser III, the design changes again: Chariots become ever larger, capable at times of carrying four passengers, and the wheels are now reinforced with eight or even sixteen spokes.

The only period in history during which the chariots of Egypt and Assyria are identical (and their deployment and portrayal identical) was during the early Neo-Assyrian epoch and during the late Eighteenth and Nineteenth Dynasties.

Innovations in military technology were rapidly seized upon by all parties — for obvious reasons. Thus a new type of siege engine or bow or armor quickly attracted the attention of suspicious and potentially hostile neighbors. And a peculiar innovation in armor design during the reign of Shalmaneser III attracts our attention: namely full-length shirts of scale armor, reaching from neck to ankles. Such extravagant protection must have been extremely weighty as well as expensive and the style was abandoned shortly after the lifetime of Shalmaneser. It was therefore a style which endured only a single generation. Yet, once again, as with cavalry, the Egyptians and their Hittite opponents seem to have anticipated the Assyrian military technicians by five centuries: For we find precisely the same kind of mail shirts depicted by Egyptian artists during the reign of Ramses II. Here the armor is worn by Ramses' Hittite opponents and their allies at the Battle of Kadesh. Interestingly, the most important allies of the Hittites at this battle were the people of Nahrin — the land of Assyria; and we can scarcely doubt that some — if not all — the soldiers sporting the full-length mail shirts in the Egyptian reliefs were Assyrians. Yet it would appear that the Assyrians and Hittites then abandoned the fashion for five centuries, re-adopted it for a generation during the time of Shalmaneser III, and then abandoned it again.

The improbability of the above scenario hardly needs to be labored, and it is evident that the warriors depicted on the bas-reliefs of Ramses II must have been contemporaries, or near contemporaries, of the Assyrian warriors portrayed on the bas-reliefs of Shalmaneser III.

Fig. 19. Shalmaneser III on a lion-hunt. The chariot design is strikingly like that employed by the Egyptians during the Nineteenth Dynasty, supposedly five hundred years earlier.

Fig. 20. Ramses II in his war chariot at the Battle of Kadesh. Note the striking similarity with the Assyrian portrayal above, particularly with regard to the design of the chariot and the pose of the horses. Note also the full-length mail shirt worn by Ramses and his Hittite and Nahrin (Assyrian) opponents.

Fig. 21. Troops of Shalmaneser III wearing full-length mail shirts. This was the only period in Assyrian history during which such armor was worn. Compare with the mail shirts worn by Ramses II and his Hittite and Assyrian opponents in Fig. 20.

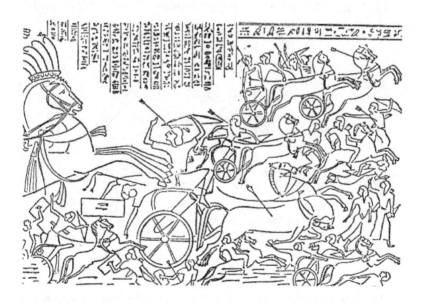

Fig. 22. Seti I battles the Hittites, from a bas-relief on his Hypostile Hall at Karnak. Note the mounted archers among the Hittite chariots. This is the first ever Egyptian portrayal of cavalrymen in action. (After illustration by Adolph Erman).

Fig. 23. Fig. Detail of one of the Hittite horsemen pictured on Seti's bas relief.

Fig. 24. Assyrian cavalry archers portrayed on the Balawat Gates of Shalmaneser III. These were, along with those of his father Ashurnasirpal II, the first Assyrian portrayals of cavalry, and they are deployed in exactly the same way as those of the Hittites portrayed in Seti I's bas relief, supposedly 500 years earlier.

Military technologies employed in Egypt or at least portrayed in Egyptian art supposedly of the 14th/13th century BC thus find their best and only real parallels in militaries technologies employed in Assyria of the allegedly 9th and 8th centuries BC — precisely 500 years later. Yet these same technologies find precise parallels in the Greek world a further two centuries down the time scale. And so, for example, the very earliest portrayal of cavalrymen in Greek art come around 600 BC.[257] Why the Greeks, ever the innovators and adapters, should have taken so long to deploy this highly-effective form of military force is nowhere remarked upon. Yet it was not just in the use of cavalry that the Greeks seemed to have lagged behind Egypt and Assyria. The Egyptians seem to have been familiar with the concept of heavily-armored infantry, the famous *hoplite* formations, seven hundred years before the Greeks.

Fig. 25. The earliest Greek portrayals of horsemen, such as this one from Boeotia, date from the early to mid-6th century BC. All the evidence suggests that the Egyptian and Assyrian portrayals of cavalry, shown above, date to the same epoch.

By the time of the Nineteenth Dynasty Egypt had, for a number of generations, been employing detachments of heavily-armored foreign mercenaries from the opposite shores of the Mediterranean named the Sardan. Various conjectures as to the country of origin of the Sardan have been made; some preferring the Mediterranean island of Sardinia, though a number of authoritative voices were raised in favor of Sardis, capital of Lydia.[258] The Sardan soldiers were to become the shock troops of the Egyptian army, and they were equipped in a way strikingly similar to the hoplites of the Hellenes

---

[257] Ibid., p. 58. Gaebel seems to be unconcerned by the astonishingly late appearance of cavalry in the Greek world as compared with Egypt and the Middle East.
[258] e.g. A. R. Burn, *Minoans, Philistines, and Greeks* (London, 1930)

allegedly seven centuries later. Thus for example the Sardan are portrayed with metal helmets, metal-studded cuirass, and double-handled shields.[259] Now double-handled shields were first introduced in the Aegean world in the 7th century,[260] and they were particularly associated with the development of hoplite battle techniques — the shield being intended to form a solid wall behind which the otherwise vulnerable hoplites would be safe. Not surprisingly, scholars were amazed to find such equipment in use in the 14th century BC.

The Assyrians too, this time two centuries before the Greeks and five centuries after the Egyptians, seem to portray warriors equipped and attired in classic hoplite fashion.

The enemies against whom the Egyptians waged war during the Eighteenth and Nineteenth Dynasties also sported some very modern-looking equipment, again recalling equipment familiar from the Greek world seven centuries later. The Hittites, for example, who are portrayed in some detail on the monuments of Ramses II, regularly carry what is clearly a variety of the classic Boeotian shield, i.e., an oval-shaped device with semi-circular apertures on either side. Now the Boeotian shield is a late development of the huge Heroic Age *dipylon* ("double-gated") shield, reaching its final form in Greece around the 7th century BC. The Medes, as we know from monuments of the Persian epoch, employed targes of identical type; but none of these are known before the 7th century.

Not only do the Egyptians anticipate the Greeks by seven centuries in their familiarity with battle techniques known to the Greeks only from the 5th or 6th centuries BC, but even their art, where it comes to the portrayal of battle, seems to predate identical work of the Greeks from the latter two centuries. Thus, for example, in various depictions of New Kingdom pharaohs in action, the king is shown on his chariot with one foot resting on the vehicle's pole, a dynamic pose which was apparently copied by the Greeks a full seven centuries later. In the words of M. A. Littauer, "The chariot warrior stands astraddle the front breastwork of the vehicle, one foot on the pole just in front of the breastwork. Since the pole here is already slightly higher than the chariot floor and since the figure leans forward, the forward leg is bent at the knee, while the other remains straight."[261] Littauer noted, evidently with a degree of puzzlement, that exactly the same motif appears on Attic black-

---

[259] See fig.3 cf. Breasted, *A History of Egypt*, p.448

[260] Herodotus, i, 171, informs us that it was the Carians who developed the double-handled shield.

[261] M. A. Littauer, "A 19th and 20th dynasty heroic motif on Attic Black-figured vases?" *American Journal of Archaeology*, (1972), 76 (2), 150-52

figured vases, like "a dinos (mixing bowl) by the potter Lydos and several neck amphorae and kraters, all from the 7th and 6th century BC."[262]

Once again, that gap of seven centuries between the culture of Egypt and that of Greece.

Fig. 26. Seti I, in his war-chariot, with foot on the chariot pole. This motif also appears in Greek art, but not until the mid-6th century BC.

The Alphabet and Phoenician Sarcophagi

In 1922, the French archaeologist Pierre Montet discovered a series of royal tombs whilst excavating the ancient site of Byblos, the biblical Gwal. The most important of these was found to belong to a King Ahiram, or Hiram, a name common enough among Phoenician royalty. A shaft cut into the rock led to a burial chamber which contained three sarcophagi. Two of these were plain and contained only bones. The third, ornately carved, belonged to Ahiram. A warning against desecrating the tomb was incised in Phoenician (Hebrew) characters at the entrance to the burial chamber, and again on the lid of the sarcophagus:

The coffin which Ithobaal, son of Ahiram, King of Gwal [Byblos], made for his father as his abode in eternity. And if any king or any governor or any army commander attacks (Gwal) and exposes this coffin, let his judicial

---

[262] Sjef Van Asten, "Further Support for a Velikovskian-like Scenario?" *Society for Interdisciplinary Studies: Chronology and Catastrophism Workshop* (2013) No. 1, p. 16

scepter be broken, let his royal throne be overthrown, and let peace flee from Gwal; and as for him, let a vagabond efface his inscriptions![263]

On one side of the sarcophagus the king is seated on a throne with winged sphinxes guarding him and courtiers facing him. The opposite side shows a procession of persons carrying offerings. Each of the two ends of the sarcophagus has figures of lamenting women.

Close by the entrance to the burial chamber, several fragments of an alabaster vase were found, one of which bore the name and royal nomen of Ramses II. There was another fragment, also of alabaster, within the chamber, and this too bore the cartouche of Ramses II. In addition, the excavators discovered a Mycenaean ivory plaque along with Cypriot pottery which however looked of 7th century date.

Not surprisingly, scholars had great difficulty in dating the tomb. The statement at the entrance to the burial chamber as well as on the sarcophagus clearly implied that the sepulcher had been excavated by the Phoenician king Ithobaal, a circumstance which, together with the style of script involved, suggested a date between the 8th and 6th centuries BC: Indeed, Ithobaal's inscription can, on stylistic grounds, be dated with a reasonable degree of accuracy and placed sometime in the first half of the 8th century. It was noted that the script employed by Ithobaal is virtually identical to that of the other Biblite kings Abibaal and Elibaal, who left two short dedications on statues of the Libyan pharaohs Sosenk I and Osorkon I.

This late dating for Ithobaal was further reinforced by the presence of apparently 7th century Cyprian pottery in the tomb. On the other hand, however, the alabaster vase of Ramses II, together with the Mycenaean ivory plaque, seemed to suggest a date of five or six centuries earlier, in the early 13th century.

On the strength of the latter material, Montet, the tomb's discoverer, dated it to the 13th century. On the other Dussaud, a leading French orientalist, agreed that the tomb dated from the 13th century but insisted that the Cypriot ware was of the 7th century. He assumed that 7th century tomb robbers broke in and left pottery there of their own age. However, even if it were possible to explain the 7th century pottery as the work of thieves, the same certainly cannot be said of the sarcophagi and the inscriptions. These, we saw, were written in Hebrew/Phoenician letters. If the tomb dated to the time of Ramses II, it seemed certain that the inscriptions must date to the same epoch. Yet inscriptions in Hebrew characters, in the time of Ramses II, supposedly the 13th century, were totally unexpected.

---

[263] Trans., W. F. Albright, *Journal of the American Oriental Society*, LXVII (1947), 155-6

A fiercely contested debate broke out among scholars with regard to the tomb. It is a debate which has never been resolved. On the one hand were the epigraphists, who could not concede that the inscriptions in the tomb were of a time as early as the 13th century. The letters of the dedications, as well as the language used, were found to be almost identical to those of the Mesha stela (contemporary with Shalmaneser III — supposedly c. 850 BC) and the Hezekiah letters chiselled into the rock wall of a water conduit of the Shiloah spring near Jerusalem, of supposedly 700 BC. The Ahiram dedications, they argued, must have been written sometime between these two dates.

On the other hand were the archaeologists, who insisted that the vase of Ramses II had to take precedence and that the tomb could not possibly therefore date after the 13th century BC. "From the discovery of the two alabaster vases inscribed with the name of Ramses II in the tomb of Ahiram, we can deduce beyond any uncertainty that the tomb, the sarcophagus and its inscription date from the thirteenth century before our era."[264]

Thus the opinion of an archaeologist. An eminent epigraphist, however, begged to differ: "It is strange that there should be agreement on this dating of the thirteenth century because of two fragments with the name of Ramses II, though there is not the slightest reason for such dating. After the tomb of Ahiram was robbed in the eighth to seventh century and stood open, grave robbers in a new visit deposited in it vases from some other tomb, a more ancient one. It follows that the tomb and the inscriptions were made before the seventh to eighth century, but when can be determined only by the epigraphists, who must not pay the slightest attention to the vases with the name of Ramses II."[265]

As Velikovsky noted in his consideration of this tomb, the first of the above experts assumed that the Cyprian vases had been brought into the tomb by thieves, whilst the second accepted this explanation but had the thieves also bring in the Ramses II vase.[266]

But the problem was not to be so easily solved: For the ornament of the sarcophagus, which Ithobaal clearly states he had fashioned, was typical of Phoenician work from the time of Ramses II. "The evidence of the ornament on this coffin seems decisive as to date. It cannot be later that the thirteenth century. The forms of the letters have induced the epigraphists to doubt the

---

[264] R. Dussaud. "Topographie historique de la Syrie antique et medieval," *Syria* V (1924), 142

[265] W. Spiegelberg, "Zur Datierung der Ahiram-Inschrift von Byblos," *Orientalistische Literaturzeitung* XXIX (1926) cols. 735-7

[266] Velikovsky, *Ramses II and his Time*, p.84

excavator's conclusions, and some play has been made with the sherds found in the tomb. The epigraphic argument is not sound."[267]

And thus the arguments raged to and fro. The epigraphists tried, as Velikovsky noted, to reduce the date of the tomb as much as the chronology would allow, bargaining for every decade, whilst the archaeologists, convinced of the absolute certainty of Egyptian dates, bargained with equal ardor in the opposite direction. However, another problem, not generally mentioned in the debate, is that sarcophagi as such were not otherwise attested in Phoenician burials until the 5th century or the latter 6th century, at the earliest. The next Phoenician sarcophagus known to archaeology, after that of Ahiram, is that of Tabnit, King of Sidon around 490 BC. This latter is heavily Egyptian in design and inscribed with both hieroglyphs and Phoenician letters. The latter text is said to display a "remarkable" similarity to the Shebna Inscription from Jerusalem which, however, is generally dated to the 7th century.[268] In 1999 Sabatino Moscati, an authority on Phoenician archaeology, was moved to remark on the fact that "after Ahiram new sarcophagi are only found in the fifth century."[269] He was later to add that "this sarcophagus [of Ahiram] is a unique case since no others have appeared prior to the 6th-5th century."[270]

Barnett, another authority, noted not too many years earlier how the sarcophagus of Ahiram "obviously reproduces in stone a contemporaneous wooden chest decorated with carved panels; it is the earliest example of what later became the established type of Phoenician funerary furniture, continuing with little change through stone sarcophagi such as the late 6th and early 5th century pieces from Amathus, Tamassos, and Athienou on to the Satrap of Alexander sarcophagi and that of the 'Mourning Women' at Carthage."[271]

Again and again material from Phoenicia, which is easily compared chronologically with material from the Greek world, shows that the world of the Late Bronze Age, specifically contemporary with the Egyptian Eighteenth and Nineteenth Dynasties, should rightfully be placed in the 7th and

---

[267] Sidney Smith, *Alalakh and Chronology* (London,1940), p.46

[268] Christopher B. Hays, "Re-Excavating Shebna's Tomb: A New Reading of Isa 22, 15-19 in its Ancient Near Eastern Context," *Zeitschrift für die Alttestamentliche Wissenschaft*; (2010). "The similarity of the inscription to that of Tabnit of Sidon (KAI1.13, COS2.56) is remarkable, extending even to the assertion that there are no precious metals within."

[269] S. Moscati et al, *The Phoenicians* (New York, 1999), p. 355; cited by L. M. Greenberg, "The Lion Gate at Mycenae Revisited," *Society for Interdisciplinary Studies: Proceedings of Conference 'Ages Still in Chaos'* (September, 2002).

[270] Ibid.

[271] R. D. Bennett, "Phoenician-Punic Art," in *Encyclopedia of World Art*, XI (New York, 1966), p. 307. Cited from Greenberg. loc cit.

6th centuries BC rather than the 15th and 14th centuries, to which it is presently assigned.

One more point — Frankfort, interestingly enough, noted that the carved lions which act as supports for the Ahiram sarcophagus "seem to anticipate Syro-Hittite sculpture of the eighth century BC."[272] Syro-Hittite or Neo-Hittite culture is of course dated by its relationship to Assyrian history. On this ground it (and the Ahiram sarcophagus) seems to belong to the 8th century. Thus material which is Egyptologically dated to the 14th century is at the same time Assyriologically dated to the 8th and classically dated to the 6th centuries.

This same phenomenon is encountered again and again, wherever we look at the art and material culture of the region.

The non-existence therefore of any Phoenician tradition of sarcophagi interment between Ahiram and the 6th or 5th century presents conventional historiography with an immense problem. Even assuming that Ahiram's burial be dated to the 9th or 8th century, as is now generally agreed, this still leaves a gap of two to three centuries between his monument and the next Phoenician example of such. But the problem is easily resolved when we accept that far from being an iron-cast measuring rod, Egyptian chronology as it stands has no scientific basis whatsoever. Ramses II did not reign in the early 13th century; he reigned in the 6th. Nonetheless, he really was contemporary with the Neo-Assyrian kings normally dated between 850 BC and 700 BC, just as the epigraphic evidence suggested. As we shall see, he was a contemporary of Shalmaneser III's son Shamshi-Adad V, and his grandson Adad-Nirari III — all of whom rightfully belong, like Ramses II himself, in the 6th century.

As to Ithobaal, he was a contemporary not only of Ramses II, but of Jeroboam II of Israel, his close neighbor. Ramses II, it remains to be shown, was an ally of the latter two kings, and he labored hard during his entire reign to re-establish Egypt's hegemony in the region; a hegemony which the kings of Israel and Byblos, long oppressed by the expansionist policies of Syria, were more than happy to accept.

When Ahiram died, the pharaoh sent funerary presents to his son Ithobaal, and these were placed in the deceased king's tomb. This would probably have occurred mid-way through the reign of Ramses II, contemporary with either Adad-Nirari III or Shalmaneser IV of Assyria/Media. The two later Biblite kings Abibaal and Elibaal (contemporaries of Sosenk I and Osorkon I), whose writings offered an almost precise match for those of

---

[272] H. Frankfort, *The Art and Architecture of the Ancient Orient* (Penguin, New York, 1988), p. 271 Cited from Greenberg, loc cit.

Ithobaal, reigned under the Neo-Assyrian kings Sargon II and Sennacherib — who themselves need to be brought forward in the time scale into the Persian period.

Semitic Influences on the Egyptian Language

Scholars are frequently amazed at the extent to which Asiatic words and terminology, more specifically Hebrew words and terminology, penetrated the Egyptian language during the Nineteenth Dynasty. Thus for example in the epic *Poem of Pentaur*, commemorating the deeds of Ramses II, a number of Phoenician (or Hebrew) words are used instead of their Egyptian equivalents. In this context we may mention the word *katzin*, for "officer," *sesem* (*sous*), for "horse,"[273] and the *naarim*, who saved Ramses at the Battle of Kadesh, is "youths" in Hebrew. We know of units of specialized troops by the same name employed in the armies of the kings of Israel from the time of Ahab.[274]

But it would appear that the Egyptians of Nineteenth Dynasty times took a very active interest in all things Hebrew. There appears even to have been what we could only describe as a "Hebrew College" in the country, designed to train Egyptian scribes in the use of the Hebrew/Phoenician language. A well-known letter of the period, that of the scribe Hori, reveals very clearly the extent of knowledge of Hebrew. Hori, it appears, had been insulted by another scribe named Amenemope, to whom the letter is addressed. Amenemope had charged Hori with ignorance, and Hori replied with a sarcastic letter proving his own learning and exposing the ignorance of his opponent. The field of knowledge in which Hori claimed to be an authority was Palestinology.

The contents of the missive show that Hori certainly knew his stuff. The letter mentions many geographical locations in Palestine, and such is the knowledge displayed that it is believed that it may actually have been composed in Palestine. Hori would thus have been an official of the pharaoh stationed at the court of a client king in Palestine.

Even more impressive than the knowledge of Palestinian geography is the numerous Hebrew words listed by the scribe. Thus we have mention of *kemakh*, "flour," of *koz*, meaning "bramble" and *asheph*, a "quiver." There is even an entire Hebrew sentence: *Avadta kmo ari, mahir noam* — "You have perished like a lion, said the speedy scribe."

---

[273] Emmanuel De Rouge, *Oeuvres diverses* Vol.V (Paris, 1914), pp.318-343
[274] I Kings 20:14-19. See also J. Macdonald, "The Na'ar in Israelite Society," *Journal of Near Eastern Studies* 35 (1976), p. 169

Now since Ramses II, and therefore the scribe Hori, is placed in the early 13th century BC by orthodox chronology, we must expect that the Hebrew words and phrases used in Hori's letter would display obvious archaisms. Actually, it is assumed that since this is the 13th century there cannot have been any Hebrews in Palestine at all, and the Hebrew in Hori's letter is the language of the Canaanite natives of the mid-second millennium. Yet the astonishing thing is that Hori's Hebrew is identical, in minute detail, to the Hebrew employed in Palestine during the period of the later monarchies, say around the time of Isaiah. Thus Hori used the words *sofer yodea* for a learned scribe and *mahir* for a speedy scribe. This last word appears throughout the document, as it was Hori's intention to point out the duties of a *mahir*, who must be able to record conversations as they occur — much like a short-hand secretary. As Velikovsky noted, "A pen of a mahir," or "a pen of a speedy writer," is found in the opening passage of Psalm 45. Scribes were a professional class from the days of the first Jewish kings in Palestine, but, as Velikovsky notes, the idea of a "speedy scribe," or one who could write down words as they were spoken, "is a late development in the art of writing."[275]

Textbook chronology therefore requires us to believe that the language of Palestine remained completely unchanged for the six or seven hundred years separating the time of Hori from the epoch in which scholars would expect to have found written the advanced Hebrew that he used, i.e., the 8th/7th century BC. It is the equivalent of finding a document from the time of Chaucer written in modern English! Yet such an implausible, not to say fantastic, idea is passed over in the textbooks without comment.

The letter of Hori was written in hieratic Egyptian,[276] but, as we shall now see, texts written in alphabetic Hebrew script, and a late development of the script at it, have also been found associated with material dating to the time of Ramses II.

Scarabs and Pottery

Throughout the entire region of Syria/Palestine, scarabs belonging to the pharaohs of the New Kingdom are regularly found in strata associated with the Hebrew monarchies and the Neo-Assyrian kings. These artefacts should have provided historians with first-class material on how to date the Eighteenth and Nineteenth Dynasties, yet their significance was and is explained away by two recurring propositions: (a) That the scarabs are copies of artefacts many hundreds of years old, and: (b) That they are genuine but "heir-

[275] Velikovsky, *Ramses II and his Time*.
[276] Papyrus Anastasi I, ed. and trans., A. H. Gardiner, *Egyptian Hieratic Texts* I (Leipzig, 1911)

looms" handed down for centuries and finally deposited in strata where they do not rightfully belong.

Neither of these explanations holds water and are further contradicted, as we shall see, by the evidence of pottery and art/culture, which also regularly place material contemporary with Egypt's New Kingdom in a context many centuries after their assumed proper date.

From the earliest days of scientific archaeology, in the nineteenth century, excavators found an abundance of scarabs belonging to pharaohs such as Thutmose III, Amenhotep II and Ramses II right throughout Syria/Palestine. At the beginning, their occurrence was honestly noted and reported. Thus for example A. H. Layard spoke of scarabs of Thutmose III and Amenhotep III in Neo-Assyrian remains constructed by Ashurnasirpal II in the Khabur region of Syria.[277] Layard made no comment upon this, save to remark that the artefacts confirmed the close links between ancient Egypt and Assyria. Later, however, when the chronologies of Egypt and Assyria became more set in stone, the awkward pieces tended to be ignored, and an abridged version of Layard's book, now available on the internet, fails to mention them at all. Nonetheless, scarabs of the New Kingdom continued to be discovered throughout Syria/Palestine, and these have caused immense problems for conventional history.In the last years of the nineteenth century, F. J. Bliss and R. A. S. Macalister conducted extensive excavations at Tel es-Safi and other sites in Palestine. During these digs they found thirty scarabs of Thutmose III, Amenhotep III and other New Kingdom pharaohs in levels they recognized as belonging to the time of the Hebrew kings. However, the significance of their discoveries was lost. They wrote: "Evidently some of them [the scarabs], if not all, are mere Palestinian imitations of imported specimens, and are therefore of no value in fixing the date of the associated objects. It is an elementary archaeological canon that under the most favorable circumstances scarabs alone can give a major limit of date only; when the element of copying, perhaps long subsequent to the engraving of the original exemplar, is introduced, the chronological importance practically disappears."[278]

To this comment, Velikovsky replied: "Scarabs were presents of the pharaohs; they were also the official seals of the reigning monarch used in Egypt and the dependent countries; their impressions have been found in Palestine on the handles of jars that had contained oil or wine, and also on stones used as weights. Why should the impressions for legal and other official purposes have been imitations of seals of ancient pharaohs?"[279]

---

[277] Layard, op cit., p. 282
[278] F. J. Bliss and R. A. S. Macalister, *Excavations in Palestine (1898–1900)* (London, 1902), p. 152
[279] Velikovsky, *Ramses II and his Time*, p. 240

Why, indeed?

A great many more New Kingdom scarabs were found throughout Palestine in subsequent years; all seemed to occur in strata five centuries or so younger than the pharaohs named on them. The explorers of Jericho, Sellin and Watzinger, wrote: "It is beyond doubt that all scarabs found are of genuine Egyptian workmanship of their time, not one a foreign or late imitations."[280] Again: "It has already been frequently established in the Palestinian excavations that the old scarabs were worn centuries later as unintelligible amulets, and therefore, when we find them, we obtain but a *terminus a quo* [earliest possible date]."[281] Consequently, "We are compelled ... to assume that it was a custom in Palestine to use old scarabs ... at a time when there was no longer any understanding of their original meaning."[282]

So, the anomalous scarabs were explained away by Bliss and Macalister as imitations or fakes, and by Sellin and Watzinger as genuine but mere heirlooms. What about the possibility that they may have been contemporary with the comparatively late strata in which they were found? This was never even considered.

Both "explanations" could be conveniently used for the discovery of a scarab of Thutmose III on the floor of the palace of Omri and Ahab in Samaria, a city which did not even exist until the time of the latter two monarchs.[283] On this occasion however the discoverers plumped for the "imitation" or "fake" explanation, declaring that "This [find] may be a local imitation of an Egyptian scarab."[284]

Thus clue after clue to the real chronology of the ancient Near East was missed.

Archaeologists, tied as they are to the conventional system, regard the end of the Bronze Age — Late Bronze 3 — to have occurred in Syria/Palestine around 1200–1150 BC, and the Iron Age, beginning with Iron I, to have commenced immediately thereafter. However, if the chronology proposed in the present work is correct, we might expect the so-called Iron Age I strata — a relatively impoverished period in Palestinian history — to have commenced at a later date. Indeed, since Iron I is the point in Palestinian history during which Egypt ceases to be the major cultural influence, to be replaced thereafter by Assyria, we might expect it to commence around the time of the Neo-Assyrian kings Shalmaneser V and Sargon II (conventionally

---

[280] E. Sellin and C. Watzinger, *Jericho* (Berlin, 1913), p. 157
[281] Ibid.
[282] Ibid.
[283] G. A. Reisner, C. S. Fisher, and D. G. Lyon, *Harvard Excavations at Samaria, 1908-1910* Vol. 1 (Cambridge, 1924), p. 377
[284] Ibid.

late-8th/early-7th century), who asserted Assyrian control over the region and carried out mass deportations of the inhabitants of Israel, with the latter being replaced by settlers from the East.

The transition from what is called Late Bronze to Early Iron is marked by a fairly dramatic deterioration in levels of culture and by the destruction of a number of important cities, among them Hazor, Gezer, Lachish and Debir. Since the ruin of these settlements is normally dated to the late 13th or early 12th century, the destruction is normally regarded as the work of the invading Israelite tribes. However, it has been demonstrated that the new Iron Age culture, which appears after the destructions, is merely an impoverished form of that of the Late Bronze Age[285] and that "there is no reason to attribute it to a nation of newly-arrived settlers apart from the *a priori* assumption that the settlement of Israel was taking place at this time."[286]

If the Late Bronze Age really is contemporary with the earlier Israelite kingdoms (down roughly as far as Uzziah/Azariah in Judah and Pekah in Israel), then the destruction of the above-named cities can only have been the work of the Assyrian kings Tiglath-Pileser III and his successors Shalmaneser V, Sargon II and Sennacherib; and indeed the cities damaged at this juncture are actually named in the records of these kings and in the Bible. Thus 2 Kings 15:29 reports that Tiglath-Pileser III attacked and reduced Hazor (conventionally dated to 733 BC), whilst the end of Late Bronze Age Gezer was likely to have been the work of the same campaign, when the Assyrian armies attacked Philistia. The conquest of Gezer is depicted in reliefs from Tiglath-Pileser III's palace at Nimrud.[287] The end of Late Bronze Lachish would be the work of Sennacherib (conventionally 701 BC), his conquest of the city being recorded in 2 Kings 18:14 and in his own reliefs.

Similar correlations could be suggested for a whole series of other sites displaying evidence of destruction at this time, among them Megiddo, Debir, Beth-Shan, Ashdod, Aphek and Beitin. In all these cases, the Iron Age culture which followed these destructions was an impoverished form of what had gone before, clearly representing a scattered population's efforts at recovery in the wake of the destruction of the major cities and death and possibly deportation of large numbers of the people. Even more to the point, the new Iron Age culture now displays, for the first time in the region, the unmistakable influence of Assyria. Hitherto the prevailing influence throughout Syria and Palestine had come from Egypt.

---

[285] J. B. Pritchard in J. P. Hyatt (ed.), *The Bible in Modern Scholarship* (London, 1965), pp. 320-1.
[286] J. Bimson, "Can There be a Revised Chronology Without a Revised Stratigraphy?" *Society for Interdisciplinary Studies: Proceedings, Glasgow Conference* (April, 1978), 18.
[287] H. Tadmor, "Philistia under Assyrian Rule," *Biblical Archaeology* 29 (1966), 89, n. 15.

The most striking evidence for this was revealed at Timna, an ancient copper-mining site in the Arabah. The predominant pottery at the site, named "Edomite," was decreed to be transitional LBA-Iron Age, and accordingly dated to the 12th century by most archaeologists, including the influential Yohanan Aharoni and Beno Rothenberg. However, the site's excavator, Nelson Glueck, begged to differ. He insisted that the town must date to the Sargonid Age (8th/7th century) because he had already found identical "Edomite" pottery at Tell el-Kheleifeh (possibly ancient Ezion-geber), where it is clearly dated — through inscriptional material and Assyrian pottery — to the 8th–6th centuries BC. A prolonged and acrimonious debate ensued: Aharoni and Rothenberg insisting, on the strength of New Kingdom Egyptian finds at the site, that the Timna material be dated no later than the 12th century; Glueck and his ally William Albright equally insistent (on the strength of the Sargonid material) that the settlement be dated to the 8th and 7th centuries.[288] So great is the prestige of Egyptology that most authorities finally found in favor of Aharoni and Rothenberg, and they continued to date Late Bronze Timna to the 12th century. Yet Glueck never capitulated; and on the contrary pointed to various other transitional LBA/Iron Age sites in Palestine where artifacts, especially pottery, of clearly Sargonid design, were located together with material otherwise dated to the 12th and 11th centuries.

Much of the evidence for dating the first Iron Age towns of Palestine to the Sargonid epoch was brought together by John Bimson. Though Bimson later repudiated the chronological scheme outlined by him in the 1970s, the work he did then was invaluable and has never been refuted. In the "Ages in Chaos?" Conference at Glasgow in 1978, Bimson pointed to a number of crucial facts about transitional LBA/Iron Age Palestine:

At Tell Deir Alla, in the Jordan Valley, the final LBA settlement, supposedly destroyed at the start of the 12th century, yielded several plates of scale armor which, according to Bimson, offer a precise match for the scale armor worn by soldiers of Sennacherib at the siege of Lachish.

At the same site the first Iron Age town (supposedly 11th/12th century) yielded a child's feeding-bowl, of pottery, which was compared by the archaeologist Franken to an almost identical bowl, in metal, from a tomb of 7th century Gordion in Anatolia.

In many of the rather impoverished Iron Age II cities of Palestine, which Bimson dated to the time of Sennacherib, scarabs of a pharaoh Menkheperre are commonly found. Bimson noted that Menkheperre was one of the names

---

[288] N. Glueck, "Some Ezion-Geber/Elath Iron II Pottery," *Eretz-Israel* 9 (1969), p. 54, and N. Glueck, *The Other Side of the Jordan* (London, 1970), pp. 73, 93-4.

of the Ethiopian King Shabataka, and that the supposedly "Solomonic" cities where these scarabs occurred should be dated to his time (contemporary with Sennacherib).

A number of architectural features found in the Iron II cities of Hazor, Megiddo, Gezer, and elsewhere, and supposedly dating from the 10th century BC, are strongly reminiscent of designs otherwise found in buildings of the 7th and 6th centuries.

The evidence from Israel then seems to be fairly consistent with that from other regions, which suggests that the demise of the so-called Late Bronze Age (Egyptian New Kingdom) needs to be brought forward by five centuries to make it contemporary with the advent of the major expansion of Neo-Assyrian military power under the Sargonids. The stratigraphy then presents the following picture:

Palestinian Stratigraphy

Stratum	Predominant Cultural Influence
Late Bronze I	Egypt — early 18th Dynasty
Late Bronze IIA	Egypt — late 18th Dynasty
Late Bronze IIB	Egypt — 19th Dynasty
Iron Age I	Sargonid Assyria (circa 750 BC)

The Nimrud Ivories and the Tombs of Enkomi

In the ruins of Calah, the new capital erected by Ashurnasirpal II, excavations began in the mid-nineteenth century, finding an abundance of *objets d'art* — specifically fragments of carved ivory — which often displayed a pronounced Egyptian influence. These are the so-called Nimrud Ivories. The difficulty arose in the fact that many of the Egyptian-style pieces displayed motifs and concepts which only entered Egyptian art in the latter years of the Eighteenth Dynasty. The first ivories were discovered by Layard, and these were augmented throughout the late 19th and early 20th centuries, with the most recent additions to the collection discovered in excavations under the auspices of the British School of Archaeology, begun in 1959 by Max Mallowan and continued by David Gates. Once again, many of the new pieces struck the excavators as belonging to an earlier epoch, with one report suggesting that the archaeologists had stumbled upon an ancient "antique shop." Others suggested that the ivories were carved in a deliberately archaizing style in order to make them appear older. Hence an article in the *New York Times* of 1961 spoke of an "ancient swindle."[289] In Mallowan's own words, one of the pieces, which portrayed a hero spearing a griffin, was "No doubt Syrian," and was "of peculiar interest for its relationship with a stone carving from Ras Shamra/Ugarit of the fourteenth century BC." The plaque, he continues, "is a testimony to the long continuity of iconography which here can be demonstrated to cover a span of at least five centuries. The posture is also familiar in Egypt and occurs in the iconography illustrating the combat of Horus and Seth."[290]

Across the Mediterranean from Syria, on the island of Cyprus, archae-ologists and art historians encountered a similar problem. Here, towards the end of the 19th century, at a cemetery near Enkomi, site of an ancient metropolis, a team from the British Museum conducted extensive excava-tions. A large burial ground with numerous undisturbed sepulchers was uncovered. Many of the finds, particularly the ivories, bore striking resem-blances to artwork from Assyria, there assigned to the 9th and 8th centuries BC. Thus for example a carving of a man slaying a griffin is remarkable "for the helmet with chin strap which he [the man] wears. It is a subject which appears frequently on the metal bowls of the Phoenicians, and is found in two instances among the ivories discovered by Layard in the palace at Nimroud."[291] The date of the palace is given as 850–700 BC.

Numerous other artistic indicators pointed in the same direction. Most remarkable, however, was a silver ring engraved on the bezel "with a design of a distinctly Assyrian character — a man dressed in a lion's skin standing before a seated king to whom he offers an oblation. Two figures in this costume may be seen on an Assyrian sculpture from Nimroud of the time of Assurnazirpal (884–860), and there is no doubt that this fantastic idea spread rapidly westward."[292]

These Assyrian-looking pieces however immediately posed a real problem, for the date of the cemetery was quickly established both by the occurrence in them of artifacts of clearly Mycenaean Greek provenance and by the discovery of several Egyptian objects of late Eighteenth and/or early Nineteenth Dynasty origin. Among these were a scarab bearing the cartouche of Tiy, the wife of Amenhotep III, as well as several gold necklaces of a type typical of the late Eighteenth and Nineteenth Dynasties.[293] Expedition leader A.S. Murray was in no doubt that the cemetery was in use for only a rela-

---

[289]"Ancient Swindle is Dug up in Iraq," *New York Times*, November 26, 1961
[290] Max Mallowan, *The Nimrud Ivories* (London, 1978), p. 56
[291] All quotations from A. S. Murray, "Excavations at Enkomi" in A. S. Murray, A. H. Smith, H. B. Walters, *Excavations in Cyprus* (London, British Museum, 1900).
[292] Ibid.
[293] Ibid.

tively short period of time. "In general," he said, "there was not apparent in the tombs we opened any wide differences of epoch. For all we could say, the whole burying-ground may have been the work of a century."

Now the Mycenaean material, together with that of the Egyptian New Kingdom, should have settled very quickly the age of the cemetery. Even by 1896, the year of the excavations, the chronology of the Eighteenth and Nineteenth Dynasties was well established, or so it seemed. There should really have been no doubt as to the placing of the tombs in the 14th century BC. But Murray soon began finding things which made him question the prevailing wisdom. Quite apart from the occurrence of objects of 9th/8th Assyrian appearance, other artefacts, particularly those that could be connected with the Greek world, pointed to an even more recent date, specifically to the 7th and 6th centuries BC. Murray cited, as one example among many, a vase, typical of the burials at Enkomi. The dark outlines of figures on the vase are accompanied by dotted white lines, making the contours of men and animals appear to be perforated. The feature is very characteristic of Enkomi pottery; and yet, "The same peculiarity of white dotted lines is found also on a vase from Caere [in Etruria], signed by the potter Aristonothos which, it is argued, cannot be older than the seventh century BC. The same method of dotted lines is to be seen again on a pinax from Cameiros [on Rhodes] in the [British] Museum, representing the combat of Menelaos and Hector over the body of Euphorbos, with their names inscribed. That vase also is assigned to the seventh century BC. Is it possible that the Mycenae and Enkomi vases are seven or eight centuries older?"[294]

The connection between a vase of the Mycenaean Age and Aristonothos of the 7th century caused "a remarkable divergence of opinion, even among those who defend systematically the high antiquity of Mycenaean art."

Other features of the vase pointed in the same direction. The workmanship and design of sphinxes or griffins with human forelegs on the object illustrated "its relationship, on the one hand, to the fragmentary vase of Tell el-Amarna (see Petrie, *Tell el-Amarna*, Plate 27) and a fragment of fresco from Tiryns (*Perrot and Chipiez*, VI, 545), and on the other hand to the pattern which occurs on a terracotta sarcophagus from Clazomenae [in Ionia], now in Berlin, a work of the early sixth century BC."

It wasn't only pottery that caused problems. Many metal objects, including some of bronze, silver and gold, raised serious questions: "Another surprise among our bronzes is a pair of greaves.... It is contended by Reichel that metal greaves are unknown in Homer. He is satisfied that they were an invention of a later age (about 700 BC)."

---

[294] Ibid.

One of the Enkomi tombs revealed a collection of gold pins. "One of them, ornamented with six discs, is identical in shape with the pin which fastens the chiton [tunic] on the shoulders of the Fates on the François vase in Florence (sixth century BC)." A pendant "covered with diagonal patterns consisting of minute globules of gold soldered down on the surface of the pendant" was made by "precisely the same process of soldering down globules of gold and arranging them in the same patterns" that "abounds in a series of gold orna-ments in the British Museum which were found at Cameiros in Rhodes" and which were dated to the seventh or eighth century.

Porcelain told the same story. A porcelain head of a woman "seems to be Greek, not only in her features, but also in the way in which her hair is gath-ered up at the back in a net, just as in the sixth century vases of this shape." Greek vases of this shape "differ, of course, in being of a more advanced artistic style, and in having a handle. But it may be fairly questioned whether these differences can represent any very long period of time."

Surveying the glass, Murray noted: "In several tombs, but particularly in one, we found vases of variegated glass, differing but slightly in shape and fabric from the fine series of glass vases obtained from the tombs of Cameiros, and dating from the seventh and sixth centuries, or even later in some cases. It happens, however, that these slight differences of shape and fabric bring our Enkomi glass vases into direct comparison with certain specimens found by Professor Flinders Petrie at Gurob in Egypt, and now in the British Museum. If Professor Petrie is right in assigning his vases to about 1400 BC, our Enkomi specimens must follow suit." It appears that he had found certain fragmentary specimens of this particular glassware beside a porcelain necklace, to which belonged an amulet stamped with the name of Tutankhamen, that is to say, about 1400 BC.

He came to the conclusion that the "Phoenicians manufactured the glass ware of Gurob and Enkomi at one and the same time." Consequently, "the question is, what was that time? For the present we must either accept Professor Petrie's date (about 1400 BC) based on scanty observations collected from the poor remains of a foreign settlement in Egypt, or fall back on the ordinary method of comparing the glass vessels of Gurob with those from Greek tombs of the seventh century BC or later, and then allowing a reasonable interval of time for the slight changes of shape or fabric which may have intervened. In matters of chronology it is no new thing for the Egyptians to instruct the Greeks, as we know from the pages of Herodotus."

In his discussion of the Enkomi material, Velikovsky noted that here Murray came close to the real problem, "but shrank from it." He did not dare revise Egyptian chronology, and without taking this bold step, he was unable to solve the conundrum. He pleaded for a late date for the Enkomi tombs, but in the face of the apparently unassailable evidence from Egypt, he could put forward no sound argument. His proposal to reduce the time of the Mycenaean Age was rejected by the scholarly world, because this would infallibly also have meant the down-dating of the Eighteenth and Nineteenth Egyptian dynasties by the same margin and into the same period of time — i.e., the 7th and 6th centuries BC. Such a proposition was unthinkable, as Murray's famous contemporary Arthur Evans, the excavator of Knossos in Crete, pointed out. Evans admitted that "nothing is clearer than that Ionian art [of the 7th/6th century] represents the continuity of Mycenaean tradition," and that some objects, such as the porcelain figures "present the most remarkable resemblance, as Dr Murray justly pointed out, to some Greek painted vases of the sixth century BC." Nevertheless, he insisted that the weight of evidence must favor the manifold connections between the Mycenaean Age and Egypt of the Eighteenth and Nineteenth Dynasties. Were not the flasks of the Enkomi tomb almost as numerous in Egyptian tombs of the Eighteenth Dynasty? A gold collar or pectoral inlaid with glass paste, found in Enkomi, had gold pendants in nine different patterns, eight of which are well-known designs of the time of Akhnaton, "but are not found a century later." A metal ring of Enkomi, with cartouches of the heretic Akhnaton, was especially important, because "he was not a pharaoh whose cartouches were imitated in later periods."

There could, then, be no separation of the Enkomi tombs from the late Eighteenth and early Nineteenth Dynasties; but these were unquestionably to be dated to the 14th century BC. In time, Murray's objections were forgotten, and the Enkomi burials are today confidently dated between the 15th and 14th centuries BC.

So, the material excavated at Enkomi could be dated Egyptologically to the 14th century BC, Assyriologically (and biblically) to the 9th/8th century BC, and classically (in Greek terms) to the 7th/6th century BC, and thus demonstrate in a striking way the proposition advanced in these pages for a double down-dating of Egyptian history: by 500 years to make it compatible with biblical and Assyriological history and by a further two centuries to make it compatible with that of the Greeks.

CHAPTER 7: IN THE DAYS OF SETI I AND RAMSES II

An Egyptian "Renaissance"

As shown, abundant evidence exists to show that the end of the Eighteenth Dynasty and the extinction of Akhnaton's line was far from peaceful, and that civil war as well as foreign invasion marked the age. Horemheb was apparently installed in power with Asiatic assistance and it would seem that, to begin with, Egypt under its new "Tanite" line was a client of Assyria/Media.

Horemheb's energies appear to have been taken up with attempts to restore order in Egypt. It is likely that his seizure of the throne was regarded by many as a usurpation, and we cannot doubt his own claims that disorder and lawlessness stalked the land. After about eight years Horemheb went to meet the gods, and his place was taken by the little-known Ramses I, apparently a close relative of the vizier Seti who had earlier celebrated a 400th anniversary. Ramses I seems to have reigned little more than a few months before he too met his fate and was replaced on the throne by his son, who took the name Seti I.

Right from the beginning Seti I saw his task as first and foremost the re-establishment of Egypt as a major power. During the time of the Aton heresy and its immediate aftermath, a state of near-anarchy had prevailed in Egypt's vassal territories in Syria/Palestine. This was a situation that could not be tolerated indefinitely, as it posed a direct threat to Egypt herself. Quite apart from the loss of tax revenues from the more northern states, the abject powerlessness into which Egypt appeared to have fallen would perhaps in future provide an irresistible temptation to aggressors from still further afield. With this in mind, Seti I described his first year as year 1 of the "repetition of birth," year 1 of the "Renaissance," and set out with his armies to re-establish Egyptian hegemony in those Asian territories closest to home. As we examine Seti I's life and military career, we shall find that he was, as we would expect from the chronology already established, a contemporary of the Syrian king Hazael as well as Hazael's opponents, the biblical kings Jehoahaz and Jehoshaphat. He was also, of course, a contemporary of the "Assyrian" (i.e., Mede) king Shalmaneser III. In the present chapter we shall see how both Seti I and his successor Ramses II interacted with all these supposedly "Iron Age" kings who are said to have flourished over five centuries later. But we shall find that the kings of Israel in particular, most especially Jehoahaz, Joash, and Jeroboam II, were clients and active allies of the pharaohs of the Nineteenth Dynasty.

Fig. 27. Seti I, who launched Egypt's "Renaissance" during the Nineteenth Dynasty, from his tomb in the Valley of the Kings.

Having said all that, it is worth repeating a fact stressed continuously throughout much of the present work: namely, that the "Iron Age" kings of Israel and Neo-Assyria are currently dated according to biblical time scales which, however, are not correctly aligned with those of the classical world; the former being too long by two centuries. Thus, all the kings and potentates of Judah, Israel and Assyria currently dated between the 9th and 8th centuries BC need to be brought down the time scale a further two centuries into the 7th and 6th centuries BC.

The people and events to be dealt with in the present chapter all belong, in fact, to the 6th century, to the declining years of Mede power and the epoch immediately preceding the rise of Persia. Thus the Hittite Great Kings Hattusilis III and Tudkhaliyas IV will be revealed as the well-known Lydian rulers Alyattes and Croesus, who vied for control of the Near East with the Egyptians and the Medes.

The Egyptian–"Assyrian" Alliance

After the death of Suppululiumas, the Hittite Empire had to face a resurgent Assyria under Ashuruballit I, who launched a series of devastating raids against Hittite possessions in northern Syria as well as against the Anatolian heartland. This is not conjecture but is recorded in both Hittite and Assyrian documents. It is made abundantly clear by the war annals of Suppiluliumas's son Mursilis II, which were discovered at Boghaz-koi. These reveal that Mursilis had to face "incessant" Assyrian pressure.[295] In this prolonged war Assyria had the support of Egypt. From Mursilis' annals we learn that in his second year he sent a military chief to Sarri-sin-akh, prince of Carchemish (evidently the same person as Sangara/Sankhara mentioned by Shalmaneser III), with an order to resist the king of Assyria: "When the Assyrian comes, you will battle with him." In the seventh year of the annals, mention is made of some agreement to which the king of Egypt was a party, and although the lines are mutilated, it is clear that an alliance was concluded by the king of Assyria with the king of Egypt against Mursilis. At the approach of the king of Egypt, some Syrian potentates crossed over to the side of Mursilis' enemies. Mursilis wrote to the garrison in Carchemish that if the Egyptian army entered Nuhasse in Syria, he should be informed immediately, "and I shall come and battle against them." However, the Egyptian army did not arrive.

Two years later, in the ninth year of Mursilis, hostilities flared again. We hear that "the king of Assur conquered the land of Carchemish." Mursilis marched to the region and freed it, installing the son of Sarri-sin-akh on the throne of Carchemish. Some important portions of the text are damaged, but its editor was able to reconstruct them, and his conclusion was that "Mursilis, in his ninth year met his adversary, Ashur-uballit, on the Euphrates line."[296] The Hittite king does not actually name his Assyrian opponent, though it is likely that the modern editor was probably correct in his assumption that

---

[295] Goetze, "Anatolia from Shuppiluliumash to the Egyptian War of Muwatallish," loc cit., p. 121

[296] A. Goetze, "Die Annalen des Mursilis," *Mitteilungen, Vorderasiatisch-aegyptische Gesellschaft*, XXXVII (1932), 2

Ashuruballit (Ashurnasirpal) still sat on the throne of Assyria, whether or not he was personally present on the battlefield. If, however, Ashurnasirpal II shared a long coregency with his son Shalmaneser III, as we suspect, it is likely that it was the latter who was present on the Euphrates.

It is agreed that the events spoken of by Mursilis almost certainly took place during the reign of Horemheb, and he was "the Egyptian" whom the Hittite king warned his allies against. But what could have prompted this Egyptian–Assyrian alliance? Certainly the Hittites under Suppiluliumas and Mursilis II posed a real threat to the interests of both Assyria and Egypt in Syria, and this by itself could have encouraged the two powers to co-operate. However, as we saw in Chapter 5, there are very good grounds for believing that Horemheb was actually placed on the Egyptian throne by forces from Assyria — or at least with help from Assyria. How else to explain the clear Mesopotamian influence displayed in Horemheb's proclamations, as well as the great flood of Asiatic cultural traits arriving in Egypt during his time?

The pro-"Assyrian" (i.e., pro-Mede) policy of Horemheb continued during the reigns of his successors Seti I and Ramses II, and the ongoing hostilities with the Hittites, which continued intermittently during the next decade, flared up again in the final years of Seti I, who was to lead huge armies northward in support of his "Assyrian" ally. Yet in order to under-stand the great war waged against the Hittites by Seti I and Ramses II, we need to be clear about the correct chronological placement of these men. Seti I and Ramses II, we have seen, would have to be, under the historical scheme proposed in the present study, contemporaries of Shalmaneser III and his son Shamshi-Adad V. These latter, normally placed in the late-9th and early 8th centuries BC, were actually Mede Great Kings of the early 6th century. It was during the reigns of these two men that the war between Lydia and the Medes, mentioned repeatedly in the classical historians, was to erupt into one of the greatest conflicts of the ancient world.

Sardanapalus and the Battle of the Nations

Towards the end of Shalmaneser III's reign, the entire Assyrian heart-land, no doubt with the support of the Hittites (Lydians), rose against the Medes. This was not, supposedly, an insurrection of conquered territories but a revolt of the major centers of Assyria itself, including the cities of Ashur, Nineveh, Arbela, and Arrapha, as well as six of the provinces of the north-west and isolated districts here and there in other provinces.[297]

---

[297] Olmstead, op cit., pp.153-4

The revolt against Shalmaneser III is one of the great mysteries of ancient times. Why, it has been asked, should the people of Assyria so unanimously rise against their legitimate king, a man who had successfully led their armies in war after war; a man who had enriched the land with booty and tribute from far and wide; a man who had made Assyria the wealthiest and most powerful kingdom in the known world? No other comparable rebellion against a divinely-appointed king of antiquity is known. Various explanations have been offered. Most bizarrely, perhaps, it has been suggested that Shalmaneser may have become the victim of a desire to resurrect the Sacrificial King cult, which Frazer claimed to have observed amongst primitive peoples.[298] It has otherwise been suggested that the crown prince became jealous of the favors bestowed upon the *turtanu* (Major General) Daian Ashur and staged the rebellion to forestall his usurpation of the throne.[299] Neither of these explanations, nor any of the others offered, has proved convincing or has gained widespread support. However, the rebellion provides not the slightest mystery as soon as we realize that Shalmaneser III was not an Assyrian but a Mede, whose Assyrian satrapy had become a mainstay of his empire.

Documents of the time tell us that the rebel leader was Ashur-da'in-apla, a son of Shalmaneser but apparently not his heir. Now Ashur-da'in-apla bears a name identical to that of Sardanapalus, whom Herodotus, Diodorus, and various other classical authors describe as the last native Assyrian king. Since the decipherment of the cuneiform script in the nineteenth century, scholars have made repeated efforts to identify Sardanapalus from the native documentary sources. In time it came to be widely accepted that Ashurbanipal, the last major Neo-Assyrian monarch, be identified with Sardanapalus.[300] However, there have always been problems with this equation. Quite apart from the fact that a "b" in one name had to be changed to a "d," it is simply not true to say that Ashurbanipal was the last Neo-Assyrian king; his empire showed no signs of collapse until well after his death.

It has of course always been known that the only character from the cuneiform documents whose name could unquestionably be associated with Sardanapalus was the rebel Ashur-da'in-apla; but the two men were never linked because the "traditional" biblical chronology, along whose lines Assyrian history was reconstructed, placed Shalmaneser III and Ashur-da'in-apla in the latter 9th century BC, whereas the classical sources insisted that Sardanapalus had lived near the end of the 7th century. However, since

---

[298]   e.g. H. W. F. Saggs, *The Greatness that was Babylon* (London, 1962), pp.100-1
[299] Olmstead, op cit., p.155
[300] Ibid., p.109

Shalmaneser III and Ashur-da'in-apla actually lived at the turn of the 7th century, there is in reality no chronological difficulty.

All very well, it may be said; but if Ashur-da'in-apla, a son of Shalmaneser, is the same as Sardanapalus, how can he be regarded as a native Assyrian? The answer may be that Ashur-da'in-apla was the son of one of Shalmaneser's concubines, a woman of the Old Assyrian (i.e., Akkadian) royal line. Ashur-da'in-apla could thus have promoted himself as a native prince intending to restore Imperial Assyria. This would certainly explain the unanimity with which the major cities of the land (some of whom had been very well treated by Shalmaneser III) supported him.

At least one ancient source, Ctesias of Cnidus, whose work is quoted by Xenophon, informs us that the last king of an independent Assyria was a rebellious satrap of a Mede king named Cyaxares. Ctesias describes a devastating conflict in which the Assyrian rebel threw together a mighty coalition against the Great King. According to Xenophon, the rebel satrap (who is not named) enlisted the support first of Syria, Arabia and Hyrcania, and then of Lydia, Phrygia and Cappadocia.[301] The latter three regions, it should be noted, formed the territory of what we now call the Hittite Empire. In this epic struggle for mastery of the Near East, called the Battle of the Nations by Ctesias, only Persia remained loyal to the Medes. It was said that the support of the Persian king, named Cambyses by Xenophon but Atradates by Ctesias, was crucial to the outcome and that the Assyrian was defeated in a great battle not far from his capital city.

The evidence would suggest that this last Assyrian king was none other than Ashur-da'in-apla, the defeat of whose rebellion is undoubtedly reflected in the classical traditions of the defeat and death (by fire, and his own hand) of Sardanapalus.

It remains to be noted that the Egyptians too participated in the Battle of the Nations, when first Seti I and later his son Ramses II led great armies against the people of Naharin (Assyria) and their Hittite/Lydian allies.

Egypt and the Battle for Assyria

When the people of Assyria rebelled against Shalmaneser III (identifiable for us as the Mede king Cyaxares — the second monarch of that name), an event which we date to the first quarter of the 6th century BC, the Egyptians threw in their lot with the Medes, whilst the Lydians (Hittites) under Muwatallis II joined forces with the native Assyrians. These events are clearly reflected in the military career of Seti I, who must, if the chronology

---

[301] Xenophon, *Cyropaedia* i, v, 3

proposed in these pages is correct, have reigned contemporaneously with the final fifteen years or so of the reign of Shalmaneser III — and therefore with the beginning of the Assyrian rebellion.

That the Egyptians were already allied to the "Assyrians" (i.e., Medes) is proven, and we saw earlier how Mursilis II refers to this alliance in his autobiography. During his first years as pharaoh Seti I spent much time and energy consolidating Egyptian control in Palestine and southern Syria. Here he was acting, as we shall see at the end of the present volume, specifically on behalf of Egypt's old ally and client-state, the Northern Kingdom of Israel. After order had been restored to those regions nearest Egypt, Seti moved into Syria and eventually clashed with the Hittites. Historians see this as an inevitable consequence of Egypt's ongoing drive to restore authority throughout the territories once controlled by the pharaohs of the Eighteenth Dynasty. However, bearing in mind the Assyrian–Egyptian alliance referred to by Mursilis II in his autobiography, we can reasonably assume that, in fighting the Hittites in northern Syria, Seti I was acting on behalf of his "Assyrian" (i.e., Mede) friend and ally.

The campaign in northern Syria is recorded on Seti's Hypostile Hall at Karnak, where we find that the pharaoh claims to have captured the city of Kadesh. This is the same Kadesh in whose environs Ramses II fought a great battle just five or six years later. Velikovsky argued in great detail that this Kadesh had to be Carchemish, a proposition accepted by the present author. (Note: If Kadesh of northern Syria is not Carchemish, then we have to assume that the Egyptians never noticed the existence of the latter highly important strategic stronghold, for nowhere do they use the name Carchemish).[302] Seti asserts that he took control of Kadesh from the Hittites, though the veracity of this claim is called into question by the fact that Ramses II had to fight to retake it just five or six years later.

Whatever the truth, we can state with some certainty that in the ninth or tenth year of his reign, Seti I led a huge Egyptian army into the north of Syria, where he came into conflict with the Hittites, a people who had a long history of hostility to the rulers of Assyria and with whom they were almost certainly then in conflict. That these events were part of the "Battle of the Nations" mentioned by Ctesias of Cnidus is put beyond reasonable doubt by the manifold varieties of evidence already examined which place the Egyptian Nineteenth Dynasty contemporary with the Neo-Assyrian epoch stretching from the reign of Shalmaneser III through to Tiglath-Pileser III.

---

[302] Note however, this Battle of Kadesh is not the same as the Battle of Carchemish, fought by pharaoh Necho and mentioned in biblical and other sources. The enemy of the Egyptians at this time, Nebuchadrezzar of Babylon, was the same man as Artaxerxes III of Persia. This is a topic examined in some detail in my *Ramessides, Medes and Persians.*

Shamshi-Adad V and Semiramis

We have stated that Sarduri I of Urartu already claimed the title of Great King, and as such we have identified him with Mursilis II of Hatti. Shalmaneser III largely broke the power of this king, and his successor, Ishpuini, ruled over a much reduced empire. Thus Ishpuini of Urartu would have been one and the same as Muwatallis II of Hatti (Lydia), who had inherited a much-weakened Hittite Empire after years of incessant Assyrian (Mede) pressure. This drawn-out and exhausting war with Assyria, we have seen, is referred to in the Autobiography of Mursilis.

Yet before the end of his estimated twenty-one-year reign, events moved dramatically in favor of Mursilis II. Suddenly the Assyrian pressure on Hatti-Land was relaxed, and when he died, Mursilis bequeathed to his heir Muwatallis II an ascendant kingdom, on the brink of mastery of the Near East. What, historians have asked repeatedly, could have caused this sudden reversal of fortunes? From the perspective of our new chronology, the revived fortunes of Hatti are no mystery. The Hittites benefited from the support of a new and powerful ally: The numerous and warlike people of Assyria, who rose in rebellion against their Mede masters.

In this, as in so many other details, the histories of the supposed 14th and 9th centuries offer a precise match.

Historians are unanimous that the Assyrian rebellion greatly weakened the Neo-Assyrian state of the 9th century, and the powerful empire founded by Ashurnasirpal II and Shalmaneser III became, under Shamshi-Adad V, a mere shadow of its former self; subordinate to the power of Urartu in the north. This reign represented the nadir of the Neo-Assyrian kingdom's fortunes, and we find Ishpuini of Urartu, whose regnal years roughly coincided with those of Shamshi-Adad V, claim that he had conquered the "Ashurini land" (i.e., Assyria). He gloried in the titles "Great King" and "King of the Universe."[303]

That such a catastrophic circumstance should have evaded the attention of the Neo-Assyrian chroniclers is hardly surprising, though they do admit to the loss of virtually the whole of Assyria during the rebellion of Sardanapalus. It is almost certain that the conquest of Assyria referred to by Ishpuini recalls the events of the great rebellion and the Battle of the Nations. We can scarcely doubt that Sardanapalus was closely allied with Hatti/Urartu/Lydia; and indeed we recall that Ctesias of Cnidus specifically relates that he was.

---

[303] Olmstead, op cit., p.161

Shamshi-Adad V, who is to be identified with the Mede king Arbaces (named by Ctesias as the conqueror of Sardanapalus), claimed to have defeated the rebellion of Sardanapalus within a couple of years of ascending the throne; yet it is known that he never succeeded in re-establishing the authority of Nineveh west of the Euphrates: Indeed, that was a region into which he never ventured. Other circumstances would make us suspect that much, if not most, of the Assyrian heartland also remained outside his control.

It is evident then that this weak period in the history of the Neo-Assyrian kingdom precisely parallels the collapse of "Middle Assyrian" fortunes during the reigns of Ashuruballit's grandson, who is named Arik-den-ili on some documents.[304] His reign saw the re-emergence of the Hittite Empire under Muwatallis II and Hattusilis III as the dominant power in the region. Evidently then, if we are on the right track, Ishpuini of Urartu was an alter ego of Muwatallis; an equation which in any case is already forced upon us by the prior identification of Ishpuini's father Sarduri with Muwatallis' father Mursilis II. Thus Shamshi-Adad V/Arbaces must have been a contemporary also of Seti I of Egypt, whose war against Muwatallis heralded the beginning of a mighty struggle between Hatti/Lydia and Egypt that carried over into the reigns of both these kings' successors.

In order to secure the defeat of Sardanapalus, it would appear that Shamshi-Adad had to enlist both Babylonian and Egyptian assistance. To this end he married an apparently Babylonian princess named Sammuramat. This of course was the famous Semiramis of classical legend.

The figure of Semiramis looms large in the pages of the ancient authors. By them she is presented as a character of larger than life proportions. A Babylonian queen of extraordinary talents, she is credited with a multitude of wonderful achievements. Many of the cities of Mesopotamia, it is said, were adorned by her with great monuments. She was said, for example, to have constructed the famous Hanging Gardens of Babylon. Her extraordinary career, we are told, encompassed epic endeavors in the manliest of arts, that of war; and among other exploits her armies are said to have conquered Egypt and invaded India. (Diod. ii.15-20) In terms of the prominence of her character she may be placed on a par with — or even above — the other great characters of the ancient Near East: with Sardanapalus of Assyria, with Cyrus of Persia and with Croesus of Lydia. In later years she shared the fate

---

[304] Although we have identified the so-called Middle Assyrians as alter egos of the Mitannians, historians, working within the contraints of accepted chronology, assume that the Assyrian kings against whom Mursilis II and Hattusilis III waged war were Middle Assyrians. They were not, of course; they were they early Neo-Assyrians who all, of course, bore typically "Middle Assyrian"-type names. Hence the confusion.

of other prominent characters of early times; her legend transmuting into virtual myth, with the queen herself deified. In these stories she was said to have been the wife of Ninos, the semi-mythical founder of Nineveh, whom the Hebrews associated with Nimrod and who is now reckoned to be none other than the god Ninurta.

Whilst the historical Semiramis, whose name is read as Sammur-amat in the cuneiform (Sumerian "gift of the sea"), was admittedly an extraordinary woman, historians are nevertheless puzzled by her prominence in ancient literature. True, she lived in a turbulent time. Her marriage to the king of Assyria is widely believed to have been designed to forge an alliance to crush the ongoing revolt in Assyria itself. Shamshi-Adad V, it appears, died whilst quite young, perhaps killed in battle. In any event, the crown prince, the future Adad-Nirari III, was then too young to assume the responsibilities of kingship, and so Semiramis acted as regent for a period of four years, ruling, to all intents and purposes, as king. During this time she made dedications in her own name, placing them before that of her son. A memorial stele was found at Ashur along with the kings and high officials of the country, an honor quite exceptional for a woman.

So, the life of the historical Semiramis was undoubtedly marked by great events; and she was self-evidently a remarkable woman. Yet for all that, her legendary reputation far exceeds (so we are told) the historical reality. Stories of far-flung conquests, as in Egypt and India, are viewed as pure fantasy, and the overwhelming scale of her reputation is regarded as most mysterious, probably to be explained by the normal propensity of the story-teller for exaggeration.

Such is not the opinion of the present writer. In view of the reconstruction of history presented here, it will be obvious that whilst some elements of the Semiramis legend are fantastic, the historical figure which inspired them was truly an extraordinary and outstanding individual; an individual so unusual in terms of career and personality that the exaggerations of later story-tellers become very understandable. The true significance of Semiramis' life and career has now been effectively effaced from the history books because the chronology of the ancient Near East, the time scales erected by historians upon which to place events and cultures, is fictitious. Characters and happenings which were in fact contemporary have been placed centuries apart, with the result that their significance and relationship to each other has been lost. When, however, the sequence of time and events is put right, Semiramis re-emerges as the outstanding character of her age. For the career of Semiramis took in some of the greatest events ever to occur in the ancient Near East. Upon the death of her husband she ruled alone, for four years, the mighty empire of the Medes; an empire that did indeed stretch from the borders of Egypt on one side to those of India on the other.

Fig. 28. Shamshi-Adad V, also known by the Mede name Arbaces; husband of Semiramis and conqueror of his brother Sardanapalus, satrap of Assyria. He was a contemporary and ally of Seti I and Ramses II.

Ramses II and Alyattes of Lydia

By his fifth year Ramses II was actively engaged in the great struggle for control of the civilized world that was still raging. He led a mighty army to the Euphrates, evidently in support of Shalmaneser III's son Shamshi-Adad V. But the young pharaoh was foolhardy and inexperienced, and his men marched straight into a well-prepared trap. Ramses II was lucky to escape from Kadesh with his life, and the Hittites, led by the crown prince Hattusilis, scored a major victory.

The Battle of Kadesh is probably the best-known military engagement of pre-classical times and certainly the best documented. Although an epic poem, the so-called "Poem of Pentaur," was composed to commemorate the event, there is a paucity of information regarding events leading up to it. If, however we are on the right track, we can be fairly sure that the engagement was part of the ongoing struggle between the Hittites (Lydians) and their allies and those of the "Assyrians" (Medes) and theirs. From the surviving records it is evident that at the time Hittite control extended throughout Assyria proper, or at least that the Assyrian people were part of a confederacy which united them with the Hittites: In the register of Hittite allies at the battle, Naharin (i.e., northern Mesopotamia/Assyria) is listed second after the Hatti-Land itself.[305] These Naharin folk were the Assyrian rebels against whom both the recently-deceased Shalmaneser III and his son Shamshi-Adad V waged war. The latter asserted that within two or three years the Assyrian rebels had been defeated and the *status quo* restored. That this was untrue is evident enough. Shamshi-Adad V was never able to assert his authority west of the Euphrates and on the contrary, the Hittites/Lydians were now firmly entrenched in the region around Carchemish, where their client states formed a wedge dividing the Egyptians in the south from their Mede allies in the northeast. Throughout his entire reign, the cities of northern Syria paid tribute to the Hittites under king Hattusilis III. To make matters worse, after little more than a dozen years on the throne, Shamshi-Adad died and his wife Semiramis assumed the regency for four years. The traditions surrounding Semiramis' name suggest that her reign for far from pacific; and though no military exploits of hers are recorded in the Assyrian inscriptions, this is easily explained by the apparent hostility of her son Adad-Nirari III.

Meanwhile the war dragged on. The Egyptian and "Assyrian" (Mede) rulers had a very definite program in mind: Egypt would take pressure off the Medes by attacking Hattis's (Lydia's) allies in Syria, whilst the Medes, for their part, would hold the line against Lydian ambitions in northern Mesopotamia, whilst contributing to the effort against Lydia's allies in Syria where possible.

Hattusilis, who ascended the Hittite/Lydian throne shortly after the engagement at Kadesh, is one of the best-known monarchs of antiquity. However, placed in the 13th century BC by his association with Egypt's Nineteenth Dynasty, he loses his proper context and importance. Inasmuch as we have identified the Hittite Empire with that of the Lydians of the 6th

---

[305] Alan Gardiner, *The Kadesh Inscriptions of Ramesses II* (London, 1975), pp. 57ff.

century, it is evident that Hattusilis should be identified with a monarch of the latter kingdom. Indeed, given the reconstruction of events proposed thus far, and given the fact that Hattusilis was the penultimate Great King of a united Hatti Empire, there is only one person he could be equated with: Alyattes, father and predecessor of Croesus, last king of Lydia.

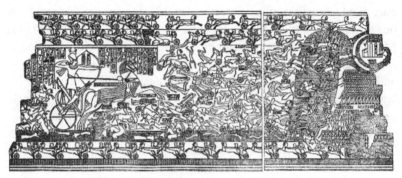

BATTLE SCENE FROM THE GREAT KADESH RELIEFS OF RAMSES II ON THE WALLS OF THE RAMESSEUM.

Fig. 29. The Battle of Kadesh, fought between Ramses II and Alyattes, who was at that time still the Crown Prince of the Lydian Empire.

Classical sources inform us that Alyattes was a mighty king who waged war against many of his neighbors, and who subjugated most of the Aegean coast of Asia Minor. How then does this correspond with what we know of Hattusilis? We know that Hattusilis maintained and extended Hittite control over western Asia Minor, and his victories in the far west are commemorated in various surviving documents. The list of Hittite allies at the battle of Kadesh "mentions several peoples who all ... are hitherto already familiar and recognizable from the Hittite imperial records as being the names of peoples of Western and Central Anatolia."[306] The writer of these words, R. D. Barnett, offers the following identifications of these names:

Drdny	=	Dardanoi (Homeric name for Trojans).
Ms	=	Mysia (a region of Asia Minor).
Pds	=	Pitassa (either Pedasa, near Miletus, or Pedasos, in the Troad).
Krks	=	Karkisa (Caria).
Lk	=	Lukka (Lycia).

---

[306] R. D. Barnett "The Sea Peoples: Anatolians at the Battle of Qadesh," in *The Cambridge Ancient History*, Vol.2 part 2 (3rd ed.), p.360

If these identifications are broadly correct, and virtually no authority denies it, then the Hittites were at that time in control of most of western Asia Minor.

Herodotus informs us that early in his career Alyattes moved to strengthen Lydian control over the west, a control established by his immediate predecessors. As part of this policy, we are told, he attacked the Greek port of Miletus, continuing a war initiated by his father Sadyattes.[307] By our reckoning, Sadyattes must of course be the same as Hattusilis' father Mursilis, and we must expect this king to be involved in military action on the Aegean coast. Sure enough, Hittite records tell us that Mursilis attacked and conquered a city on the Aegean coast named Millawanda, or Millawata (generally agreed to be Miletus),[308] a settlement which had been the property of the king of Ahhiyawa (generally agreed to be Achaea — i.e., Greece).[309] From the records of Mursilis we find that the king of Ahhiyawa at this time was called Antarawas, a name that has been identified with the Greek Andreus. Twelve years later he names another king of Ahhiyawa, this time Tawagalawas, who is also known as "the Ayawalawas." This has been interpreted as Eteocles the Aeolian.[310]

Yet these clear references to Greek settlements in Hittite documents of supposedly the 13th century BC have caused the utmost embarrassment to scholars, since the Ionic and Aeolian colonies are not dated by anyone earlier than the 10th or 9th century BC. But if we are actually in the 6th century BC, there is no problem, and Greek settlements, as well as a Greek city of Miletus, are entirely to be expected.

During the time of Mursilis the province of Arzawa, the Lydian heartland, rebelled. Uhha-zitish, the rebel leader, was defeated in a great battle and pursued to the town of Apasa, identified with Ephesus. Mursilis followed him to Apasa, but Uhha-zitish had fled "across the sea," no doubt to Greece.[311]

Thus it would appear that during and directly preceding the reign of Hattusilis, the Hittites were busy consolidating their hold over the peoples of the Aegean coast, a situation which agrees precisely with what we know of the Lydian kingdom in the time of Alyattes and his immediate predecessors.

[307] Herodotus, i, 17
[308] Barnett, "The Sea Peoples: Anatolians at the Battle of Qadesh," loc. cit., p.362 "Miletus is widely thought to be the Millawanda of the Hittites."
[309] Goetze, "Anatolia from Shuppiluliumash to the Egyptian War of Muwatallish," loc cit., p.122
[310] Burn, op cit., p.121
[311] Goetze, "Anatolia from Shuppiluliumash to the Egyptian War of Muwatallish," loc cit.

Herodotus mentions the fact that one of Alyattes' greater successes was his conquest of Smyrna,[312] and sure enough, a stela of Mursilis, Hattusilis' father, stands at Karabel, just outside the city.[313]

Fig. 30. Hattuslis (Alyattes) presents his daughter to Ramses II.

[312] Herodotus, i,16
[313] Burn, op. cit., pp.134-5

In the end, Alyattes failed to conquer Miletus,[314] which would explain why Hattusilis makes no mention of a successful war against Millawanda. He recalls with pride however his successful fifteen-year war against the Gasga (whom we equate with the Scythians),[315] a fact which recalls Alyattes' achievement of driving the Cimmerians out of Asia.[316]

Alyattes, we have seen, was also involved in prolonged warfare on his eastern front against the Medes. In the records of Assyria, these wars are recalled in the various campaigns waged by Adad-Nirari III, Shalmaneser IV and Ashur-Dan III against the Great King of Urartu, Argishti. Peace was however briefly restored in this region when a major battle was interrupted by an eclipse.

One final point. The name written in the cuneiform of Boghaz-koi as Hattusilis is composed of two elements: Hattus-ili, meaning "he of Hattusa," or simply "of Hattusa," the "ili" component indicating the genitive. As with Lydian, the "ili" element normally formed a suffix to the noun. However, as is the case with many other languages, it is possible that on certain occasions the genitive may have been added as a prefix. Thus "Ili-hattus" or "Ali-hattus" may have been how the name was commonly pronounced. In short, it is possible, even likely, that Hattusilis and Alyattes (Greek Aluattes) are the same name.

Adad-Nirari III (Astyages the Mede)

According to the scheme proposed in these pages, Hattusilis III must have been a contemporary and adversary of Shamshi-Adad V, whose reign was short, and of Adad-Nirari III. Now it is known that Hattusilis was indeed contemporary with an Assyrian king named Adad-Nirari (with whom he corresponded), but it is believed that this Adad-Nirari lived five centuries before the famous grandson of Shalmaneser III.

It is generally supposed that Assyria underwent a period of renewed military expansion under Adad-Nirari III and that he re-established Assyrian military pre-eminence in the region in a way comparable to that enjoyed under Shalmaneser III. This is assumed on the basis of two inscriptions. In one of these, Adad-Nirari III claims to have reconquered all the states west of the Euphrates that had been lost in the final years of Shalmaneser III and had remained independent throughout the reign of Shamshi-Adad V.

---

[314] Herodotus, i,16
[315] Goetze, "Anantolia from Shuppiluliumash to the Egyptian War of Muwatallish," loc. cit., p.260
[316] Herodotus, i,16

As to the numerous hostile kings who had rebelled in the time of my father Shamshi-Adad and had withheld the regular [tributes], [the terror-inspiring glam]our overshadowed them [and] upon the command of Ashur, Sin, Shamash, Adad [and] Ishtar, my trust [inspiring] gods, they seized my feet [in submission].[317]

The above document certainly gives the impression that Adad-Nirari III was a ruler to compare with Shalmaneser III, and that impression is further reinforced by another inscription, which records Adad-Nirari's conquest of Damascus (a feat never accomplished by Shalmaneser III) and his reception of tribute from Joash of Israel.[318] But if Assyria was the major power in Syria during the reign of Adad-Nirari, he certainly cannot have been a contemporary of Hattusilis; for we know that in his epoch the Hittite Empire was dominant, and Hittite armies waged a prolonged war with Egypt for supremacy in Syria. Thus if Adad-Nirari III's claims are correct, or if the impression they convey of military dominance in the region is accurate, he must indeed have lived long after Hattusilis III, as conventional history believes.

But just how powerful a king was Adad-Nirari III?

In recent years scholars have begun to look beyond the bombast of the Assyrian inscriptions and have come to the conclusion that, far from regained pre-eminence, Assyria was "despite outward appearances ... in decline" during and after the reign of Adad-Nirari III.[319] We are told that "it was Adad-nirari's fate to see it [the decline] spread and inaugurate the dark period between the early and late Neo-Assyrian empire."[320] His expeditions across the Euphrates were little more than raids, and he never succeeded in reducing the Hittite states of northern Syria. Furthermore, his attack on Damascus is now deemed an opportunistic venture aimed at acquiring easy plunder — a venture that avoided major confrontation with the Hittite states of north Syria, who were now firmly within the sphere of Urartian influence. "Adad-nerari III reacted to the strategic problem by campaigning mainly in south Syria, an easier target than north Syria, partly from the terrain, but principally because this would not directly involve Urartu."[321] We know now that during the reign of Adad-Nirari "there was a powerful state of Urartu controlling the whole region westwards from south of Lake Urmia to Melid, with states from Melid southwards as far as Carchemish

---

[317] Luckenbill, op. cit., i, 734
[318] H. W. F. Saggs, *The Might that was Assyria* (London, 1984), p.81
[319] Grayson, "Ashur-dan II to Ashur-Nirari V (934-745 BC.)," loc cit., p.271
[320] Ibid.
[321] Saggs, op cit., p.81

completely under Urartian influence, and further south a fairly solid coalition under the domination of an anti-Assyrian Damascus."[322]

The mighty Urartian state, which virtually encircled Assyria on its
northern and western frontiers, and which included the Hittite states of
Syria in its confederation, must have been one and the same as the Hittite
Empire of Muwatallis II and Hattusilis III. We know that during the time
of Adad-Nirari III two kings sat on the throne of Urartu; one for a comparatively short period, the other enjoying a much longer reign. The first of these,
a powerful ruler named Menua, must have been an alter ego of Muwatallis II,
whilst his successor, an even more powerful king named Argishti (or Argisti),
must be regarded as identical to the powerful and long-lived Hattusilis III.[323]

We are told by historians that Menua developed "the process of conquest,
especially in the south east [around Lake Urmia], by means of systematically
planned lines of fortresses and defensive posts, a strategy later revived by
the Romans."[324] We hear also that "The Assyrians, until they had regained
their strength, could do little to oppose him,"[325] and, significantly enough,
that "Under Menua the pressure on Parsua [i.e., Persia] continued."[326] This
mighty king, who described himself as the "Great King" and "King of the
Universe, "who established a system of conquest later copied by the Romans,
and who undertook "immense" building activity,[327] can scarcely be identified
with anyone other than Muwatallis II, the Great King who made Hattiland
the dominant force in the ancient east, and who, in his final years, smashed
the pretensions of Egypt in Syria when his army bested the might of Ramses
II at the Battle of Kadesh.

At the time of this momentous engagement, Muwatallis had already associated his son Urhi-Teshub with him on the throne; but Urhi-Teshub never
wore the crown; he was deposed, probably very shortly after Muwatallis'
death, by his uncle Hattusilis, who banished him first to Nuhasse in northern
Syria, and then to a destination across the sea, very probably Cyprus.

Strange then how we read that Menua "followed his father's pattern
in exercising a joint rule with his son Inushpua ... but for some reason he

---

[322] Ibid.

[323] I have of course already identified Menua's predecessor Ishpuini as the alter ego of
Muwatallis. However, Urartian kings, like the Assyrians, frequently used more than one·
name, as we shall see with regard to Tiglath-Pileser III. Both Ishpuini and Menua were
regarded as conquerors of the Assyrian homeland, a circumstance that places both firmly
in the time of Muwatallis II.

[324] Barnett, "Urartu," loc. cit., p.343

[325] Ibid.

[326] Ibid., p.341

[327] Ibid., p.343

did not succeed to the throne."[328] Inushpua did not succeed to the throne because he was the same person as Urhi-Teshub, the crown prince deposed by Hattusilis, the Great King of Hatti and Urartu, who also called himself Argishti.

The parallels between Argishti I and Hattusilis III are rather obvious. As Argishti I was the penultimate ruler of an independent Urartu, so Hattusilis III was the penultimate ruler of an independent Hatti Land; and just as Hattusilis had a very long reign, during which the Hittite Empire reached its peak of power, so under Argishti I, "Urartu reached its virtual zenith in extent, prestige and power."[329] In such circumstances the king of Urartu/Hattiland would naturally treat with contempt any attempt by an Assyrian ruler to presume to place himself on an equal footing. Thus Hattusilis addressed this angry missive to Adad-Nirari:

With respect to brotherhood ... about which you speak — what does this brotherhood mean? ... with what justification do you write about brotherhood? And for what reason should I write to you about brotherhood? Were perhaps you and I born of the same mother? As my [father] and my grandfather did not write to the king of Ashur [about brotherhood], even so must you not write [about brotherhood and] Great-kingship to me.[330]

If Hattusilis was the same person as Alyattes, the penultimate king of Lydia, then active warfare did indeed take place during his reign against the Median kings of Assyria. We may be justified also in identifying Adad-Nirari III with Astyages of the Greek authors, the last Great King of the Medes, during whose time the war with the Lydians came to an end.

However, it would appear that the Hellenic historians amalgamated the identities of a number of Mede kings under the names Astyages and Cyaxares: For the simple fact is that between Adad-Nirari III and Tiglath-Pileser III (whom we shall identify with the Persian Cyrus), there were three lesser Neo-Assyrian kings: Ashur-Nirari V, Ashur-Dan III and Ashur-Nirari V, and Shalmaneser IV. Some, or all, of these kings must have been ephemeral, and their lack of monuments suggests extreme weakness and instability. Furthermore, it is unlikely that they could have ruled Assyria for the thirty-five years assigned to them in the monuments.

Nevertheless, it was during the reign of one of these lesser monarchs, Ashur-Dan III, that a major eclipse of the sun, *shamash-atalu*, is recorded, in the eponym year of Bur-Sagale. This eclipse was almost certainly the same as that mentioned by Herodotus and placed by him near the end of the Mede

---

[328] Ibid., p.341
[329] Ibid., p.347
[330] A. Goetze "The Hittites and Syria (1300-1200 BC.)," in *The Cambridge Ancient History,* Vol.2 part 2 (3rd ed.), p.258

epoch.[331] The "father of history" tells us that a major conflict between Lydians and Medes was aborted after the sky was darkened by a total eclipse. In the immediate aftermath of this event, a treaty of friendship was negotiated between Alyattes and a Mede ruler named Cyaxares. The kings of Cilicia and Babylon acted as intermediaries.[332] It is probable that the Lydians simultaneously made friends with the Medes' allies, the Egyptians. Interestingly, Herodotus informs us that the peace between Lydia and Media was cemented by the marriage of Alyattes' daughter Aryenis to Cyaxares' son Astyages. If Hattusilis and Alyattes are the same person, then he married more than one daughter to a foreign potentate at this time, for the peace with the Medes must have come in parallel with the peace forged with the Medes' allies, the Egyptians. Sure enough, in Ramses II's 34th year we find him marrying Maathornefrerure, daughter of Hattusilis.

Croesus and His Time

We know rather a lot about Croesus because Herodotus describes his ill-starred war against Persia in some detail. Croesus' kingdom became a byword for power and wealth, yet in the ground archaeologists have found precious little evidence of this much-vaunted opulence. But of course if the Hittite Empire is actually Croesus' realm, then all is explained.

According to the reconstruction proposed here, Croesus must be one and the same as the last Great King of the Hittites, known in the cuneiform documents of Boghaz-koi as Tudkhaliyas (or Tudhaliya) IV. The Hittite Empire was at the very peak of its power when Tudkhaliyas IV ascended the throne, yet by the end of his reign it came crashing to destruction. Tudkhaliyas IV had inherited from Hattusilis a military machine second to none in the region, and from the archaeological evidence it is clear that he had maintained all the territories added to the empire by Suppululiumas and Hattusilis. What, then, could have caused the sudden and dramatic reversal of Hittite fortunes in the latter years of Tudkhaliyas's life? If we are correct, it was an ill-advised war with Persia.

Herodotus informs us that in preparation for the war, Croesus forged alliances with other kingdoms, one of which was Babylon.[333] How does this tie in with what we know of the Hittite Tudkhaliyas's policy? Sure enough, we find Tudkhaliyas in a defensive alliance with Babylon against Assyria. This alliance was concluded, it appears, very shortly before the king of Assyria,

---

[331] Herodotus, i,74
[332] Ibid., i,74
[333] Ibid., i,77

Tukulti-Ninurta, commenced hostilities with the Hittites.[334] We shall, of course, identify this second Tukulti-Ninurta with Cyrus the Great.

It would appear, incidentally, that Tukulti-Ninurta's later attack on Babylon was a direct result of the Hittite alliance; for we hear the Assyrian king accuse the Babylonian monarch of aggression against his territory.[335]

Herodotus writes that it was the Lydians who started the war. Croesus, he says, crossed the Halys river (close to Boghaz-koi),

[and] ... came to a place called Pteria, in Cappadocia ... Here he encamped, and ravaged the lands of the Syrians; and took the city of the Pterians, and enslaved the inhabitants; he also took all the adjacent places, and expelled the inhabitants, who had given him no cause for blame.[336]

In like manner, it would appear that it was Tudkhaliyas the Hittite who initiated hostilities against the king of Assyria. In a treaty with his vassal Shaushga-muwash of Amurru, the Syrian prince was called upon to furnish aid in the event of an Assyrian attack, as well as to instigate a trade blockade against Assyria;

As the king of Assyria is the enemy of My Sun, so may he also be your enemy. Your merchants shall not go to Assyria, you shall not allow his merchants in your land, neither shall they pass through your land. If, however, one of them comes into your land then seize him and send him to My Sun. As soon as the king of Assyria begins war, if then My Sun calls up troops and chariots ... so do you call up your troops and chariots and dispatch them.[337]

If we are right, the above letter is an actual command from Croesus to one of his vassals to provoke a conflict with Cyrus. The ensuing war, however, was a disaster for the Hittites, and we find the king of Assyria boasting of the capture of 28,800 Hittite prisoners.[338] This indeed was to be the first, but not the last, great victory of Tukulti-Ninurta, for his subsequent conquest of Babylon was regarded as possibly even more memorable. It should be noted, of course, that the various campaigns of this Tukulti-Ninurta offer a precise parallel, in terms of the order of events, with the military career of Cyrus.

The defeat and destruction of the Hittite Empire was long recalled by Tukulti-Ninurta, and in a triumphant summing-up of his early campaigns he boasts that he had conquered everything "as far as the frontier district of Nairi [Armenia/Anatolia] and the frontier district of Makan [Egypt] to

---

[334] R. M. Munn-Rankin, "Assyrian Military Power 1300–1200 BC," in *The Cambridge Ancient History*, Vol. 2 part 2 (3rd ed.), p.286
[335] Ibid.
[336] Herodotus, i, 76
[337] Munn-Rankin, loc cit., p.292
[338] Ibid., p.291

the Euphrates."³³⁹ The account of the Nairi war is sometimes followed by the statement that he made Azalzi and Shepardi his frontiers.³⁴⁰ Shepardi, apparently a variant of Subartu, is of course identical to Sparda, the normal Persian word for Lydia. Azalzi, it would appear, may well be a form of Sardis. Since vowels are conjectural the word may be read as Zalzi, and with the interchangeability of 'l' and 'r' this may be written Zarzi or even Sarzi.

Some scholars claim to have identified two semi-peripheral Great Kings of Hatti after Tudkhaliyas IV; yet these men, an Arnuwandash and a Suppiluliumas, belong in an earlier epoch and are misplaced in the textbooks by reason of their contemporaneity with Tukulti-Ninurta. (The identity of the "Assyrian" Tukulti-Ninurta, who smashed the power of the Hittites, is discussed at the end of the present volume). The truth is that the Hittite Empire comes to a definitive end with Tudkhaliyas IV, whose final fate is said to be unknown. If however he is the same person as Croesus, we know that, being spared execution, he accompanied first Cyrus (who was, as we shall see, identical to Tukulti-Ninurta) and then his son Cambyses (Shalmaneser) in their various campaigns throughout Asia and North Africa.

Before finishing it should be noted that as with Hattusilis = Alyattes, there is a linguistic justification for Tudkhaliyas = Croesus. Leaving aside the initial 'tud' syllable, the Hittite name is Khaliyas, which, given the interchangeability of 'l' and 'r', can be written as Khariyas. Not too different at all from the Greek Kroisos.

After the defeat of Hatti Land, Tukulti-Ninurta went on to conquer the city of Babylon, whose king he carried off in chains but later reinstated, before finally making himself king of the city.

³³⁹ Ibid., p.285
³⁴⁰ Ibid., p.286

CHAPTER 8: THE NINETEENTH DYNASTY AND THE HEBREW MONARCHIES

Seti I's Asiatic Wars

During the reign of Akhnaton, Egypt's authority in Palestine and Syria collapsed, a situation reflected in the contents of the Amarna Letters. These correspondences show, above all, how the inactivity of the pharaoh allowed Aziru, the scheming and treacherous king of Amurru (Syria), to wage destructive wars against his neighbors. From the time of Asa, whose reign must have ended just a handful of years before the composition of the Amarna Letters, the rulers of Syria intervened repeatedly in the affairs of Palestine. Asa himself "hired" the Syrian king Ben Hadad I (Hadadezer I) to attack Baasha of Israel. From this time onwards, the Syrians were involved in a protracted war of attrition with the rulers of Israel, a conflict which very nearly brought the kingdom of Israel to an end.

Egyptian neglect of its Syrian/Palestinian empire did not end with Akhnaton's death; and in fact for a while during the time of his immediate successors things grew even worse. During the reigns of Tutankhamun, Ay and Horemheb, which we synchronize with the reigns of Ahab in Israel and Jehosaphat in Judah (as well as Shalmaneser III in Assyria/Media), the kings of Syria and Moab wrought massive destruction throughout Palestine. With the accession of Seti I, however, there was again an energetic pharaoh on the throne; and right from the start he set about reasserting Egyptian control in the region. His motives for this, it appears, were not simply to further his own economic and military interests; he was also interested in helping Egypt's traditional allies in the area, the kingdoms of Judah and Israel.

But Seti never mentions any of the kings of Judah or Israel in his inscriptions. If he was such a close ally of theirs, how do we explain this omission? Even worse, how do we explain the silence of the Hebrew Scriptures, if Seti I were such an important friend?

To answer these questions, we need to look at Seti's career and military exploits in Asia. Right from the beginning of his reign, Seti was very conscious of the fact that he was overseeing a rebirth, a veritable "Renaissance," of Egypt's fortunes, and this indeed was precisely the epithet he used for his reign — quite literally the epoch of "Repetition of Birth" or "Rebirth."

Seti immortalized his military adventures, most of which were in Asia, in a series of huge bas-reliefs carved onto the north outer wall of his Hypostile Hall at Karnak. These reliefs, which are "no great works of art," nevertheless afford historians with what is almost certainly a fairly accurate record of his martial achievements. The carvings, originally in six separate segments or registers, told the story of his campaigns in Asia and against the Libyans in chronological sequence. Two of these registers, the topmost segments of the wall, are now more or less completely lost; but the four bottom sections are well preserved. Chronologically, the friezes begin at the bottom left-hand corner, where we see depicted his campaign of year 1 in southern Palestine, against the Shasu, or bedawin, and continue in clockwise order till we reach his final campaign, in year 10, against the Hittites in northern Syria.

From this as well as from other evidence, it would appear that Seti began by re-establishing Egyptian control over those parts of Asia nearest to Egypt, and gradually extended his authority northwards in subsequent years.

Seti initiated his first campaign by a punitive action against meddlesome tribesmen in southern Palestine. Before the end of that campaign, he had also dealt with enemies on the Palestinian coast and saw major action in northern Palestine, in the region of Galilee. A sphinx from Seti's funerary temple at Kurna informs us that during his stay in the latter district, the pharaoh conquered the town of Pella (Pehel) in Transjordan, and from other sources it is evident that he took Beth-Shan (known to Hellenistic authors as Scythopolis) as well as Yanoam. Along with the capture of Yanoam, the second register at Karnak depicts the submission of the princes of Lebanon, which presumably took place in the same year.

A missing third register at Karnak probably recorded a campaign through the Syrian coastal regions. This can be deduced from the sphinx at Kurna that refers to the taking of the Syrian towns of Zimyra and Ullaza. The capture of Kadesh in northern Syria, mention of which is preserved on the damaged fourth register at Karnak, may have marked a phase in the same campaign. The accompanying inscription reads: "The ascent which Pharaoh made to destroy the land of Kadesh and the land of Amor." R.O. Faulkner thought it likely that this mention of a campaign into Amor "refers not to the North Syrian coast, the conquest of which was probably dealt with to the left of the doorway, but to an inland extension of Amorite territory into the country south of Kadesh, possibly even as far south as Damascus, which seems to have fallen under Amorite influence during the revolt of Akhenaton's time."[341]

Seti's final campaign in Syria resulted in a battle with the Hittites. We do not know the location of the action, though Seti claims a victory.

From the various monuments, it is evident that the energetic Seti expended much effort in regaining for Egypt control of all the regions of Syria to the north of Galilee; i.e., to the north of what was traditionally the northern boundary of the kingdom of Israel. Whilst Seti also recorded military action in Philistia, it would seem that he never faced any enemies in central or southern Palestine, in those regions comprising the kingdoms of Israel and Judah. On two surviving stelae erected by Seti in Beth-Shan, the new king gives a fairly detailed account of his campaign in his first year, in the region of Galilee:

On this day one came to speak to his majesty, as follows: "The wretched foe who is in the town of Hamath is gathering to himself many people while he is seizing the town of Beth-shan. Then there will be an alliance with him of Pehel [Pella]. He does not permit the prince of Rehob to go outside." Thereupon his majesty sent the first army of Amon (named) "Mighty of Bows," to the town of Hamath, the first army of Re, (named) "Plentiful of Valour," to the town of Beth-shan, and the first army of Seth, (named) "Strong of Bows," to the town of Yanoam. When the space of one day had passed, they were overthrown to the glory of his majesty, the King of Upper and Lower Egypt: Men-maat-Re; the Son of Re: Seti Mer-ne-Ptah, given life.[342]

That this action took place in the province of Galilee is not in doubt. Beth-Shan is located in the south of the Plain of Esdraelon, just to the west of the Jordan, whilst Pella is almost due east on the other side of the river. Hamath cannot of course be the well-known city of that name on the river Orontes, for all the action was over in the space of one day, and it is clear that the pharaoh dispatched the three divisions of the army from a central point on the Plain of Esdraelon, probably from the garrison town of Megiddo.

---

[341] R. O. Faulkner, "The Wars of Sethos I," *Journal of Egyptian Archaeology* 33 (1947), p. 37

[342] Cited from J. Bimson, "Dating the Wars of Seti I," *Society for Interdisciplinary Studies Review* Vol.V No.1 (1980-1)

John Bimson noted that the Hebrew Scriptures (Joshua 19:35) mention a town called Hammath in the territory of Naphtali, "for which the likely site is Hamman Tabariyeh, south of Tiberias on the western side of the Sea of Galilee."[343] According to Bimson, "This may well be the Hamath of Seti's inscription. It lies 20 miles north of Beth-shan."[344]

The location of Rehob has been the subject of much discussion. However, as Bimson notes, the Old Testament mentions a Rehob somewhere to the north-west of the Sea of Galilee, on the ancient border of Israel and Phoenicia. "While the precise location of this town is uncertain, it was clearly not far from the coast, near either Acco or Achzib (cf. Joshua 19:29–30; Judges 1:31). This Biblical town is perhaps the same as the Rehob mentioned on the stela."[345]

The identity of Yanoam has also caused some speculation, though it is generally agreed that its location was the site of Tell en-Na'ameh, about ten miles south of the ancient city of Dan. However, it has been placed by some scholars on the southern shore of the Sea of Galilee, at el-Abeidiyeh.[346]

Whatever the details, it is evident that Seti's action against the "wretched foe" took place in and around Galilee, on the northern borders of the historical kingdom of Israel. This should not be forgotten when we come to consider the identity of the enemy.

Another, smaller stele from Beth-Shan shows us that the campaign against this enemy had at least another phase, when Seti's forces saw action on the other side of the Jordan, in the region of Pella and quite possibly Ramoth-Gilead. This stele, unfortunately badly damaged, tells us how plunderers on Mount Yarumtu had sought to lay waste the whole "land of Djahi" and how the forces of the pharaoh had thwarted their designs. The "land of Djahi," which the plunderers tried to conquer, has been taken to be "a vague term for Syria-Palestine" and not a precise location.[347] Nevertheless, from other Egyptian usages of the name, it would appear that Djahi "indicated the coastal strip [of Palestine] and its inland extension, the Plain of Esdraelon, which reaches eastwards along the Valley of Jezreel as far as Beth-shan and the Jordan."[348]

Yarumtu of the smaller stele is the Semitic word meaning a height or plateau, as in the familiar biblical name Ramoth. John Bimson believed that Yarumtu was actually the famous city of Ramoth-Gilead, whose probable

[343] Ibid., 17
[344] Ibid.
[345] Ibid., 18
[346] Y. Aharoni, *The Land of the Bible*, (London, 1966), p.167 Map 12
[347] J. Wilson in Pritchard (ed.) *Ancient Near Eastern Texts*, p.255 n.4
[348] Bimson, "Dating the Wars of Seti I," loc cit., p.19

site is Tell Ramith, about 25 miles west of Pella, in the mountains of Gilead. According to Bimson, "Such a location for Mount Yarumtu is very feasible from a strategic point of view."[349] A glance at a map of the region will show that "westward offensives launched from Ramoth-gilead would bring the attackers directly to Beth-shan, control of which would provide access to the Plain of Esdraelon and thence to the coastal strip."[350]

All in all, the two stela of Beth-Shan make it clear that in northern Palestine Seti I was not simply reclaiming territory for Egypt's empire: "He was acting against one group of Asiatics, who were apparently invading from Transjordan, on behalf of another."[351] But who, we might ask, was the Asiatic ally on whose behalf Seti waged war? The chronology outlined in the present work would suggest that Seti I was a contemporary of Jehu in his latter years (supposedly 842–814 BC), in whose reign "the Lord began to weary of Israel." We are told that "Hazael [of Syria] ravaged them in all the coasts of Israel, from the Jordan eastward, all the land of Gilead, and Gad, and Ruben, and Manasseh, from Aroer, which is upon the torrent Arnon, and Gilead, and Bashan."[352]

Is it possible that Seti I acted in northern Israel to stem the inroads made by Syrian raiders, and that the "wretched foe" of his inscriptions was Hazael?

The "Wretched Foe"

Numerous facts confirm for us the belief that Hazael was indeed the aggressor against whom Seti I battled in his first year. According to the numerous detailed synchronisms already established in the present work, Seti I would have ascended the throne of Egypt in about year 20 of Shalmaneser III. Since Shalmaneser records Hazael's seizure of the throne sometime between his own year 10 and 15, this would mean that Hazael had already sat on the throne of Syria for a number of years when Seti I was crowned. In short, Hazael must have been a major power in Syria at the time.

The Beth-Shan stelae clearly refer to an invasion from the east side of the Jordan, while the Scriptures tell us that in Jehu's reign Hazael occupied all of Transjordan as far south as the river Arnon. It was almost certainly from this region that he launched his further offensives across the Jordan into the heart of Israel during the reign of Jehoahaz. We have seen that the forces from east of the Jordan whom Seti defeated appear to have operated from Ramoth-Gilead (if we are correct in identifying Mount Yarumtu with

---

[349] Ibid.
[350] Ibid.
[351] Ibid.
[352] 2 Kings 10:32-3

the latter). According to John Bimson, "In the Old Testament, Ramoth-gilead was a much fought-over town in the recurring wars between Israel and the Aramaeans of Damascus, and must have had considerable strategic importance."[353] During the reign of Jehu, as we have seen, Hazael took from Israel "all the land of Gilead" along with the rest of her Transjordanian territories.[354]

The invaders halted by Seti had objectives further afield than Galilee; the whole of Palestine was threatened. They were attempting to "lay waste the land of Djahi to its full length." According to Bimson, "The capture of towns such as Beth-shan was probably an attempt to gain control of the Plain of Esdraelon, which provided access from the Jordan to the coastal strip, both to the north and (via the pass at Megiddo) the south."[355] Thus, says Bimson, "the movements and objectives of Hazael's forces exactly parallel those of the forces opposed by Seti I, so far as they can be reconstructed."[356]

Bimson also argued that Seti's grand plan in Syria/Palestine, his overall objective in all his campaigns in the region, was to halt the expansion of Syria, which he viewed as a threat not only to Egypt's interests in the region, but even to her own security. In the words of one well-known authority, "at the close of the ninth century, Hazael and Ben-hadad had imposed Aramaean rule upon vast South-Syrian territories, including Samaria, as far as the northern boundary of Philistia and Judah."[357] Thus Seti's other conquests in the region, such as Tyre and Acco, would have been aimed at breaking Hazael's power on the coastal regions. We have already noted Faulkner's suggestion that the reference to a campaign by Seti into the "land of Amor" on the damaged Karnak register refers to the "conquest of an inland extension of Amorite territory into the country south of Kadesh, possibly even as far south as Damascus."[358] Faulkner also noted that the Kurna sphinx records a conquest of the land of Takhsy, "whose southern limit may not have been very far removed from Damascus."[359] In the words of Bimson, "Since Damascus is Hazael's capital in the Old Testament and Assyrian records, these references acquire new significance in the reconstruction suggested here. Seti was trying to push back Hazael's borders, perhaps aiming at

---

[353] Bimson, "Dating the Wars of Seti I," loc cit., 20
[354] 2 Kings 13:25
[355] Bimson, "Dating the Wars of Seti," loc cit.
[356] Ibid.
[357] H. Tadmor, "Azriyau of Yaudi," *Scripta Hierosolymitana* 8 (1961), p.241
[358] Faulkner, loc cit., p.37
[359] Ibid., pp.37-8

the conquest of Damascus itself. It would appear, however, that he never achieved the latter."[360]

Further developing his theme, Bimson went on to suggest that even Seti's battle with the Hittites was merely part of his ongoing campaign to break the power of Damascus. He notes that Velikovsky's identification of Aziru of Amurru, in the Amarna letters, with Hazael of Syria (Aram), "has implication for the slightly later period now being discussed."[361] "It is known," he continues, "from two treaties, both of which survive in Hittite and Akkadian versions, that the Hittite king Suppiluliumas made a treaty with Aziras of Amurru by which Aziras became his vassal, and that the relations thus established between them continued into the reign of Suppiluliumas' son, Mursilis."[362] He calls attention to a clause in the treaty made by Suppiluliumas:

(And if somebody presses Aziras hard ... or (if) somebody starts a revolt, (if) you then wr)ite to the king of the Hatti land: 'send troops and charioteers to my aid!' I shall h(it) that enemy for (you).[363]

But Aziru, as we have seen, is not the Hazael of scriptural texts. He was rather Hazael's predecessor Ben-Hadad, either Ben-Hadad I or Ben-Hadad II, known on Assyrian monuments as Hadad-ezer, contemporary, respectively, with Asa and Jehoshaphat of Judah. Aziru's successor was named in the records of Mursilis III as DU-Teshub. Hazael and DU-Teshub were one and the same.

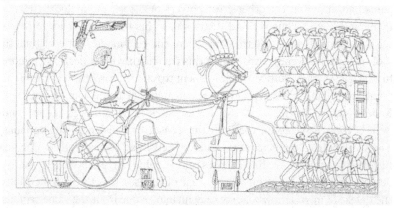

Fig. 31. Seti I with captured Syrian troops, almost certainly soldiers of Hazael.

---

[360] Bimson, "Dating the Wars of Seti I," loc cit., p.29
[361] Ibid.
[362] Ibid.
[363] Trans. A. Goetze in Pritchard (ed.) *Ancient Near East Texts*, pp.203-4

Ramses II Secures the Borders of Israel and Judah

If his inscriptions are anything to go by, it is clear that Seti achieved his major goals in Palestine and Syria, and that by the end of his reign a degree of stability was restored to the region. Nevertheless, at some stage the pharaoh seems to have suffered a major setback and to have forfeited all the terri-tory he had previously gained. Upon his accession, Ramses II had to recap-ture territory already conquered by Seti: "There can be no doubt," writes Faulkner, "that in the end Sethos [Seti] lost all his more northerly conquests. Naturally the unsuccessful fighting which followed the earlier victories remained unrecorded by the Egyptians, but it is significant that Ramesses II in his first campaign had to take Beirut by force of arms."[364] Notwithstanding such setbacks, however, there can be no doubt that Ramses II intended to build upon his father's successes and to extend Egypt's authority north-wards. This of course soon meant another direct confrontation with Hatti. It is conjectured that Mursilis III and Muwatallis must have been alarmed at the new Egyptian policy in the region inaugurated by Seti I; and there can be little doubt that both kings fully intended to honor the treaty signed between Suppiluliumas I and earlier Syrian monarchs.

Whilst all of this may be true, it is nevertheless important to remember that other forces were in play; and the mighty struggle between the Medes under Shamshi-Adad V (Arbaces) and the Assyrian rebels under Sardana-palus had drawn in the other great powers of the region, including Hatti/Lydia and Egypt. Thus we find Ramses II, in his fifth year, at loggerheads with Muwatallis in northern Syria where the celebrated Battle of Kadesh took place. The events surrounding this campaign will be dealt with more fully at a later stage. Suffice for the moment to remark that, in spite of Ramses' bombastic claims, the Egyptians were defeated. The immediate aftermath of Kadesh saw the revolt of all the Syrian states as far south as Galilee, and even beyond, if we count the Philistine coastal regions and Transjordania. The work started sixteen years earlier by Seti I had to begin all over again. In subsequent years, we find Ramses campaigning in regions fought over by Seti at the start of his reign. Thus a stele of Ramses at Beth-Shan mentions the defeat of intruders whom we may imagine came from the same regions as the plunderers bested by Seti I. If we are right, these enemies were the soldiers of Hazael.

In this interpretation then the Syrians would have had a brief respite after the Egyptian reverses at Kadesh, but they would have suffered further setbacks in subsequent years as Ramses II re-organized his forces and once

---

[364] Faulkner, loc cit., p.38

again took the offensive against Hatti's allies. Thus the king of Israel at this time (in our reconstruction, Jehoahaz), as a loyal ally of Egypt, should have benefited from Ramses' work in the region. Is this the case? Do the Scriptures record an amelioration of Israel's position in this king's reign? They do indeed. We are told in 2 Kings 13:4–5 that when the armies of Hazael had completely overthrown Israel, desperation brought a change of heart to her apostate king:

Then Jehoahaz besought the Lord, and the Lord hearkened to him; for he saw the oppression of Israel, how the king of Syria oppressed them. Therefore the Lord gave Israel a savior, so that they escaped from the hand of the Syrians; and the people of Israel dwelt in their homes as formerly.

Over the years there has been a great deal of discussion as to the identity of this "savior." One view is that the passage refers to Joash, Jehoahaz's successor, who is said to have defeated Hazael's son Ben-Hadad three times and recovered some of the lost Israelite cities (2 Kings 13:24–5): Another suggestion is that the verse refers to an even later time, that of Jehoahaz's grandson Jeroboam II, who restored Israel's Transjordanian territory and even conquered Damascus and Hamath (2 Kings 14:25–8). Neither of these views has gained wide support, owing to the fact that "this relief is apparently a response to the supplication of Jehoahaz, whereas [in this view] relief did not come until the time of Joash and Jeroboam."[365]

Several scholars, including K.A. Kitchen, have assumed that the deliverer was Adad-Nirari III of Assyria.[366] The Assyrian king does indeed boast of having captured Damascus in several of his inscriptions, and this action would certainly have given relief to Israel. It has been pointed out however that the precise date of his attack on Damascus is unknown. Until recently a date of between his sixth and eighth years (supposedly 805–802 BC) has been assumed, and this would allow Israel's respite to fall within the reign of Jehoahaz. However, Tadmor has argued that the taking of Damascus should be linked with Adad-Nirari's campaign against Mansuate, supposedly in 796 BC.[367] W.H. Shea replied to Tadmor with a strong defense of 805 BC as the date for the campaign.[368] However, in the words of John Bimson, "his argument involves dating the Rimah Stele, on which Adad-nirari records the collection of tribute from Joash of Israel to the same year. Thus Shea requires Joash to have succeeded Jehoahaz by 805 BC, which still places Adad-nira-

---

[365] J. Gray, I and II Kings: A Commentary (2nd ed., London, 1970), p.595
[366] K. Kitchen in New Bible Dictionary, J. D. Douglas ed. (London, 1962), p.58
[367] A. R. Millard and H. Tadmor, "Adad-Nirari III in Syria," Iraq 35 (1973), pp. 57-64
[368] W. H. Shea "Adad-Nirari III and Jehoash of Israel," Journal of Cuneiform Studies 30/2 (1978), pp. 101-113

ri's defeat of Damascus after the reign of Jehoahaz."[369] Therefore, Bimson concludes, "if the 'savior' of 2 Kings 13:5 acted in the reign of Jehoahaz, as the context suggests, the conventional view of events at present offers no obvious candidate."[370]

We shall shortly see however that, notwithstanding Bimson's view, Adad-Nirari also acted deliberately to protect Israel, though at a slightly later stage than the reign of Jehoahaz. In fact, as we shall demonstrate, Adad-Nirari was an ally of Ramses II, and the campaign against Hatti's vassal Damascus was intended to support his own ally Egypt during that country's mighty struggle with the Hittite Empire.

But why, the reader might ask, should Egypt work so hard to defend the kingdom of Israel? Apart from the fact that Israel was a vassal and therefore a first line of defense for Egypt herself, the pharaohs had other reasons to be friendly. Both Israel and Judah were traditional allies of Egypt, with their loyalty to the Nile kingdom enduring right to the end, when the weak pharaohs of later generations could not protect the Hebrews from utter ruin and deportation.

But Israel was a special ally. From the very beginnings of her history, the Northern Kingdom was a client of Egypt. We know from 1 Kings 11:40 that Jeroboam I, under whom Israel gained its independence from the House of David, had spent time at the Egyptian court during the reign of Shishak. We are told that Shishak attacked Judah shortly after Jeroboam's return to Palestine and his rebellion against Judah. Clearly Jeroboam and Shishak were acting as allies. In the words of Velikovsky, "From the very outset he [Jeroboam] was a political and cultural vassal of Egypt."[371]

There were still other reasons for the traditional alliance between Egyptians and Hebrews. In another place I have shown how the legend of Abraham refers to a primeval Semitic migration from Mesopotamia into Egypt, which introduced the basics of high civilization to the Nile valley right at the dawn of history. The earliest pharaohs claimed descent from these immigrants, and this was one reason for the Egyptian description of Palestine/Phoenicia as "The Divine Land." Truth is indeed much stranger than fiction.

During the remainder of his long reign, during the times (in our reconstruction) of Joash and Jeroboam II, Ramses II worked very hard to strengthen his Israelite allies, and his armies once again reached into central and northern Syria. Were the reigns of Joash and Jeroboam II periods of renewed Israelite power and prosperity? They certainly were. Of Joash we read:

---

[369] Bimson, "Dating the Wars of Seti I," loc cit., p.22
[370] Ibid.
[371] Velikovsky Ages in Chaos, Chapter 4

At the death of King Hazael of Syria his son Benhadad became king. Then king Joash of Israel defeated Benhadad three times and recaptured the cities that had been taken by Benhadad during the reign of Jehoahaz, the father of Joash.[372]

These successes were built upon, with spectacular results, by his successor Jeroboam II. We are told:

He reconquered all the territory that had belonged to Israel, from Hamath Pass in the north to the Dead Sea in the south. This was what the Lord, the God of Israel, had promised through his servant the prophet Jonah son of Amittai, from Gath Hepher.

The Lord saw the terrible suffering of the Israelites; there was no one at all to help them. But it was not the Lord's purpose to destroy Israel completely and for ever, so he rescued them through King Jeroboam.

Everything else that Jeroboam II did, his brave battles, and how he restored Damascus and Hamath to Israel, are all recorded in the History of the Kings of Israel.[373]

This then was a period of almost unparalleled power and prosperity for Israel (and for Judah, as we shall see). Together, the borders of the two Hebrew kingdoms now extended as far as in the time of David and Solomon. Had the credit for these mighty achievements been entirely Jeroboam's (and Uzziah's), we might expect the Scriptures to have devoted huge amounts of space to them. Yet the lives of Jeroboam II and Uzziah are dealt with in less than a single chapter, whereas whole books were written on the life of Israel's other great conquering king, David. This should naturally lead us to suspect whether credit for these victories was due entirely to the efforts of these two Hebrew kings. If we are on the right track, it most certainly was not.

In fact, the conquests of Joash, Jeroboam II and Uzziah correspond very closely, as John Bimson noted, with the activities of Ramses II. Thus for example we know that immediately after the Battle of Kadesh he campaigned across the Jordan, capturing territory never reached by Seti I. Whilst Ramses never actually records the taking of Damascus, he clearly campaigned extensively to the north and west of the Sea of Galilee, in the direction of Damascus. According to John Bimson, "The transjordanian town of Karnaim, mentioned in Amos 6:13 as a place the Israelites boasted they had taken, is 'Identified with Sheikh-Saad, north-east of Ashtaroth, where an inscription bearing the name of Ramses II was found.'"[374]

---

[372] 2 Kings 13:24-5
[373] Ibid., 14:25-8
[374] J. Bimson, "Israel in Egypt," *Society for Interdisciplinary Studies Review*, Vol. IV No.1 (1979)

The Kingdom of Judah too, as noted, went through a remarkable renaissance at this period. Uzziah extended his rule into Philistine territory (2 Chronicles 26:6-7) and into Edom, where he rebuilt the town of Elath (Chron. 26:2). In addition, he was said to have received tribute from the transjordanian Ammonites (Chron. 26:8). In Bimson's words, "These expansions of power also correspond with Ramesses II's sphere of action, which included Philistia (his capture of Ashkelon is depicted in a relief at Karnak), Edom (Luxor reliefs), and both Moab (Luxor reliefs) and Bashan (Ashtaroth-Karnaim inscription), between which lay the territory of the Ammonites."[375]

According to Bimson, "These striking correspondences suggest that Ramesses II was not merely acting in Egypt's interests but in the interests of Israel and Judah. He may even have acted in concert with one or both of these kingdoms on some of the above occasions."[376]

The action mentioned by Ramses II against Moab is of particular interest. The Moabites had inflicted great harm on both Israel and Judah during the reign of Ahab. The Scriptures inform us that later, at a time coinciding with the death of the prophet Elisha, and during the reign of Joash, the Moabites again crossed the Jordan and attacked Israel (2 Kings 13:20). Apparently, they were acting in concert with the Syrians. The very fact that Ramses II makes such a point of celebrating victories over this people, as well as the other traditional enemies of the Hebrews — Syrians, Philistines and Edomites — without mentioning the peoples of Israel and Judah at all, would make us suspect strongly that he was acting on their behalf.

In the second decade of his reign, the hand of Ramses II was greatly strengthened by the successes of his "Assyrian" (Mede) allies, and Adad-Nirari III acted in Syria as an ally of Egypt, with the aim of destroying the Syrian power-base of their common enemy, Hattusilis III (Alyattes).

The "Israel Stele" of Merneptah

If the chronology proposed on these pages is correct, Ramses II would have been a contemporary of kings Amaziah and Azariah (Uzziah) of Judah and of kings Zechariah, Menahem and Pekahiah of Israel. As such, his son and heir Merneptah (more accurately, Merenptah) would have reigned contemporaneously with Azariah's successor Jotham and with Pekahiah's successor Pekah. It was during the reigns of these kings that Tiglath-Pileser III of Assyria began to intervene directly in the affairs of southern Syria and Palestine. During the reign of Tiglath-Pileser, the Assyrians began the depor-

[375] Ibid.
[376] Ibid.

tation of the population of the Northern Kingdom of Israel, a process that would be completed by his successor Shalmaneser V, and it is evident that in this period the military power of Assyria was drawing dangerously close to Egypt. As such, we must wonder whether any of this is reflected in the records surviving from the time of Merneptah.

It so happens that pharaoh Merneptah is best known for the "Israel Stele," an inscription discovered by Flinders Petrie in 1896, whose main purpose was the glorification of the pharaoh's achievement in saving Egypt from Libyan invasion. By rights, the inscription should therefore really be called the "Libya Stele." In the text, Merneptah is called:

the Sun, driving away the storm which was over Egypt, allowing Egypt to see the rays of the sun, removing the mountains of copper from the neck of the people ...

That Egypt had been directly threatened with conquest is obvious. The lines preceding the mention of Israel are:

One comes and goes with singing, and there is no lamentation of mourning people. The towns are settled again anew; as for the one that ploweth his harvest, he shall eat it. Re has turned himself to Egypt; he was born, destined to be her protector, the King Merneptah.

The concluding lines of the inscription follow at this point:

The kings are overthrown, saying: "Salam!" Not one holds up his head among the Nine Bows. Wasted is Tehenu, Kheta is pacified, plundered is Pekanan [i.e., "the Canaan"], with every evil, carried off is Askalon, seized upon is Gezer, Yenoam is made as a thing not existing. Israel ('-s-r-'-r) is desolated, his seed is not; Palestine (H'-rw) has become a widow for Egypt. All lands are united, they are pacified; everyone that is turbulent is bound by King Merneptah, given life like Re, every day.

The inscription is of course named the "Israel Stele" for these lines, which are widely believed to constitute the one and only mention of the Israelites in Egyptian hieroglyphic literature.

In 1978 John Bimson made a detailed study of the stele and concluded that the despoliation and pacification of Syria and Palestine described on the monument was the work not of Merneptah himself but of Tiglath-Pileser III. Bimson was able to show, in some detail, that both Assyrian and biblical sources could be made to concur with the stele in identifying Tiglath-Pileser as the author of Palestine's woes. According to Bimson, the "outcome of [Tiglath-Pileser's first] ... two incursions into the West corresponds exactly with the Asian events referred to on the 'Israel stele'."[377] As well as the claim

---

[377]   J. Bimson, "An Eighth-Century Date for Merneptah," *Society for Interdisciplinary Studies Review* Vol. III No. 2 (1978), p. 58.

that "Hatti is pacified" (which Tiglath-Pileser did indeed pacify), the stele tells us that "the Canaan is plundered with every evil." There follow a number of specific statements about that region. Two Philistine cities, Ashkelon and Gezer, are mentioned, and both these cities also occur in the annals of Tiglath-Pileser. Next we hear of Yenoam, which, Bimson notes, is a region of Israel. Both Tiglath-Pileser and the Book of Kings refer to Assyria's despoliation of this area and how the inhabitants were carried captive to Assyria. In 2 Kings 15: 29, for example, we read:

In the days of Pekah king of Israel there came Tiglath-pileser king of Assyria, and took Ijon, and Abel-beth-maachah, and Janoah, and Kedesh, and Hazor, and Gilead, and Galilee, all the land of Naphtali, and carried them captive to Assyria.

All of the above territories constitute the northernmost regions of the Kingdom of Israel, and it was within them that Yenoam or Yanoam, mentioned both by Merneptah and Tiglath-Pileser, was situated. "There can be no doubt" says Bimson "that this devastation is the "laying waste" of Israel to which the stele refers after the mention of Yenoam."[378]

Bimson of course does not actually prove that Merneptah and Tiglath-Pileser III were contemporary, but he certainly shows that they could well have been. The Egypt of Merneptah was a much-diminished power, an empire that had already relinquished all pretense to influence in Syria/Palestine, areas long regarded as Egypt's rightful sphere. The main purpose of the Israel Stele, we recall, is to record how Merneptah had saved Egypt in a *defensive* war against the Libyans. This alone should preclude the notion, commonly accepted in the scholarly community, that the despoliation of Palestine (as well as the pacification of Hatti) mentioned in the text was the work of Merneptah. Such a feat, worthy of a Thutmose III or a Ramses II, would have been immortalized in a grander way than upon a paltry stele.

We know in any case, from other sources, that the pacification of Hatti mentioned on the inscription was the work of an Assyrian king. Merneptah reigned during the destruction of the Hittite Empire whose last king, Tudkhaliyas IV, we have already identified with Croesus. The end of Hittite power at this time can, we have seen, be linked to the activities of the Assyrian Tukulti-Ninurta, a man whom we shall also demonstrate used the appellation Tukulti-apil-esharra, Tiglath-Pileser.

An air of impending doom seems to pervade the "Israel Stele." The pharaoh records the destruction of Hatti and the nations of Syria and Palestine simply as a matter of fact, and the only sense of pride or self-glorifica-

---

[378]   Ibid.

tion we detect is that Egypt, alone among the nations, still survives. That, however, was an achievement whose days were numbered.

In *Ramses II and His Time*, Velikovsky equated Ramses II's heir Merneptah with the king known to Herodotus as Apries, who reigned just before the Persian conquest. The present author concurs with this identification and we shall now see how Merneptah/Apries alludes in one of his most famous monuments to the despoliation of Syria/Palestine, as well as the kingdom of Lydia (Hatti), by the nascent power of Achaemenid Persia.

APPENDICES

The Medes

Herodotus relates how the Medes, having borne the yoke of Assyrian rule for many years, rose in revolt under a leader named Deioces and how, after many vicissitudes, they established themselves as an independent nation. Under their next king, Phraortes, they began to subdue "all of Asia," people by people.[379] Then they moved against the Assyrians, "especially those Assyrians who held Nineveh." These Assyrians, we are told, had "formerly ruled all of Asia," though by now they were "quite isolated, all their allies having dropped away from them."[380] Nevertheless, "in themselves they were as strong as ever, and when Phraortes fought them, he himself was killed, after a reign of twenty years, and also much of his army."[381] It was under Phraortes' successor, Cyaxares, that the Medes finally "made the Assyrians their subjects, apart from the province of Babylon." From this point onwards, the Medes were the greatest power in the known world. Ancient writers commonly referred to them as the "mighty Medes" and made it plain that the conquest of Assyria was an epic event that changed the course of history.

For all that, and in spite of the claims of the ancients, modern scholars are astonished by the apparent non-appearance of any "Mede Empire" in the archaeological record. So complete is this Mede disappearing act that in recent years not a few orientalists have come to doubt the very existence of

---

[379] Herodotus, i, 102
[380] Ibid.
[381] Ibid.

such an entity as the Mede Imperium. A conference in Padua in 2001, called to discuss this very topic, came to the conclusion (as the Proceedings demonstrated) that the Mede Empire was virtually non-existent archaeologically; at least in the Late Iron Age strata in which it was sought. Papers included M. Roaf, "The Median Dark Age"; R. Schmitt, "Die Sprache der Meder — eine grosse Unbekannte" ('The Language of the Medes — a Great Unknown'); and John Curtis, "The Assyrian heartland in the period 612–539 BC." All the scholars contributing expressed exasperation at the difficulties in trying to "pin down" the historical Medes. Roaf for example stated, "This survey of the evidence, both textual and archaeological, for the Medes between 612 and 550 BC has revealed almost nothing. Media in the first half of the sixth century is a dark age."[382] In a similar vein, John Curtis laments that, "It has to be admitted at the outset that there is not the slightest archaeological indication of a Median presence in Assyria after 612 BC."[383]

From the point of view of the reconstruction presented in these pages, however, the existence of the Mede Empire is not in question and it has, on the contrary, left abundant traces of its existence. This is the so-called "Bronze Age" kingdom of Mitanni, commonly placed in the 15th century BC — a full seven and a half centuries before the real epoch of the Medes in the 7th century BC.

As Chapter 1 has shown, the Mitanni folk make their first appearance in history when Parattarna, the son of a man named Shuttarna, succeeded in establishing his control of much of northern Mesopotamia, where he installed client kings with Hurrian names in various cities. It was left, however, for a successor, probably a son, named Shaushtatar, to complete the conquest of the region and establish Mitanni as a world power. Shaushtatar, who would be remembered as the first Great King of Mitanni, won everlasting fame for his conquest of Assyria, whose cities he plundered and stripped of their treasures. These were carried off to adorn his own capital Washukanni, though many of them were later returned to Assyria in the time of Ashuruballit I. From the reign of Shaushtatar, all kings of Mitanni were Great Kings, and their prestige and power were known throughout the entire civilized world. Egyptian pharaohs eagerly sought wives from the Mitanni royal family, and the Mariyanna, the chivalric class of Mitannian society, held high office in the kingdoms of Syria and Palestine.

---

[382] "Continuity in Empire (?) Assyria, Media, Persia: Proceedings of the International Meeting in Padua," (26th–28th April, 2001) *History of the Ancient Near East. Monographs* V. Padova. S.a.r.g.o.n., 2003 Giovanni Lanfranchi, Michael Roaf, Robert Rollinger (eds) R. Roaf "The Median Dark Age," 12

[383] Ibid., John Curtis, "The Assyrian heartland in the period 612-539 BC,"165

The Old Assyrian kingdom overthrown by Shaushtatar was of course the Assyrian Empire overthrown by the Medes, an event which we must place around 700 BC. (Shaushtatar was a contemporary of Thutmose III of Egypt). Shaushtatar, in whom we see Cyaxares (actually Cyaxares I) of the Greek and Hellenistic authors, was to be the first in a mighty dynasty that comprised at least ten Mitanni/Mede emperors, who would dominate much of the ancient orient until their overthrowal by Cyrus of Persia in 546 BC. Assyria itself was to become one of the most important satrapies of the Mitanni/Mede Empire, and the Indo-Aryan conquerors actively imitated the customs and preserved the imperial traditions of their Semitic subjects. It is virtually certain that Shaushtatar himself and the Mitanni/Mede Great Kings who followed him possessed Assyrian royal titles, though, it is claimed, these are unknown.

Nevertheless, a mighty conqueror named Shamshi-Adad I, whom conventional history places three centuries before Shaushtatar, seems to be a very good candidate for identification with the first Mitanni/Mede king in Mesopotamia. Shaushtatar's immediate predecessor, Parattarna or Parsatatar (in whom we see Phraortes), waged an inconclusive war against the Old Assyria kingdom, and it would appear that Shamshi-Adad I should be regarded as Parattarna/Phraortes' alter ego. Sure enough, Shamshi-Adad I also waged an inconclusive war against the Akkadian king Naram-Sin (who was in fact identical to the Old Assyrian king Naram Sin), and it was left to his successor Ishme-Dagan to complete the job of defeating the Assyrians. Thus it would appear that Ishme-Dagan is the Assyrian alter ego of Shaushtatar, whilst Shamshi-Adad I is the Assyrian name for his predecessor Parattarna. The other "Middle Assyrian" kings who follow Ishme-Dagan are nothing more than alter egos of the Mitannians.

Tukulti-Ninurta I and Tukulti-Ninurta II

An Assyrian king named Tukulti-Ninurta provides the link between the Bronze Age Middle Assyrians and the Iron Age Neo-Assyrians. I refer to Tukulti-Ninurta II, father of Ashurnasirpal II. This man, as David Rohl rightly guessed, is identical to Tukulti-Ninurta I, last of the Middle Assyrians. However, although this statement is correct, it needs qualification: For there were indeed two Tukulti-Ninurtas, and the king normally identified as Tukulti-Ninurta I — namely the man who defeated the Hittites and conquered Babylon — is *not* the same person as the father of Ashurnasirpal II. As a matter of fact, Tukulti-Ninurta I and Tukulti-Ninurta II are placed in reverse order in the texbooks; the second Tukulti-Ninurta should actually be placed around 70 years before Tukulti-Ninurta I. Things are made even worse by the fact the lives and careers of the two men have been hopelessly confused.

Where historians in general, as well as revisionist writers such as David Rohl, went wrong was in their failure to understand that the "Middle Assyrians" were alter egos of the Mitannians. This being the case, the last recognizable Great King of Mitanni — Tushratta — who was murdered by his son Shattiwaza, is identical to Tukulti-Ninurta, last important king of the Middle Assyrians, who was murdered by his son Ashurnasirpal. Proof of their single identity comes in the fact that both Tushratta and Tukulti-Ninurta (I) are said to have been contemporaries of a Hittite great king named Suppiluliumas. Since Tukulti-Ninurta I is believed to have lived almost a century after the Suppiluliumas who corresponded with Akhnaton and Tushratta, it is supposed that there were two Suppiluliumas. This, however, is an error; there was only one. He reigned contemporary with Tushratta and with Tushratta's Semitic alter ego Tukulti-Ninurta (I).

About 80 years after Suppiluliumas and Tushratta/Tukulti-Ninurta, another Assyrian (or apparently Assyrian) king adopted the title Tukulti-Ninurta. It was this second Tukulti-Ninurta who conquered the Hittite Empire under Tudkhaliyas IV, whom we have already identified as Croesus of Lydia. It was the same Tukulti-Ninurta who conquered Babylon under its king Kashtiliash and who deported the latter in chains to Ashur. Thus the second Tukulti-Ninurta has to be identical to the Persian Cyrus the Great. It was this man too who was honored in the famous Tukulti-Ninurta epic poem. The second Tukulti-Ninurta brought to an end the earlier branch of the Neo-Assyrian (i.e., Median) dynasty and, to complicate matters further, also called himself Tukulti-apla-esharra, better known as Tiglath-Pileser III.

That Tukulti-Ninurta, the conqueror of the Hittites and Babylon, was the same person as Tukulti-apla-esharra (III), is hinted also by the fact that the two names have identical meanings. Tukulti-Ninurta is translated as "my trust is in Ninurta" whilst Tukulti-apla-esharra" means "my trust is in the son of Ashur." Since Ninurta was the son of Ashur, it is evident that these are two versions of the same name. It would appear that in the city of Ashur and other cult-centers of this god, the king was called Tukulti-apla-esharra; in other regions of Assyria he was known as Tukulti-Ninurta.

We possess only one piece of pictorial art that can with certainty be attributed to a king Tukulti-Ninurta, a so-called pedestal displaying cult-scenes on both faces. Features of the artwork, which is clearly in classic "Neo-Assyrian" style, suggest that it was probably not fashioned before the time of Tiglath-Pileser III. Here we find the king and possibly the crown prince worshipping before a deity. In both cases, the figures are shown in a correctly-executed profile, with shoulders shown as in life, as opposed to the Egyptian-like portrayals of earlier times. This mastery of perspective was not achieved in Assyrian art until the reign of Shalmaneser III or after; and in fact the sheer excellence of the technique would indicate the epoch of Tiglath-Pileser III.

The true sequence of early "Neo-Assyrian" (in reality Mede and Persian) kings is thus:

Shalmaneser I

Tukulti-Ninurta (II)/Tushratta

Ashurnasirpal II/Shattiwaza

Shalmaneser III/Hvashatra (Cyaxares II)

Shamshi-Adad V/Arbaka (Arbaces)

Adad-Nirari III/Ishtumega (Astyages)

Ashur-Nirari V (ephemeral)

Ashur-Dan III (ephemeral)

Shalmaneser IV (ephemeral)

Tukulti-Ninurta (I)/Tiglath-Pileser III (Cyrus the Great)

The confusion of these kings and their correct sequence and relation to each other began in antiquity and has caused immense problems for modern Assyriologists. Part of the problem was the fact that the first Tukulti-Ninurta was preceded by a king Shalmaneser — Shalmaneser I — who was the son of Adad-Nirari I; whilst the second Tukulti-Ninurta was also preceded by a Shalmaneser — Shalmaneser IV — who was the son of Adad-Nirari III.

Kassites and Chaldaeans

Even as the Hittite kings of the supposed 14th and 13th centuries must be alter egos of the Urartian rulers of (supposedly) the 9th and 8th centuries, so the Kassite Dynasty of Babylonia, reputedly of the 14th and 13th centuries, must be one and the same as the Chaldaean kings who are said to have reigned in Babylonia during the 9th and 8th centuries. Thus we hold that Burnaburiash of Babylon, who wrote a number of fairly aggressive letters to Akhnaton, was identical to Nabu-apil-iddin, the Babylonian king who corresponded with Ashurnasirpal II and Shalmaneser III. Indeed, in keeping with the custom of most ancient Near Eastern dynasties, these rulers bore different names in the different cultural and linguistic regions over which they ruled. Thus this king's Kassite name was Burnaburiash, his Semitic name was Nabu-apil-iddin, and his Sumerian (i.e., Chaldaean) name was, as we shall see, Ur-Nammu.

We should then expect to find fairly close agreement between every aspect of Kassite culture of the 14th and 13th centuries and Babylonian culture of the 9th and 8th centuries. In addition, the lives and careers of the Kassite kings who followed Burnaburiash and those of the Babylonian monarchs contemporary with Ashurnasirpal II and his successors should show striking agreement. What then does the record say?

Once again, the parallels are clear and unequivocal.

The earliest known Kassite palace, located fairly close to modern Baghdad in a site called Aqar Quf (ancient Dur-Kurigalzu), presented excavators with a number of surprises. Foremost among these was the fact that the building contained artistic features uncannily similar to those encountered in the monuments of Sargon II (721 to 705 BC.): "Is it an accident that the procession of officials painted in the Kassite palace at Dur-Kurigalzu finds its nearest parallel in the palace of Sargon of Assyria at Khorsabad?"[384]

The remains of Aqar Quf's ziggurat, a 170-foot high building, is one of the best preserved in all of Mesopotamia, and it closely resembles the later structures of the Neo-Babylonian epoch. Even more strangely, however, it bears a striking resemblance to the ziggurats of the Third Dynasty of Ur, supposedly 600 years earlier: "Fronting the ziggurat is a complex of courtyards, surrounded by narrow chambers, only excavated in part but very similar in their overall plan to comparable structures at Ur, founded under the Third Dynasty."[385]

Here then we find unequivocal evidence of two of the stratigraphic gaps or hiatuses mentioned earlier. Like the Mitanni in northern Mesopotamia, who immediately follow the Akkadians though supposedly separated from them by 700 years, the Kassites in middle Mesopotamia display close parallels with Third Dynasty Ur (whose greatest kings were Ur-Nammu, Shulgi and Ibbi-Sin), though they are supposed to be separated from them by 600 years. And just as the Mitanni in the north immediately precede the Neo-Assyrians, though supposedly separated from them by 500 years, the Kassites to the south immediately precede the Neo-Assyrians, though supposedly separated from them by the same span.

---

[384] H. Frankfort, *The Art and Architecture of the Ancient Orient* (Harmondsworth, 1970), p.129
[385] J. Oates, *Babylon* (London, 1986), p.98

Kassite parallels with the Neo-Assyrian epoch extend even into the field of personal names: "In the first millennium, Kurigalzu was a not uncommon personal name. Beginning ca. 840 BC and extending into the early Achaemenid Period, there are more than a dozen references in letters and economic texts to persons bearing that name, including a scribe or scribes and the son of a provincial governor."[386]

When we look at the lives and careers of the Kassite monarchs who ruled in Babylon in the century following the reign of pharaoh Akhnaton we find, once again, impressive parallels with the kings who ruled Babylon in the century following the reigns of Ashurnasirpal II and Shalmaneser III.

Starting at the beginning, we note that the career of Burnaburiash, who corresponded with Akhnaton, displays close parallels with that of Nabu-apil-iddin, who corresponded with Ashurnasirpal II and Shalmaneser III. Both Burnaburiash and Nabu-apil-iddin were compelled to deal with a resurgent Assyria; in both cases this initially brought conflict, yet in the end both Babylonian monarchs appear to have forged close links with their Assyrian counterparts.[387]

The next Kassite king of Babylon was named Kara-khardash, son of Burnaburiash, and grandson of Ashuruballit. However, he was overthrown in a palace conspiracy and replaced by Nazibugash, "son of a nobody." But the Assyrian king (supposedly Ashuruballit, though he must have been extremely old at the time) marched into Babylonia, killed the usurper, and placed Kurigalzu, another son of Burnaburiash, on the throne.[388] Babylon was thus at this stage virtually a vassal state of Assyria.

Again, the parallels with 9th century Babylon are clear. After the death of Nabu-apil-iddin, his son Marduk-zakir-shum became king. The latter, however, was hard pressed by a usurping brother named Marduk-bel-usate. Marduk-zakir-shum was only able to hold the throne with the timely help of the Assyrian king Shalmaneser III.[389] Babylon was thus now virtually a vassal state of Assyria.

After an eventful and long reign, Kurigalzu died and was succeeded by a son named Nazimarattash. This ruler waged a bitter war against a King Adad-Nirari of Assyria and was defeated with great slaughter at a place called Kar Ishtar.[390] The Assyrian it seems had gained a decisive victory over Babylon, but instead of pressing his advantage, he reinstated Nazimarattash

---

[386] J. A. Brinkman, "Kurigalzu," *Reallexikon der Assyriologie* Vol.5 (Berlin, 1980-83), 370

[387] Johns, op cit., pp.111-12

[388] E. A. Wallis Budge and L. W. King, *Annals of the Kings of Assyria*, Vol. 1 (London, 19012), pp. xxiv-xxvii

[389] Johns, op. cit., p.112

[390] Budge and King, op cit., p.xxxii

and made a new boundary treaty. Evidently Adad-Nirari, hard pressed by an ascendant Hittite Empire under Muwatallis and Hattusilis III, needed a friendly and compliant Babylon on his southern flank.

Again, the parallels with 9th/8th century Babylon are clear. No sooner did Marduk-balatsu-ikbe, the son of Marduk-zakir-shum, take the throne than he launched Babylon into a series of wars with Assyria. His initial and unsuccessful actions against Shamshi-Adad IV seem to have been followed by equally unsuccessful campaigns against Adad-Nirari III. Whatever the exact sequence of events, by the early 8th century, we are told, the Assyrians under Adad-Nirari III had gained complete mastery over Babylon. Yet like his earlier namesake, this Adad-Nirari did not press his advantage, and was content simply to arrange new boundaries.[391] We know of course that Adad-Nirari III, hard pressed by Menua and Argishti I of Urartu, had every reason to promote friendly relations with his southern neighbors.

The Kassite lists next show a series of kings, each supposedly the son of the preceding ruler (though this is absolutely impossible), who appear to have been relatively at peace with Assyria. The fourth of these monarchs, Shagarakti-Shuriash, is of interest. He reigned thirteen years, and was the father of Kashtiliash, during whose time the throne of Babylon passed into the hands of Tukulti-Ninurta of Assyria.[392]

Once more, the parallels with 8th century Babylon are clear. After Marduk-balatsu-ikbe, there followed a series of fairly innocuous kings who appear to have maintained the peace with Assyria. However, towards the middle of the 8th century (roughly four reigns after Marduk-balatsu-ikbe), there lived a king named Nabu-shum-ishkum, who reigned thirteen years, and was the father of Nabonasser, in whose time the throne of Babylon passed into the hands of the Assyrian king Tiglath-Pileser III (Tukulti-apil-esharra). The latter was supposedly the first Assyrian monarch to "take the hand of Bel" (become king of Babylon) since Tukulti-Ninurta, five hundred years earlier.[393]

After Tukulti-Ninurta's conquest, the Kassites ruled Babylon only intermittently. Following a brief revival of their fortunes under Marduk-apil-iddin (Merodach-Baladan) I, Kassite power waned, with only two ephemeral kings appearing on the lists afterwards. The last of these was Bel-shum-iddin, who was given a reign of three years.[394]

[391] Johns, op cit., p.113
[392] Ibid., p.99
[393] See eg. Sid Smith, "The Foundation of the Assyrian Empire," in *The Cambridge Ancient History* Vol.3 (3rd ed.), p.40
[394] Johns, op cit., p.102

Precisely the same state of affairs is observed in Babylonia during the latter 8th century. A handful of native rulers briefly claimed the throne after Tiglath-Pileser's conquest. Independence was reasserted for a while by Marduk-apil-iddin III (or perhaps II), though he was eventually completely overcome by Sargon II. Only one independent king of Babylon is listed as following him. This was Bel-ibni, who was given a reign of three years.[395]

The evidence thus clearly shows that the Kassite kings were alter egos of the kings of Babylon normally dated to the 9th and 8th centuries, who were contemporaries and adversaries of the early Neo-Assyrian Empire. Yet another element of complexity is added by two other factors:

(a) As well as having duplicates, these kings (as was stressed in the first chapter) also have triplicates. Thus Nabu-apil-iddin (Nabopoladdan) of the first millennium is an alter ego of Burnaburiash of the second millennium; but he is also an alter ego of Ur-Nammu of the third millennium. The Neo-Sumerian (3rd Dynasty of Ur) kings, from Ur-Nammu through to Ibbi-Sin, are in fact alter egos of these first millennium kings of Babylon.

(b) As mentioned before, even the Neo-Assyrian (and therefore also the Urartian and contemporary Babylonian dynasties) are placed too early - by two centuries. Thus these Neo-Sumerian/Kassite/Babylonian kings are actually the Neo-Chaldaean kings of the 7th and 6th centuries, known to us from the works of the Classical authors. These were the kings who allied themselves with the Lydians (Hittites) against the Medes (early Neo-Assyrians), who were finally overcome by the Persians in 546 BC. Thus Ibbi-Sin, taken in chains to Anshan, is identical to Kashtiliash, taken in chains before Ashur, who is identical to Nabonasser/Nabonidus, taken in chains to Persia.

The following identifications are suggested:

Neo-Sumerian	Kassite	Neo-Babylonian
Ur-Nammu	Burnaburiash	Nabu-apil-iddin(Nabopoladdan)
Shulgi	Kurigalzu	Marduk-zakir-shum(Nebuchad)
Amar-Sin	Nazimarattash	Marduk-balatsu-ikbe(Belshazz.)
Shu-Sin	Shagarakti-Shuriash	Nabu-shum-ishkum

---

[395] Ibid., p.120

| Ibbi-Sin | Kashtiliash | Nabu-natsir(Nabonidus) |

Before moving on, I should stress that the Neo-Babylonian kings listed above have only a coincidental and apparent relationship to the kings normally designated under this title in the textbooks. As I have shown elsewhere,[396] there is evidence that the last Achaemenid kings, from Artaxerxes II though to Darius III, based themselves in Babylon and consciously styled themselves Babylonian monarchs, adopting royal titles that recalled the great Babylonian kings who had reigned before the conquest of Cyrus.

Arame of Urartu

In Chapter 6, we saw that one of the major opponents of Shalmaneser III was a prince named Arame. This man was apparently the ruler of numerous territories throughout northern Syria and Anatolia, and one inscription of Shalmaneser III refers to one hundred of his cities. Arame remained a persistent foe of Shalmaneser III throughout his reign, and his territories clearly formed part of a much wider Hittite confederacy. That he was a Hittite is not in doubt, for his area of influence was part of the Hittite domain. He also had the same name as an extremely prominent personage in the Hittite royal family.

The earliest reference to Arame comes in year five of Shalmaneser III: "Against the cities of Arame I drew near, Arne his royal city I captured."[397] But in spite of this and other successes, the Assyrian king failed to remove the threat posed by Arame. Ten years later, in his 15th year, Shalmaneser records further action in Anatolia against the same man. This is the last extant mention of Arame in Assyrian records, and when Shalmaneser again marches into the northern regions, in his 27th year, his opponent is named as Seduri (apparently Sarduri). Thus it is usually assumed that Arame was now dead and had been replaced on the throne by Sarduri I. Yet nowhere is the death of Arame actually recorded.

The identity of such a powerful prince is something of a mystery, and various conjectures have been offered as a solution. Some see him as the precursor, others as a subject of, the earliest Urartian king Sarduri I. Since Sarduri I has already been identified by us with Mursilis II, it is likely that Arame was either a younger brother or a son, or at least a close relative of the Hittite Great King. If this is the case, it may be worth examining the Boghaz-koi documents to see whether his name occurs in any of those voluminous texts. Whilst it is generally assumed that Arame only appears in the

[396] In my *Ramessides, Medes and Persians* (New York, 2000)
[397] Luckenbill, op cit., i, 563

inscriptions of Shalmaneser III, an excellent test of the chronology would be to see whether he is named as a contemporary of Suppiluliumas I, Mursilis II, or Hattusilis III. According to the scheme presented here, Suppiluliumas would have died sometime after the eleventh year of Shalmaneser III, and most of the latter's reign would have coincided with that of Mursilis II. Since Mursilis reigned around twenty-one years, this means that Shalmaneser III would have died near the end of Muwatallis' reign, about a year or two before the accession of Hattusilis III. We must then ask: Does Arame appear in the records of any of these Hittite rulers?

In his autobiography King Hattusilis III, the grandson of Suppiluliumas I, tells how a senior member of the ruling dynasty hatched plot to destroy his reputation. The man in question is named as Sin-Uas: "When Sin-Uas the son of Zidas saw the favor of Ishtar and also of my brother, he and his sons tried to bring imputations upon me ..."[398] At the subsequent trial, however, Hattusilis turned the tables and was able to bring accusations of religious wantonness on the part of his accuser. Finally, the Great King (Muwatallis), his brother, decided in his favor and delivered Sin-Uas into Hattusilis' hands. Hattusilis now had the power to kill his accuser, but, "Because he was a royal prince, and also an old man, I did nothing to him ... His sons I sent to Alasia [Cyprus]."[399]

In another document, which preserves the same portion of the autobiography, Hattusilis writes, "And because Arma was a relative and also a very old man, and also sick, I let him be."[400] Quite obviously, Sin-Uas and Arma were two names for the same person.

Aside from having the same name, a number of other factors would lead us to identify Arma the Hittite with Arame the Urartian. To begin with, our reconstruction would have Shalmaneser III die only about two years before the accession of Hattusilis. Certainly, the trial mentioned in the Boghaz-koi documents happened about twenty-six or twenty-seven years after the death of Suppiluliumas. (Mursilis reigned about twenty-one years, Muwatallis seven, and the trial occurred a couple of years before the death of Muwatallis.) Between therefore the first appearance of Arame in the records of Shalmaneser III (year 5) and the trial of Arma the Hittite (around year 5 of Muwatallis) something like thirty years had passed. Assuming that the Arame against whom Shalmaneser III campaigned was a mature man, perhaps in his thirties, this would mean he would have been in his sixties by the time of Muwatallis and Hattusilis. Furthermore, it is clear that the

---

[398] *Autobiography* Sec.9
[399] Ibid., Sec.10
[400] A. Goetze, *Mitteilungen, Vorderasiatisch-aegyptische Gesellschaft* XXXIV, Heft 2 (1930), 19

Arma who accused Hattusilis had a long and illustrious career as a senior Hittite ruler, probably a highly respected military commander. And if the reconstruction is correct, if Mursilis and Muwatallis were contemporaries of Shalmaneser III, Arma the Hittite *must* have seen action against him. Which of course he did.

The names of all the characters and events recorded by the Assyrians on the one hand and the Hittites on the other need to be re-examined and compared. Although we have already identified numerous correspondences, enough has been said to show the difficulties. Ancient royal personages normally had more than one name. So Arma was also called Sin-Uas. Even worse, cuneiform spellings varied from scribe to scribe, and from area to area, whilst the actual characters can be read either ideographically or phonetically. Thus for example the Great King Ura-tarhunda, who built the Storm-god's temple at Carchemish, can also be read as the Hurrian Talmi-Teshub.

Yet in spite of these difficulties, we have been able to show detailed correspondences between the social and political histories of the 14th/13th centuries and the 9th/8th, and a thorough scholarly re-examination should prove very fruitful in revealing many more.

The Princess of Bactria

At least one ancient document seems to hint at close diplomatic relations between Egypt and a great power in central Asia during the time of Ramses II. The famous Bentresh Stele, an inscription apparently dating from either the Persian or Ptolemaic age, tells the story of how the Princess Bentresh, daughter of the king of Bakhtan, was miraculously healed of a mental illness by an image of the god Khonsu which was sent from Egypt to the land of Bakhtan for that purpose. The story, we are informed, took place in the reign of Ramses II (Usermare Setepnere), after the conclusion of the long war with the "chief of Hatti."

When the daughter of the king of Bakhtan became ill, "possessed of spirits," a physician was sent from Egypt but found himself unable to effect a cure. The image of the god Khonsu was then dispatched from Egypt "that she might become well immediately," and the spirit left her. The king of Bakhtan then decided to keep the wonderful image in his own country, but being warned in a dream, he eventually allowed the priests of Khonsu to take it home.

The story of Bentresh has been the occasion of considerable debate amongst scholars. J. A. Wilson regarded it as a "pious forgery" because, whilst the text probably dates "from the 4th or 3rd centuries BC." the priests at Karnak had "cast the tale back into the reign of Ramses II," and he had "reigned in the 13th century BC."[401] Yet if Ramses II actually reigned in the 6th century, the stele may very well recall a real incident.

The identity of the land of Bakhtan also caused discussion. A number of scholars, for obvious reasons, identified it with Bactria.[402] Yet the stele itself seems to identify Bakhtan with the Land of Hatti. The elder sister of the princess Bentresh, named Nefrure in the inscription, is said to have become the chief wife, the "Great King's Wife," of Ramses II; and it is evident that this information was derived from the very real marriage of Hattusilis' daughter (who was given the Egyptian name of Maat-Nefrure) to Ramses II.

Yet there are a number of reasons why Bakhtan could not possibly be the Hittite Land.

To begin with, the journey to Bakhtan is said to have taken seventeen months. This information was evidently included to stress just how far-reaching was the prestige of Khonsu and his healing priests. But the Hatti Land was well-known to the Egyptians, and by no stretch of the imagination could a journey there have taken seventeen months, no matter how slow the mode of transport employed. Furthermore, it has been stated that nowhere else, in all of ancient literature, is the name Bakhtan applied to the Hittite land or any of its territories.

But Bactria, a region which does indeed lie at a very great distance from Egypt, has a name which can indubitably be linked to Bakhtan. The problem with this identification, of course, is that the first kingdom to control Bactria which had any contact with Egypt was that of the Medes, in the 7th and 6th centuries. Since Ramses II is placed in the 13th century, the equation with Bactria is regarded as highly suspect. Yet it would appear that Bentresh was truly a princess of that far-off country; for her name also appears in Aramaic papyri of the Persian epoch found at Elephantine,[403] a circumstance which further suggests her Iranian or central Asian origin.

Ramses II, we have already surmised, was closely allied to the Medes in the early 6th century, and the Bentresh Stele is probably a record of a real event. She would have been a daughter of the satrap of Bactria, a vassal of the Medish Great King, very probably at that time either Shalmaneser IV or Ashur-Dan III. The sending of a sacred image from Egypt to Bactria suggests fairly intimate contacts between the two countries, and this is also probably reflected in the statement of the Bentresh Stele that it was the custom of Ramses II to visit Naharim (northern Mesopotamia) every year.

[401] Wilson in Pritchard (ed.) *Ancient Near Eastern Texts*, p.29
[402] See eg. Constant de Wit, "Het Land Bachtan in de Bentresjstele," *Handeligen van het XVIIIe Vlaamse Filologencongres* (Gent, 1949), pp.80-8
[403] Wilson, loc cit., p.30n

One other ancient source spoke of a direct link between the Egypt of Ramses II and Bactria. In his lost *History of Egypt*, Hecataeus of Abdera (quoted at some length in Book 1 of Diodorus Siculus) spoke of a war waged by Ramses (whom he calls Ozymandias – i.e., "Usermaatre") against the central Asian kingdom.[404] It is impossible, of course, that Ramses II could have campaigned against Bactria, and the source of this belief is undoubtedly the various inscriptions and monuments recalling the pharaoh's protracted war with the Hittites. Nevertheless, it is surely significant that Hecataeus' Egyptian informants regarded Ramses II as contemporary with the empire of Media/Bactria, and this impression is reinforced by various other ancient authors (including Manetho), who also make kings with names like Seti and Ramses contemporaries of the Medes.

---

[404] Diodorus, i, 47, 6

EPILOGUE

Our re-examination of the period covered by *Ages in Chaos* Vol.1 has, I think it will be agreed, shown that Velikovsky got it remarkably right. The only area where he was wrong, in terms of character identifications, was in the epoch of the Amarna Letters. This was a great pity, since he was in fact so near the truth. But the attempt to make Rib-Addi of Gubla (Byblos) into Ahab of Jezreel, and the various other misidentifications offered in the same place, gave the critics the chance they needed to reject the entire work. In doing so, they threw out the baby with the bath water. Had they looked at the other types of evidence offered in the book — that of language, epigraphy, art-forms etc. — they would have understood that Velikovsky must be very nearly correct, that what was needed was some fine tuning rather than — as happened — wholesale demolition.

And so was lost an almost unique opportunity to correct the history of antiquity. The failure to take it has resulted, on the one hand, in the academic establishment continuing to patch up the cracks and explain away the anomalies which appear in ever greater quantities every year. On the other, it has resulted in "revisionist" historians creating their own, unworkable, chronologies; chronologies which fail to benefit from the remarkable insights provided in *Ages in Chaos*.

The major thrust of the foregoing work has been to show the folly of such an approach. *Ages in Chaos* must form a cornerstone in the work of reconstruction. Our big disagreement with Velikovsky is one of absolute dates. In his reconstruction, the Eighteenth Dynasty terminated around 830 BC. We however find that it actually came to a close sometime near 600 BC, with the eclipse of Akhnaton's Zoroastrian-style cult. This means, among other things, that the Nineteenth or Tanite Dynasty must have flourished in the 75 or 80 years between 600 BC and the Persian Conquest of 525 BC. Now this of course is precisely where Velikovsky himself placed the Tanite kings in his *Ramses II and His Time* — the difference being that he had separated the end of the Eighteenth Dynasty from the beginning of the Nineteenth by over two centuries; a proposition which is historically insupportable.

For us, such dissection is unnecessary, and the two great dynasties follow directly one from the other as normal.

We are thus able, to a certain degree, to rehabilitate the much-maligned *Ramses II and His Time*. The one big difference, as we have seen, is in relation to the biblical characters and events with which Ramses II should be associated.

In line with his Bible-based chronology, Velikovsky believed that Ramses II, living in the 6th century, was a contemporary of the tiny kingdom of Judah in its final death-throes, as it was crushed and devoured by the mighty Neo-Babylonian Empire. Yet it has become clear that the whole chronology of the Judean and Israelite kings is itself unnaturally extended — by over two centuries. Thus the Hebrew kings of the real 6th century are the monarchs of the divided Judean and Israelite kingdoms who are normally located in the 8th century: And it was these rulers, Jehoshaphat, Jehoram, Ahaziah, Joash and Uzziah (the kings of Judah), with whom the Nineteenth Dynasty pharaohs actually interacted.

The challenge then is to show how the history of Egypt during the Nineteenth Dynasty can be made to square with the history of the 6th century and (in terms of biblical characters and events) the 8th century. It must be shown, above all, that the Nineteenth Dynasty was terminated in 525 BC, by the Persian conquest of Egypt, a conquest well remembered for its savagery. According to conventional ideas however the Nineteenth Dynasty was followed only by a brief and relatively trouble-free interregnum before the commencement of the Twentieth Dynasty, whose greatest pharaoh, Ramses III, re-established Egypt as a great power. It remains for us therefore to demonstrate that this is not the case. We need to show that the Nineteenth Dynasty was terminated by a major Asiatic invasion, a conquest that resulted in the Nile kingdom being reduced to little more than an exploited province. And even if we can show that such a conquest occurred, such an adjustment implies that all of the remaining dynasties on Manetho's list — from the Twentieth to the Thirtieth — must be placed in the Persian Age, or in the Persian and Ptolemaic Ages. Can we find room for eleven dynasties in two hundred years of history?

The answer to that question is answered in the affirmative in the pages of *Ramessides and Persians*.

Finally, it cannot be emphasized too strongly that bringing the Eighteenth Dynasty down into the eighth and seventh centuries has dramatic consequences for the whole of ancient history. We cannot, for example, have Akhnaton die around 600 BC and leave the pyramid-builders of the Fourth, Fifth and Sixth Dynasties in the third millennium BC. The evidence suggests that this epoch, whose artisans cut iron-hard granite with mathematical precision and employed advanced Pythagorean-style geometry, must be reduced by an even greater margin of time than the New Kingdom. Astonishingly, it appears that the final Pyramid Age dynasty, the Sixth, two of whose kings were named Pepi, was identical to the Great Hyksos Fifteenth Dynasty, two of whose kings were named Apepi. In essence, this means that the Pyramid Age only ended with the rise of the Eighteenth Dynasty, around 740 BC. And this adjustment means too that the entire "Middle Kingdom," which supposedly came between the Sixth and Eighteenth Dynasties, must be completely redated. In fact, examination of the evidence makes it clear that the most important Middle Kingdom dynasty, the Twelfth, was a line of priest-kings, of Libyan origin, who "reigned" alongside the Hyksos. The last of these, Amenemhet III, threw in his lot with the Theban rebels of the early Eighteenth Dynasty and was ever afterward honored as a hero of the country. He was the great liberator "Ameny" lauded in the Neferty Prophecy.

BIBLIOGRAPHY

Books

Aharoni, Y. *The Land of the Bible* (London, 1966)

Akurgal, E. *The Birth of Greek Art* (Methuen, 1968)

Albright, W. F. *The Archaeology of Palestine: From the Stone Age to Christianity* (Baltimore, 1940)

Baikie, J. *A History of Egypt* 2 Vols. (London, 1929)

Baikie, J. *The Story of the Pharaohs* (3rd ed, London, 1926)

Bliss, F. J. and R. A. S. Macalister, *Excavations in Palestine (1898–1900)* (London, 1902)

Bonnet, H. *Die Waffen der Völker des alten Orients* (Leipzig, 1926)

Breasted, J. H. *A History of Egypt* (2nd ed. 1951)

Breasted, J. H. *Ancient Records of Egypt*, 5 Vols. (Chicago, 1906)

Budge, E. A. W. and L. W. King, eds. *Annals of the Kings of Assyria*, 2 Vols. (London, 1902)

Burn, A.R. *Minoans, Philistines, and Greeks* (London, 1930)

Carter, H. *The Tomb of Tut.ankh.Amen* Vol. 2 (London, 1923-33)

Crowfoot, J. W. and G. M. Crowfoot, *Early Ivories from Samaria* (London, 1938)

De Rougé, Emmanuel, *Oeuvres diverses* Vol.V (Paris, 1914)

De Vaux, R. *The Early History of Israel* 2 Vols. (London, 1978)

Erman, A. and H. Grapow, eds. *Wörterbuch der aegyptischen Sprache* Vol. V (Leipzig, 1926-1963)

Frankfort, H. *The Art and Architecture of the Ancient Orient* (Harmondsworth, 1970)

Gaebel, Robert E. (Cavalry Operations in the Ancient Greek World (Oklahoma, 1937)

Gardiner, A. H. *Egyptian Hieratic Texts* I (Leipzig,1911)

Gardiner, A. *The Kadesh Inscriptions of Ramesses II* (London, 1975)

Giles, F.J. *Ikhnaton; Legend and History* (Hutchinson, Australia, 1970)

Giveon, R. *Les Bedouins Shoshou des Documents Egyptiens* (Leiden, 1971)

Glueck, N. *The Other Side of the Jordan* (London, 1970)

Gray, J. *I and II Kings: A Commentary* (2nd ed., London, 1970)

Gurney, O.R. *The Hittites* (Pelican Books, 1952)

Hamilton, W.J. *Researches in Asia Minor, Pontus and Armenia* (London, 1842)

Heinsohn, G. *Die Sumerer gab es nicht* (Frankfurt, 1988)

Heinsohn, G. *Perserherrscher gleich Assyrerkönige?* (Frankfurt, 1992)

Heinsohn, G. *Wann lebten die Pharaonen?* (Frankfurt, 1990)

James, P. et al. *Centuries of Darkness* (London, 1991)

Johns, C. H. W. *Ancient Babylonia* (Cambridge, 1913)

Krieger, P. (trans of S. Schott) *Les chants d'amour de l'Egypte Ancien* (Paris, 1956)

Layard, A.H. *Discoveries in the Ruins of Nineveh and Babylon* (London, 1853)

Lepsius, C.R. (E. Naville ed.) *Denkmäler aus Aegypten und Aethiopien* (Leipzig, 1897)

Luckenbill, D. D. *Ancient Records of Assyria and Babylonia* 2 Vols. (Chicago, 1926)

MacQueen, J. G. *The Hittites* (London, 1975)

Mallowan, Max. *The Nimrud Ivories* (London, 1978)

Maspero, G. *History of Egypt* 13 Vols (London, 1906))

Montgomery, J. A. *Arabia and the Bible* (Philadelphia, 1934)

Morenz, S. *Egyptian Religion* (Cornell University Press, 1973)

Moscati, S. et al, *The Phoenicians* (New York, 1999)

Murray, A. S., Smith, A. H. and Walters, H. B. *Excavations in Cyprus* (London, British Museum, 1900)

Naville, E. *The Temple of Deir el-Bahari* Part III (London, 1907)

Niemi, T. M., Ben-Avraham, Z., and Gat, J. (eds.) *The Dead Sea: The Lake and Its Setting* (Oxford, 1997).

Oates, J. *Babylon* (1986)

Olmstead, A.T. *A History of Assyria* (New York, 1923)

Petrie, F. *A History of Egypt* 3 Vols. (London, 1905)

Petrie, F. *The Making of Egypt* (London, 1939)

Pfälzner, P. *Mitannische und Mittelassyrische Keramik* (Berlin, 1995)

Pritchard, J. (ed.) *Ancient Near Eastern Texts* (Princeton, 1950)

Rawlinson, G. *History of Ancient Egypt* 2 Vols. (London, 1881)

Reisner, G. A. Fisher, C. S. and Lyon, D. G. *Harvard Excavations at Samaria*, 3 Vols. (Cambridge, 1924)

Robins, G. *The Art of Ancient Egypt* (British Museum Press, 1997)

Saggs, H.W.F. *The Greatness that was Babylon* (London, 1962)

Saggs, H.W.F. *The Might that was Assyria* (London, 1984)

Sellin, E. and Watzinger, C. *Jericho* (Berlin, 1913)

Smith, S. *Alalakh and Chronology* (London,1940)

Sweeney, E. *Ramessides, Medes and Persians* (New York, 2000)

Sweeney, E. *The Genesis of Israel and Egypt* (London, 1997)

Velikovsky I. *Peoples of the Sea* (New York and London, 1977)

Velikovsky, I *Ramses II and his Time* (New York and London, 1978)

Velikovsky, I. *Ages in Chaos* (New York and London, 1952)

Velikovsky, I. *Oedipus and Akhnaton* (New York and London, 1960)

Whitfield, P. (ed.) *Longman Illustrated Animal Encyclopaedia* (London, 1988)

Woldering, I. *Egypt: The Art of the Pharaohs* (London, 1962)

Woolley, L. *Carchemish III* (London, 1952)

Yahuda, A. *The Language of the Pentateuch in its Relation to Egyptian* (Oxford, 1933)

Articles

Abdel-Aziz Saleh "Some Problems Relating to the Pwenet Reliefs at Deir el-Bahari," *Journal of Egyptian Archaeology* 58 (1972)

Albright, W. F. "An Archaic Hebrew Proverb in an Amarna Letter from Central Palestine," *Journal of Near Eastern Studies* 89 (1943)

Albright, W. F. "The Amarna Letters from Palestine," in *The Cambridge Ancient History* Vol.2 part 1 (3rd ed.)

Barnett, R. D. "The Sea Peoples: Anatolians at the Battle of Qadesh," in *The Cambridge Ancient History*, Vol.2 part 2 (3rd ed.)

Barnett, R. D. "Urartu," in *The Cambridge Ancient History* Vol.3 part 1 (3rd ed.)

Barth, H. "Versuch einer eingehenden Erklärung der Felssculpturen von Boghaskoei in alten Kappadocien," *Monatsberichte der Königlichen Preussischen Akademie der Wissenschaften* (Berlin, 1869)

Bennett, R. D. "Phoenician-Punic Art," in *Encyclopedia of World Art*, XI (New York, 1966)

Bimson, J. "Can There be a Revised Chronology Without a Revised Stratigraphy?" *Society for Interdisciplinary Studies: Proceedings, Glasgow Conference* (April, 1978)

Bimson, J. "Dating the Wars of Seti I," *Society for Interdisciplinary Studies: Review* Vol.V, No.1 (1980-1)

Bimson, J. "Hatshepsut and the Queen of Sheba: A Critique of Velikovsky's Identification and an Alternative View," *Society for Interdisciplinary Studies Review* 8 (1986)

Bimson, J. "Israel in Egypt," *Society for Interdisciplinary Studies: Review* Vol. IV, No.1 (1979)

Birch, K. in *Society for Interdisciplinary Studies: Catastrophism and Chronology Workshop* No. 2 (1987)

Breasted, J. H. "A City of Ikhenaton in Nubia," *Zeitschrift für Aegyptische Sprache* 40 (1902/1903)

Brinkman, J. A. "Kurigalzu," *Reallexikon der Assyriologie* Vol.5 (Berlin, 1980-83)

Butzer, K. W. "Physical Conditions in Eastern Europe, Western Asia and Egypt Before the Period of Agriculture and Urban Settlement," in *The Cambridge Ancient History* Vol.1, part 1 (3rd ed)

Curtis, J. "The Assyrian heartland in the period 612-539 BC" in "Continuity in Empire (?) Assyria, Media, Persia: Proceedings of the International Meeting in Padua", (26th — 28th April, 2001) *History of the Ancient Near East. Monographs* V. (Padova. S.a.r.g.o.n., 2003) Giovanni Lanfranchi, Michael Roaf, Robert Rollinger (eds)

Danelius, E. "Did Thutmose III Despoil the Temple in Jerusalem?" *Society for Interdisciplinary Studies: Review* Vol. II, No.3 (1977/78)

Danelius, E. "The Identification of the Biblical 'Queen of Sheba' with Hatshepsut, 'Queen of Egypt and Ethiopia,'" *Kronos* I, 4 (1977)

Danelius, E. and H. Steinitz, "The Fishes and other Aquatic Animals on the Punt Reliefs at Deir el Bahri" *Journal of Egyptian Archaeology* 53 (1967)

De Wit, Constant, "Het Land Bachtan in de Bentresjstele" *Handeligen van het XVIIIe Vlaamse Filologencongres* (Gent, 1949)

Dhorme, P. "Premiere traduction des textes pheniciens de Ras Sharma," *Revue Biblique* Vol. 40, No. 1 (1931)

Dhorme, P. "Un nouvel alphabet semitique," *Revue Biblique* Vol. 39, No. 4 (1930)

Drower, M. S. "Syria Before 2200 BC," in *The Cambridge Ancient History* Vol.1, part 2 (3rd ed.)

Drower, M. S. "Syria c. 1550 — 1400 BC" in *The Cambridge Ancient History* Vol.2 part 1 (3rd ed.)

Dussaud, R. "Topographie historique de la Syrie antique et medieval," *Syria* V (1924)

Ewing, Rev. W. "Syria" in *Countries of the World* Vol.6 (Waverley Books, London, 1933)

Faulkner, R. O. "The Wars of Sethos I," *Journal of Egyptian Archaeology* 33 (1947)

Gadd, C. J. "Assyria and Babylon c.1370-1300 BC." in *The Cambridge Ancient History* Vol. 2, part 2 (3rd ed.) p.27

Glueck, N. "Some Ezion-Geber/Elath Iron II Pottery," *Eretz-Israel* 9 (1969)

Goetze, A. "Anatolia from Shuppiluliumash to the Egyptian War of Muwatallish," in *The Cambridge Ancient History* Vol.2, part 2 (3rd ed.)

Goetze, A. "Die Annalen des Mursilis," *Mitteilungen, Vorderasiatisch-aegyptische Gesellschaft*, XXXVII, 2 (1932).

Goetze, A. "The Hittites and Syria (1300-1200 BC.)," in *The Cambridge Ancient History*, Vol. 2 part 2 (3rd ed.)

Goetze, A. "The Struggle for Domination of Syria (1400-1300 BC.)" in *The Cambridge Ancient History* Vol.2, part 2 (3rd ed.)

Grayson, A. K. "Ashur-dan II to Ashur-Nirari V (934-745 BC.)" in *The Cambridge Ancient History* Vol. 3, part 1 (3rd ed.)

Greenberg, L. M., "A Linguistic Note on the Land of Punt," *Society for Interdisciplinary Studies, Review* No. 1 (2018).

Greenberg, L. M., "The Land of Punt, Redux," *Society for Interdisciplinary Studies, Review* No. 2 (2018)

Greenberg, L. M., "The Lion Gate at Mycenae Revisited," *Society for Interdisciplinary Studies: Proceedings of Conference 'Ages Still in Chaos'* (September, 2002)

Handwerk, B. "King Tut's New Face: Behind the Forensic Reconstruction," *National Geographic* (June, 2005)

Hawkins, J. D. "The Neo-Hittite States in Syria and Anatolia," in *The Cambridge Ancient History* Vol.1, part 3 (2nd ed)

Hayes, W. C. "Egypt: From the Death of Amenemmes III to Seqenenre II," in *The Cambridge Ancient History* Vol.2, part 1 (3rd ed.)

Hayes, W. C. "Egypt: Internal Affairs from Tuthmosis I to the Death of Amenophis III," in *The Cambridge Ancient History* Vol.2, part 2 (3rd ed)

Hays, Christopher B. "Re-Excavating Shebna's Tomb: A New Reading of Isa 22, 15-19 in its Ancient Near Eastern Context," *Zeitschrift für die Alttestamentliche Wissenschaft*; (2010)

Heinsohn, G. "Who were the Hyksos?" *Sixth International Congress of Egyptology* (Turin, 1991)

Hrozny, B. "Une Inscription de Ras-Shamra en langue Churrite," *Archiv Orientalni* IV (1932)

James, P. "Chronological Problems in the Archaeology of the Hittites," *Society for Interdisciplinary Studies Review* Vol.VI (1982)

Kupper, J. R. "Northern Mesopotamia and Syria," in *The Cambridge Ancient History* Vol.2, part 1 (3rd ed)

Lewy, J. "The Sulman Temple in Jerusalem," *The Journal of Biblical Archaeology* 59 (1940)

Littauer, M. A. "A 19th and 20th dynasty heroic motif on Attic Black-figured vases?" *American Journal of Archaeology*, 76, No. 2 (1972).

Lorton, D. "Hatshepsut, the Queen of Sheba, and Immanuel Velikovsky" (1984) www.geocities.com/Athens/Academy/1326/hatshepsut.html

Luke, H. C. "Palestine," in *Countries of the World* Vol.5 (London, 1933)

Maccoby, H., "The Queen of Sheba and the Song of Songs," *Society for Interdisciplinary Studies, Review* Vol. IV, No. 4 (Spring, 1980)

Macdonald, J. "The Na'ar in Israelite Society," *Journal of Near Eastern Studies* 35 (1976)

Malamat, A. "Hazor, 'The Head of all those Kingdoms,'" *Journal of Biblical Literature* Vol. LXXIX (1960)

Millard, A. R. and H. Tadmor, "Adad-Nirari III in Syria," *Iraq* 35 (1973)

Munn-Rankin, J. M. "Assyrian Military Power 1300-1200 BC." in *The Cambridge Ancient History* Vol.2, part 2 (3rd ed.)

Newberry, P. E. "Three Old Kingdom Travellers to Byblos and Punt," *Journal of Egyptian Archaeology* 24 (1938)

Nibbi, A. "The Shipwrecked Sailor Again," *Göttinger Miszellen* 24 (1977)

Porter, R. "Recent Developments in Near Eastern Archaeology," in *Society for Interdisciplinary Studies: Review* 2, (2002)

Rohl, D. and B. Newgrosh, "The el-Amarna Letters and the New Chronology," *Society for Interdisciplinary Studies: Chronology and Catastrophism Review* No. I (1988)

Rullkoetter, J., and Nissenbaum, A., "Dead Sea asphalt in Egyptian mummies: Molecular evidence," *Wissenschaften* (December, 2004)

Sayed, A. M. "Discovery at the Site of the 12th Dynasty Port at Wadi Gawasis on the Red Sea Shore," *Revue d'egyptologie* 29 (1977)

Shea, W. H. "Adad-Nirari III and Jehoash of Israel," *Journal of Cuneiform Studies* 30/2 (1978)

Smith, Sid. "The Foundation of the Assyrian Empire," in *The Cambridge Ancient History* Vol.3 (3rd ed.)

Spiegelberg, W. "Zur Datierung der Ahiram-Inschrift von Byblos," *Orientalistische Literaturzeitung* XXIX (1926)

Stewart, D., "Hatshepsut is the Queen of Sheba," December, 2008 at www.don-stewart-research.blogspot .

Stiebing, W.H. "A Criticism of the Revised Chronology," *Pensee* Vol.3 No.3 (Autumn, 1973)

Tadmor, H. "Azriyau of Yaudi," *Scripta Hierosolymitana* 8 (1961)

Tadmor, H. "Philistia under Assyrian Rule," *Biblical Archaeology* 29 (1966)

Van Asten, Sjef. "Further Support for a Velikovskian-like Scenario?" *Society for Interdisciplinary Studies: Chronology and Catastrophism Workshop* No. I (2013).

Velikovsky, I. "The Correct Placement of Haremhab in Egyptian History," *Kronos* IV, No.3 (1977)

Virolleaud, C. "Les Inscriptions cuneiforms," *Syria* X (1929)

Von Soden, W. "Der Aufstieg des Assyrereiches als geschichtliches Problem," in *Der alte Orient* Vol. 31, No.12 (1937)

Classical Texts

Diodorus Siculus, *History of the World*

Herodotus, *The Histories*

Josephus, *Against Apion*

Josephus, *The Jewish War*

Sophocles, *Antigone*

Xenophon, *Cyropaedia*

Abbreviations

ANET = *Ancient Near Eastern Texts*

CAH = *The Cambridge Ancient History*

SIS = *Society for Interdisciplinary Studies*

INDEX

A.

Abdastartus, 23, 99-101
Abdi-Ashirta, 23, 94, 99-101, 103, 104
Abdi-Hiba, 93, 94, 96, 99, 101, 103, 105, 106, 116
Abdi-Khiba, 93
Abibaal, 100, 172, 175
Abimelech, 101
Abimilki, 101
Acco, 103, 212, 214
Achaea, 200
Achaemenid, 119, 223, 231, 234
Adad, 130, 203
Adad-Nirari, 27, 108, 144, 150-152, 154, 175, 196, 198, 202-205, 217, 218, 220, 229, 231, 232
Adad-Nirari III, 27, 152, 154, 175, 196, 198, 202-205, 217, 220, 229, 232
Addudani, 106
Adnah, 106
Adonis, 131
Adrastus, 130, 131
Aeolia, 19
Ahab, 5, 20, 94-96, 100, 104, 106, 113, 114, 117, 176, 179, 209, 220, 239
Ahaziah, 240
Ahhiyawa, 200
Ahiram, 26, 171, 173-175

Ahmose, 29, 30
Ahura-Mazda, 119, 120, 122, 146
Akhet-Aton, 114, 120, 131
Akhnaton, 5, 7, 10, 13, 15, 17, 24, 26, 27, 40, 80, 91, 93, 97, 98, 105, 107, 110-112, 114-116, 120-129, 131-134, 139, 142, 144-146, 149, 152, 155, 186, 187, 209, 228, 229, 231, 239, 241
Akurgal, Ekrem, 23, 24
Al Kuds, 69
Alabastronpolis, 142
Alalakh, 174
Alasia, 235
Aldred, Cyril, 134
alter ego(s), 24, 38, 96, 99, 103, 108, 111, 122, 125, 153, 159, 161, 195, 204, 227, 228, 233
Alyattes, 18, 19, 109, 155, 189, 197, 199-202, 205, 206, 208, 220
Amalekites, 5, 9, 29, 30
Amanus, 108
Amarna, 5, 7, 10, 13, 15, 16, 24, 80, 91, 92, 94-107, 109-113, 115, 117, 121, 124, 128, 132, 134, 143, 146, 209, 215, 239
Amasiah, 106
Amathous, 131
Amaziah, 107, 220
Amenemhab, 87
Amenemope, 26, 176

Amenhotep I, 29

Amenhotep II, 60, 97, 99, 178

Amenhotep III	, 7, 10, 23, 46, 80, 91, 93, 96-101, 105, 121, 122, 125, 126, 128, 145, 152, 155, 178, 183

Amenophis, 60, 128-131

Amon, 37, 50, 53, 71, 95, 124, 125, 132, 135, 136, 142, 211

Amor, 211, 214

Amurru, 23, 94, 99, 101, 104, 111, 207, 209, 215

Anatolia, 6, 9, 13, 15-18, 24, 108, 149, 152-156, 159, 162, 181, 189, 199, 200, 207, 234

Ankhesenamun, 137, 138

Anshan, 233

Antigone, 127, 138-140

Apepi I and II, 241

Apion, 20, 23, 94, 100, 128

Arabia, 30, 35, 39, 44, 47, 49, 50, 57, 61, 67, 87, 192

Arabs, 30, 65

Aram, 109, 215

Aramaeans, 214

Arame, 154, 234, 235

Araunah, 78, 79

Arbaces, 152, 195, 197, 216, 229

Arbela, 190

Ardys, 155

Argistis I, 154

Argos, 131

Arik-den-ili, 195

Arma, 235, 236

Armenia, 17, 207

Arnuwandash, 208

Arpad, 154

Artatama, 121, 152

Artaxerxes II, 234

Aruna, 76-79, 83

Arvad, 111

Arzashkum, 154

Arzawa, 18, 19, 200

Arzenu, 69

Asa, 5, 79, 95, 97-99, 102, 103, 116, 209, 215

Asar, 56

Ashdod, 180

Ashguza, 16

Ashkelon, 220, 222

Ashkenaz, 16

Ashur, 13, 109, 190, 191, 196, 203, 205, 228, 233

Ashurbanipal, 7, 24, 25, 191

Ashurnasirpal, 6, 23, 108, 111, 122, 145-147, 149-152, 156, 158, 163-165, 168, 178, 182, 189, 190, 194, 227-231

Ashurnasirpal II, 6, 23, 108, 111, 122, 145, 146, 149-152, 156, 158, 163-165, 168, 178, 182, 190, 194, 227, 229-231

Ashuruballit, 107, 108, 111, 144-147, 150, 152, 189, 190, 195, 226, 231

Asia Minor, 17-19, 58, 155, 199, 200

Asiatics, 53, 54, 74, 76, 83, 84, 135, 136, 140, 141, 145, 147, 213

Assyria(ns), 3, 6, 7, 9, 12-15, 17, 21, 23, 24, 26, 27, 37, 54, 58, 70, 94, 104, 107-109, 119, 122, 129, 130, 135, 136, 144-147, 149-156, 160, 161, 163-170, 175, 178-184, 187-198, 202-209, 214-217, 220-222, 225-232, 234, 236

Astarte, 143

Astata, 104

Astyages, 18, 152, 202, 205, 206, 229

Aton, 120, 132, 187

Avaris, 29, 67, 129, 144

Awarkus, 24

Ay, 100, 107, 123, 127, 129, 134, 135, 137-142, 144, 147, 209

Azalzi, 208

Azariah, 7, 180, 220

Aziru, 94, 95, 99, 101, 103-105, 115, 117, 209, 215

Azitawatas, 24

B

Baal, 143

Baalbazer, 100

Baasha, 5, 97, 99, 102-104, 116, 209

Babylon(ia), 6, 7, 16-18, 23, 24, 46, 58, 104, 108, 144, 151, 191, 193, 195, 206-208, 225, 227-234

Bactria, 236-238

Baghdad, 10, 230

Bakhtan, 236, 237

Bashan, 213, 220

Batroun, 94

Batruna, 94

bear, 40, 59, 79, 85, 87, 92, 111, 145, 191, 230

Beketaten, 125

Bel, 10, 232

Benhadad, 117, 219

Ben-Hadad, 95, 96, 103-105, 117, 214, 215, 217

Bentresh, 236, 237

Beth Horon, 78

Beth-Shan, 180, 210-214, 216

Bimson, John, 22, 31-36, 38, 41, 44, 45, 49, 53, 56, 57, 62, 65, 66, 180, 181, 211-215, 217-222

Biridia, 102, 103

Boeotian shield, 170

Boghaz-koi, 15, 17-19, 153, 154, 159, 189, 202, 206, 207, 234, 235

Botrys, 93, 94

Breasted, James Henry, 44, 47, 53, 54, 58, 70, 71, 73, 77, 83, 120, 132, 141, 170

Bronze Age, 11, 12, 22, 65, 66, 81, 82, 115, 174, 179, 180, 182, 226, 227

Budge, Wallis, 231

Burnaburiash, 229-231, 233

Byblos, 24-26, 41-45, 54-56, 67, 73, 74, 111, 112, 131, 171, 173, 175, 239

C

Caesarea, 59

Calah, 146, 163, 164, 182

Cambyses, 152, 192, 208

camel-leopard, 57

Canaan(ites), 25, 64, 69, 70, 73, 74, 81-83, 91, 93, 94, 96, 102, 110, 177, 221, 222

Cappadocia, 192, 207

Carchemish, 24, 104, 108, 111, 154, 156, 158-162, 189, 193, 198, 203, 236

Caria, 19, 199

Carmel Ridge, 77

Caucasus, 13, 16

cavalry, 23, 78, 144, 163-165, 168, 169

Champollion, 20

chariots, 6, 47, 76, 84, 109, 164, 165, 167, 207

Cilicia, 18, 26, 206

Cimmerians, 15, 202

Creon, 127, 129, 137, 139, 140

crocodile, 59

Croesus, 17-19, 155, 189, 195, 199, 206-208, 222, 228

Ctesias, 109, 192-195

cuneiform, 6, 10, 11, 15, 18, 26, 36, 88, 109, 111, 113, 159, 160, 191, 196, 202, 206, 217, 236

Cush(ites), 37

Cuthi, 16

Cyaxares, 7, 14, 15, 109, 152, 192, 205, 206, 225, 227, 229

Cypriot(s), 131, 172

Cyprus, 46, 110, 183, 204, 235

Cyrus, 14, 16, 17, 152, 195, 205, 207, 208, 227-229, 234

D

Damascus, 74, 79, 83, 104, 109, 117, 203, 204, 211, 214, 215, 217-219

Danelius, Eva, 37, 38, 54, 59, 60, 78-80, 84, 85

Dardanoi, 199

Darius III, 234

Dark Age, 22, 155, 156, 226

David, 20, 22, 25, 29-31, 34, 45, 46, 50, 56, 62, 65, 74, 78, 81, 89, 93, 98, 104, 182, 218, 219, 227, 228

Deioces, 225

Didymeus, 110

Diodorus, 57, 128, 129, 191, 238

Divine Land, 33, 41, 56, 62, 63, 218

Djahi, 212, 214

Djefti, 77
Djeser-kau, 88, 89
Dumasqa, 104
Dur-Kurigalzu, 230

E

Ecbatana, 14
Edom(ites), 59, 60, 74, 83, 181, 220
Elah, 5, 99, 102, 103, 105, 116
elephants, 57, 58, 67, 87
Elibaal, 172, 175
Elisha, 220
Enlil-Nirari, 145
Ephesus, 23, 94, 99, 200
epigoni, 123, 129, 139, 142
Eriphyle, 130, 131
Esarhaddon, 24
Esdraelon, 77, 80, 211-214
Eteocles, 123, 127, 130, 200
Ethbaal, 94, 100
Ethiopia, 30, 33, 35, 37, 38, 65, 66, 127-129, 131, 132, 135
Euphrates, 58, 70, 81, 83, 104, 109, 146, 189, 190, 195, 197, 198, 202, 203, 207, 208
Exodus, 30, 93
Ezion-geber, 181

F

frankincense, 47-49

G

Gabala, 131
Gad, 213
Galilee, 210-212, 214, 216, 219, 222
Gasga, 15, 16, 202
gazelle, 58, 59
Gem-Aton, 132
Genesis, 38, 49, 56, 92, 124
Gilead, 49, 213, 214, 222

giraffe, 56-58, 60
Glasgow Conference, 23, 26, 180
Greece, 3, 6, 121, 124, 127, 131, 144, 170, 171, 200
Greek(s), 6, 23, 36, 37, 40, 43, 45, 48, 110, 111, 119, 123, 124, 126-131, 137-139, 142, 147, 164, 169-171, 174, 183-186, 200, 202, 205, 208, 227
Greenberg, Lewis M., 35, 43, 63, 174, 175
Gubla, 112, 239
Gutians, 16
Gwal, 171, 172

H

habatu, 16
Habiru, 16, 94
Hadad-ezer, 104, 115, 215
Haemon, 139
Halys, 9, 17, 18, 207
Hamadan, 14
Hamath, 211, 212, 217, 219
Hamite(s), 56, 60
Hammath, 212
Hanigalbat, 108
Hapu, 128, 131
Har Kodsho, 79
Hathor, 45, 49, 55, 60, 63, 67
Hatshepsut, 5, 20-22, 29-38, 40, 41, 44, 45, 47-51, 53-57, 59, 60, 62-67, 69-73, 75, 76, 80, 81, 84, 87, 100, 125, 137
Hatti, 17, 54, 96, 104, 107-111, 152-154, 194, 195, 199, 205, 208, 215-218, 221-223, 236, 237
Hattina, 108, 154
Hattusas, 155, 162, 163
Hattus-ili, 202
Hattusilis III, 19, 150, 155, 189, 195, 198, 202-205, 220, 232, 235
Hazael, 95, 104, 109, 188, 213-217, 219
Hazor, 11, 180, 182, 222
Hebrew, 5, 16, 20, 21, 25, 26, 38, 39, 48, 57, 69, 70, 79, 88, 89, 91-98, 103, 104, 106, 110, 113, 120, 130, 144, 171, 172, 176-178,

209, 210, 212, 219, 240

Hecataeus, 238

Heinsohn, Gunnar, 4, 10, 12, 21, 25

Heraclid(s), 18

heresy, 128, 129, 132, 187

heretic, 121, 123, 133, 144, 186

Herihor, 25

Herodotus, 14, 15, 18, 24, 38, 70, 87, 128, 131, 170, 185, 191, 200-202, 205-207, 223, 225

Hilani-house, 23, 26, 158

hippopotamus, 58

Hiram, 99, 100, 171

Hittite(s), 5, 6, 9, 13, 15-19, 23, 24, 26, 27, 82, 108, 109, 137, 138, 144, 145, 149-168, 170, 189, 190, 192-195, 198-200, 203-208, 210, 211, 215, 218, 222, 227-229, 232-238

Horemheb, 23, 26, 100, 107, 109, 129, 136, 139-144, 146, 147, 155, 158, 164, 187, 190, 209

Horon, 78

Horus, 24, 56, 84, 88, 120, 137, 142, 183

Hurrian(s), 13, 103, 110, 152, 153, 161, 226, 236

Huy, 135

Hyksos, 5, 9-12, 29, 30, 67, 119, 128-130, 143, 147, 164, 241

Hypostile Hall, 23, 167, 193, 210

I

Iahzibada, 107

Ibbi-Sin, 230, 233, 234

iconography, 39, 40, 183

Iehozabad, 107

India, 57, 58, 149, 195-197

Indo-European, 18, 61

Indra, 13

Ini Teshub, 161

Ionia(ns), 19, 110, 184, 186

Iran(ians), 12, 13, 120-122, 152, 155, 237

Iron Age, 12, 22, 65, 66, 114, 115, 179-182, 188, 226, 227

Irqata, 92

Isaiah, 21, 37, 92, 177

Ishhupre, 24

Ishme-Dagan, 152, 227

Ishtar, 10, 13, 154, 203, 231, 235

Israel(ites), 3-5, 9, 11, 20, 22, 29, 30, 33, 34, 36, 47-50, 56, 62, 64, 69, 73-81, 84, 93-100, 102-105, 110, 112, 115-117, 119, 124, 130, 146, 149, 175, 176, 180, 182, 188, 193, 203, 209-214, 216-222, 240

Ithobaal, 171-173, 175, 176

Ithobalos, 94

J

Jaman, 110

James, Peter, 22, 24, 26, 31, 35

Jebus(ites), 78, 79, 81, 93, 94

Jehoahaz, 188, 213, 217-219

Jehoram, 240

Jehoshaphat, 5, 20, 25, 95-99, 102, 106, 107, 188, 215, 240

Jehozabad, 106, 107

Jehu, 109, 146, 213, 214

Jenin, 103

Jeroboam I, 34, 69, 77, 102, 218

Jerusalem, 20, 23, 25, 30, 48, 60, 69, 70, 74, 78-85, 89, 92-99, 101-103, 105, 107, 173, 174

Jezreel Valley, 77

Joash, 95, 188, 203, 217-220, 240

Joppa, 73, 76-78

Jordan, 16, 47-49, 57, 67, 74, 84, 181, 211-214, 219, 220

Joseph, 20, 49, 58

Josephus, 20, 23, 33, 35-39, 66, 78, 84, 94, 100, 128, 129

Joshua, 16, 92, 93, 212

Judah, 5-7, 73, 74, 77, 81, 84, 93, 95-99, 102, 103, 105, 180, 188, 209-211, 214-216, 218-220, 240

K

Kadesh, 23, 25, 46, 69, 70, 73, 74, 76, 77, 79, 82-84, 98, 109, 165, 166, 176, 193, 197-199,

204, 210, 211, 214, 216, 219

Kandalanu, 7

Kar Ishtar, 231

Karabel, 19, 201

Karaduniash, 104

Karnaim, 219

Karnak, 23, 50, 53, 69, 70, 73, 77, 78, 83-87, 142, 144, 164, 167, 193, 210, 211, 214, 220, 236, 237

Kashtiliash, 228, 232-234

Kassite(s), 17, 229-233

Katuwas, 24, 159, 161

Khatti, 111

Khenthenopher, 50, 55

Kheta, 44, 221

Khoisan, 62

Khonsu, 236, 237

Khorsabad, 230

Khwashatra, 7, 14

Khyan, 10

Kilamuwa, 23, 26, 158

Kurigalzu, 231, 233

Kurtiwaza, 151, 152

L

Labayu, 91, 96, 99, 101-103, 105, 116

Lachish, 79, 180, 181

Lebanah, 48

Lebanon, 41-45, 49, 54-56, 59, 63, 67, 73, 74, 85, 87, 111, 135, 210

lioness, 40

lions, 58, 67, 175

Lorton, David, 31, 34, 36, 41, 42, 44, 45, 49-52, 56, 62

Luwian, 18

Luxor, 220

Lycia, 19, 199

Lydia(ns), 6, 17-19, 154, 155, 169, 189, 190, 192, 194, 195, 197-200, 202, 205-208, 216, 223, 228, 233

M

Mackey, Damien, 58

Madai, 14

Mahallata, 111

Makan, 207

Makeda, 33, 34, 38

Makera, 33, 34, 38

Malatya, 154, 157

Manasseh, 213

mandragora, 86

Manetho, 6, 20, 101, 127-131, 144, 147, 238, 240

Mansuate, 217

Marduk-apil-iddin, 24, 232, 233

Mari, 11

Mariyanna, 13, 61, 152, 226

Matiene, 14

Mattan-Baal, 100

Mattiwaza, 151

Mede(s), 7, 12-15, 17, 18, 20, 23, 35, 108, 109, 119, 120, 123, 145, 151, 152, 155, 170, 188-195, 197, 198, 202, 205, 206, 216, 220, 225-227, 229, 233, 234, 237, 238

Median, 14, 17, 205, 226, 228

Megiddo, 50, 58, 73, 74, 76, 77, 103, 113, 180, 182, 211, 214

Melid, 154, 203

Memphis, 23, 140, 141, 143, 164

Menander, 23, 94, 99-101, 103

Menkheperre, 75, 85, 88, 89, 181

Meritaten, 127, 138, 142

Merneptah, 24, 26, 27, 111, 161, 220-223

Merodach-Baladan, 24, 232

Meroe, 55

Mesha, 113, 173

Mesopotamia, 10-12, 15-17, 27, 46, 56, 58, 119, 144, 153, 155, 164, 195, 198, 218, 226, 227, 230, 237

Methusastartus, 100, 101

Middle Assyrians, 150-152, 195, 227, 228

migdol, 79

Miletus, 199, 200, 202

Millawanda, 200, 202
Mita, 9, 14
Mitanni(ans), 5, 9, 12-15, 17, 23, 46, 54, 83, 119-123, 144, 149-153, 155, 195, 226-228, 230
Mitra, 13
Mizraim, 57, 144
Moab(ites), 209, 220
Montet, Pierre, 171, 172
Montu, 84
Morenz, Siegfried, 43
Mursilis, 15, 18, 108, 150, 153-155, 158, 189, 190, 193-195, 200, 201, 215, 216, 234-236
Musri, 57, 109, 144-146
Mutnodjmet, 142
Muwatallis, 155, 192, 194, 195, 204, 216, 232, 235, 236
Mykty, 76-80, 83
myrrh, 44, 47-49, 53, 60, 67
Myrsilos, 18

N

Nabonasser, 232, 233
Nabonidus, 233, 234
Nabu-apil-iddin, 229-231, 233
Naharin, 44, 192, 198
Nairi, 153, 154, 207, 208
Naphtali, 212, 222
Naphuria, 7, 91
Naram Sin, 9, 10, 227
Nazibugash, 231
Nazimarattash, 231, 233
Nebuchadrezzar, 6, 193
Necho, 193
Nefertiti, 122, 125
Nefrure, 237
negroes, 56, 57, 60
Neith, 37, 142
Neshili, 18
New Kingdom, 3, 4, 10, 11, 19-21, 25, 30, 34, 45, 65, 82, 88, 113, 170, 177-179, 181, 182, 184, 241

Nibbi, Alessandra, 57
Nicodemus, 111
Nikaule, 37, 38
Nikdem, 110
Nikmed, 110, 111
Nikmepa, 23, 26, 27, 158
Nikomedes, 110, 111
Nile, 10, 29, 43, 58, 59, 63, 81, 131, 218, 240
Nimmuria, 7, 91
Nimrod, 196
Nimrud, 180, 182, 183
Nineveh, 13, 23, 94, 190, 195, 196, 225
Ninos, 196
Ninurta, 196, 228
Niqmaddu, 110
Niqmepa, 158
Nubia, 33, 35-37, 39, 52, 55, 65, 70, 124, 132, 133
Nuhasse, 116, 189, 204

O

Oedipus, 5, 40, 121, 123-127, 137, 139
Old Assyrian(s), 9, 12, 14, 17, 119, 151, 192, 227
Old Babylonian(s), 58
Old Testament, 4, 20, 21, 29, 36-38, 91, 106, 212, 214
olibanum, 48
Omri, 102, 105, 106, 109, 112-114, 116, 117, 179
Ophir, 61
Orontes, 58, 73, 82, 83, 104, 108, 211
oryx, 57
Osarsiph, 129, 147
Osiris, 43, 49, 56, 63, 67
Osorkon I, 172, 175
ostrich, 58

P

Palestine, 10, 11, 13, 15, 16, 23, 24, 29, 30, 33, 40, 42-47, 49, 50, 52, 56-59, 61, 64-67,

69, 70, 73-77, 81-87, 91, 92, 94, 95, 97-99, 102, 106, 107, 112, 113, 130, 135, 136, 146, 147, 176-181, 187, 193, 209-214, 216, 218, 220-223, 226

Papis, 128, 131

Parattarna, 9, 12-14, 152, 226, 227

Parsatatar, 12, 227

Parsua, 204

Pausanias, 131

Pehel, 210, 211

Pella, 210-213

Pelusium, 129

Pepi I and II, 241

Perehu, 61

Persia(ns), 6, 13, 14, 16, 17, 19, 21, 23, 35, 37, 58, 109, 119, 120, 122, 132, 145, 151, 152, 170, 176, 189, 192, 193, 195, 204-206, 208, 223, 226-229, 233, 234, 236, 237, 240, 241

Petrie, Flinders, 25, 39, 40, 56, 184, 185, 221

Philistia, 70, 71, 79, 180, 211, 214, 220

Phoenicia, 33, 43-45, 49, 56, 67, 110, 174, 212, 218

Phraortes, 14, 15, 152, 225, 227

Phrygia, 192

Polyneices, 123, 127, 129, 138

pottery , 10, 112, 114, 115, 150, 172, 177, 178, 181, 184

prenomen, 37, 88

Psalms, 120

Pteria, 207

Pul, 7

Punt(ites), 33, 34, 41-57, 59-67, 70, 71, 85, 87

Pwenet, 49, 56

Pygmalion, 100

Pyramid Age, 30, 241

Q

Quti, 16

R

Ramoth, 212

Ramses I, 187

Ramses II, 3, 4, 6, 20, 21, 23, 24, 26, 27, 82, 89, 98, 109, 111, 143, 161, 165-167, 170, 172, 173, 175-178, 187, 188, 190, 192, 193, 197, 199, 201, 204, 206, 216, 218-220, 222, 223, 236-238, 240

Ras Shamra, 109, 183

Rawlinson, George, 88

Red Sea, 41, 55, 62, 64, 65

Rehob, 211, 212

Rehoboam, 25, 34, 69, 76, 77, 80, 84, 96-98

Rekhmire, 87

Retenu, 42, 47, 50, 86, 135

Retjenu, 69, 70, 77, 85, 86, 136

Rezenu, 69

rhinoceros, 56-58, 60, 67, 146

Rhinocolura, 129, 144

Rib-Addi, 92, 93, 95, 96, 239

Ruben, 213

S

Sa.Gaz, 16, 103

Saba, 35-37, 39

Sadyattes, 155, 200

Sais, 37

Saka, 16

Salem, 93

Samaria, 48, 95, 101, 102, 112-117, 130, 179, 214

Sammuramat, 195

Sangara, 108, 158, 189

Sankara, 158-161

Sanskrit, 13, 14

Sapalulme, 108

sarcophagi, 171, 172, 174, 175

Sardan, 169, 170

Sardanapalus, 109, 190-192, 194, 195, 197, 216

Sardis, 169, 208

Sarduris II, 154

Sargon, 9, 10, 12, 22, 119, 152, 176, 179, 180, 230, 233

Sargon II, 22, 152, 176, 179, 180, 230, 233

Sarre-Kushukh, 156, 159-161

Sarre-sin-akh, 159-161

Saul, 20, 29

scarab(s), 179, 183

Scyth(ians), 14-17, 202, 210

Scythopolis, 210

Sekhmet, 40, 124

Semiramis, 194-198

Semite(s)/Semitic, 7, 9-11, 56, 57, 60, 61, 65, 79, 103, 110, 111, 130, 143, 144, 150, 176, 212, 218, 227, 228, 230

Sennacherib, 24, 176, 180-182

Senwosret, 37, 87, 88

Sesostris, 45, 70, 85, 87, 88

Sethos, 24, 211, 216

Seti, 23, 24, 26, 60, 100, 107, 109, 132, 143, 155, 158, 164, 167, 168, 171, 187, 188, 190, 192, 193, 195, 197, 209-216, 218, 219, 238

Seti I, 23, 26, 60, 100, 107, 109, 155, 158, 164, 167, 168, 171, 187, 188, 190, 192, 193, 195, 197, 209-216, 218, 219

shabak, 40

Shabaka, 39, 40, 132

Shabataka, 39, 181, 182

Shagarakti-Shuriash, 232, 233

Shagaz, 16

Shalmaneser III, 23, 27, 57, 96, 100, 104, 107, 108, 110, 111, 122, 145-147, 149, 150, 152-155, 158, 163-168, 173, 175, 188-194, 197, 198, 202, 203, 209, 213, 229, 231, 234-236

Shalmaneser IV, 175, 202, 205, 229, 237

Shamshi-Adad, 151, 152, 158, 175, 190, 194-198, 202, 203, 216, 227, 229, 232

Shamshi-Adad V, 152, 158, 175, 190, 194-198, 202, 216, 229

shashak, 89

Shaushtatar, 12-14, 152, 226, 227

Sheba, 5, 20, 30-40, 51, 56, 57, 59, 62, 64, 66, 69, 71, 73, 75, 85, 89, 100

Shechem, 91, 93, 95, 96, 101, 102, 114, 115

Shepardi, 208

Shepherd Kings, 9, 10, 147

Shewa, 37

Shiloah, 173

Shishak, 5, 21, 23, 34, 35, 69, 70, 75, 76, 84, 87-89, 97, 98, 218

Shulgi, 230, 233

Shulman, 94

Shuttarna, 152, 226

Sidon, 111, 174

Simyra, 112, 115

Sinai, 41, 47, 57, 59, 67

Sipylus, 19

Siwa, 37

Smenkhare, 121, 123, 125, 127, 129, 130, 133, 134, 138, 139, 142, 147

Smyrna, 19, 201

Solomon, 20-23, 25, 30, 31, 33-36, 38, 39, 41, 56, 61, 62, 64, 65, 69, 70, 74-76, 81, 84, 85, 87, 89, 94, 96-100, 102, 219

Solymites, 129, 130

Somalia, 54, 55, 64-67

Sosenk I, 172, 175

Sparda, 208

sphinx, 39, 40, 124, 210, 214

Stewart, Don, 38

stratigraphy, 22, 23, 115, 180, 182

Subartians, 109, 144

Subartu, 109, 208

Sukhis, 24, 159-161

Sumur, 95, 96, 112, 115, 116

Suppiluliumas I, 15, 26, 27, 96, 110, 149, 151, 153, 155, 156, 159, 216, 235

synchronisms, 4, 5, 21, 30, 213

Syria, 9-13, 15, 16, 23, 24, 26, 40, 42, 44, 46, 47, 50, 52, 56-59, 61, 65, 67, 70, 73, 74, 81, 82, 85-87, 91, 94-96, 99, 101, 103, 104, 106-108, 110, 111, 115-117, 130, 131, 136, 146, 147, 154-156, 158, 159, 173, 175, 177-180, 183, 187, 189, 190, 192, 193, 198, 203-205, 209-211, 213-223, 226, 234

T

Taanach, 77, 80
Tagi, 92
Tanis, 142, 143
Tanit, 142
Tanite(s), 142, 187, 240
Theba, 29, 37, 39, 40
Thebes, 1, 36, 37, 39, 40, 50, 51, 55, 63, 64, 66, 67, 71, 84, 105, 114, 119, 120, 123, 124, 127, 129, 130, 132, 139, 142, 144
Thutmose III, 5, 21-23, 25, 30, 34, 35, 42, 44, 47, 49-52, 54, 55, 61, 62, 64, 66, 67, 69-88, 96-99, 130, 178, 179, 222, 227
Thutmose IV, 13, 42, 97, 99, 121, 165
Tiberias, 212
Tiglath-Pileser III, 7, 21, 22, 24, 27, 111, 152, 154, 156, 157, 159, 161, 165, 180, 193, 204, 205, 220-222, 228, 229, 232
Tiresias, 128, 129, 139
Tirhakah, 132
Tiy, 121, 125, 183
Transjordania, 216
Tudkhaliash IV, 23, 24
Tukulti-apil-esharra, 222, 232
Tukulti-Ninurta, 24, 150-152, 155, 207, 208, 222, 227-229, 232
Tukulti-Ninurta I, 24, 150-152, 227-229
Tunip, 82, 92
Tushpa, 154
Tushratta, 13, 122, 151, 152, 228, 229
Tutankhamun, 100, 107, 112-114, 123, 127, 130, 133-140, 144-146, 209
Tydeus, 130
Tyre, 23, 99, 101, 111, 214

U

Ugarit, 23, 26, 109-112, 158, 183
Unqi, 154
Urartu, 13, 108, 152-155, 194, 195, 202-205, 232, 234
Ura-tarhundas, 159, 160
Urhi-Teshub, 204, 205
Urukki, 24

Urusalim, 80, 93, 102
Usertasen, 87, 88
Usikheprure, 24
Uzziah, 7, 180, 219, 220, 240

V

Van, 154, 171, 237
Varuna, 13

W

Washukanni, 13, 14, 226
Wenamon, 24, 25

X

Xenophon, 192

Y

Yanoam, 210-212, 222
Yarumtu, 212, 213
Yazilikaya, 17, 153, 162, 163
Yemen, 66

Z

Zalzi, 208
Zannanzash, 138
Zaphata, 79
Zarathustra, 119, 120, 123
Zefti, 77
Zephathah, 79
Zerah, 79, 97, 98
Zichri, 106, 107
Zimri, 103
Zincirli, 23, 26
Zoroaster, 119, 120, 122
Zuchru, 107
Zumur, 116
Zurata, 103

Printed in the United States
By Bookmasters